Opportunity Time

Opportunity
Time

LINWOOD HOLTON

University of Virginia Press • *Charlottesville and London*

University of Virginia Press
© 2008 by the Rector and Visitors of the University of Virginia
All rights reserved
Printed in the United States of America on acid-free paper

First published 2008

9 8 7 6 5 4 3 2 1

LIBRARY OF CONGRESS CATALOGING-IN-PUBLICATION DATA

Holton, A. Linwood (Abner Linwood), 1923–
    Opportunity time / Linwood Holton.
        p.   cm.
    Includes index.
    ISBN 978-0-8139-2720-6 (cloth : alk. paper)
    1. Holton, A. Linwood (Abner Linwood), 1923–   2. Governors—Virginia—
Biography. 3. Virginia—Politics and government—1951–74. Virginia—Social policy.
I. Title.
    F231.3.H65A3 2008
    975.5'043092—dc22
        [B]   2007045615

To our children, and their children,
with the hope that they will have as much fun in their lives
as Jinks and I have had in our long life together

Contents

Acknowledgments

I do not exaggerate when I say that this book would not exist but for the friendship, interest, persistence, skill, and patience of Kathy Lyles Plotkin. She began her contributions when she voluntarily took pictures and produced a montage of them in 1965. She is especially proud of the image of me asleep in the back seat of a Ford between campaign stops—suggesting maybe that sleeping candidates can't be expected to win!

She was the producer of a television program in Roanoke during the 1969 campaign, but she watched with special interest as her husband was elected to the Virginia Senate in the midterm elections. Years later, having published a book of her own and having established her own business, Wordworks, she nudged me in 2002 to quit thinking these vague thoughts about maybe some-day writing a book and *get on with it!* Her promised assistance was given at every step of a long effort: she edited every chapter, made suggestions for revisions, supplied technical expertise, transcribed the work to one of these modern word processors, and above all, kept my feet to the fire! For all of that, and more, I am much indebted to Kathy Plotkin.

Equally important was the help of my wife of over fifty years, Jinks. I dictated most of this from memory to a hand-held tape recorder, and she did the initial transcription to manuscript pages. She also suggested differences in emphasis, corrected my sometimes faulty recollections, and again, above all, encouraged me to finish the job.

My friend Paul Gaston, Emeritus Professor of History at the University of Virginia and important mentor of a former student (our son Woody), read the nearly finished manuscript and made valuable, detailed comments.

My law firm in Richmond, McCandlish Holton, and especially our firm administrator, Kelly Lyda, gave encouragement and tangible assistance, making many copies of various parts of the manuscript.

Jennifer McDaid, an archivist at the Library of Virginia, made a valiant though futile effort to find a copy of the picture of Chief Justice Burger without his halo. There may be a copy in the Warren Burger Papers, but Ms. McDaid learned that the collection is closed to researchers until 2026.

My children, their spouses, and some of their offspring served as cheerleaders, for which I am especially grateful.

On August 31, 1970, one era in American history ended; another of enduring promise began. David Brinkley opened his evening newscast on NBC-TV that night with a dramatic video from Richmond, Virginia, and the *New York Times* on its front page the next morning ran a photograph that captured this moment of national shift. There was more to this story than an ugly conflict averted and a political leader's path defined.

The action photograph shows a new governor and his smiling teenage daughter striding down a sidewalk. It is the first day of school. She is white. All the other students in the picture are black, and the high school is under a court order to integrate that morning. In a state that once closed its public schools rather than integrate them, in a region seething with resentment over court-ordered school busing, a southern governor is declaring, by example, "The age of defiance is past." And his children are walking with him.

I was then a young television reporter in Virginia just out of college, closer in age to the students warily entering Kennedy High School that historic morning than to Governor Linwood Holton, whose political career I was covering. As I write, I can still hear the steel in his voice as he read an inauguration pledge, only a few months before that first day of school, "to make Virginia a model in race relations." The Holton years were part of a sweep of national change. Virginia and the South were a compelling American story in the early 1970s. The Civil Rights Act was being enforced. Dr. Martin Luther King was dead, and racial embers burned. Across the nation, federal courts were telling school boards that students must be bused to distant schools so that blacks and whites could go to class in more balanced numbers. Progressive southern governors, including one named Jimmy Carter, were in the national spotlight and on the cover of *Time*.

In Virginia, as in many southern states, political power was solidly in the hands of one conservative party, the Democrats. Virginians voted Democratic for the courthouse and the state house, but Republican for the White House. In Virginia, the moderates were the Republicans, concentrated in the western half of the state, where I was a reporter and where Linwood Holton had established his political base. "The Mountain Valley Boys," I heard them called, were from the Blue Ridge Mountains and Shenandoah Valley, not from the tobacco fields of "Southside" or the capital of the Confederacy, Richmond.

Linwood Holton's historic election as the first Republican governor in one hundred years had harnessed together the civil rights community, state organized labor, and voters no longer comfortable with Virginia's legacy of "Massive Resistance" to integration. Busing wasn't the driving issue in the Virginia campaign, but as soon as Governor Holton took office, the federal court order to bus Richmond students hit him in a very personal way.

Around the Holton family dinner table at the Governor's Mansion that summer of 1970, his four children were full of questions and understandable doubts as they faced the certainty of attending integrated schools. Their parents recall hearing such questions from them as: Would they be bused? Would they be stared at? What about making friends? Would they be safe? The court had ruled that the governor's residence was not city property, so the Holtons could have chosen any school for these four. But for Governor Holton, that fateful day in 1970 was what he still calls "Opportunity Time."

I have watched the Holton "kids" ever since, and I marvel each time I see them. Years after I left Virginia to become an ABC News White House correspondent covering presidential campaigns, I remember being herded with other reporters up a back stairway to get in place for the Democratic nominee's arrival. Our shepherd was a lanky teen with a fury of curly hair. It was Dwight Holton, the same child I had played tetherball with behind the Governor's Mansion in Richmond more than a decade before. Later, he went to work in the Clinton West Wing, and later still, he married the White House National Security Council press secretary Mary Ellen Glynn.

Daughter Anne and son Woody helped integrate Mosby Middle School the day their sister Tayloe was photographed entering the high school. Anne greeted me with a hug at a State Bar Association luncheon in Richmond three decades later. Like her father, Anne is a Harvard-trained lawyer. I smile at the circle of life—a governor's daughter now First Lady, living again in Virginia's classical executive mansion, the wife of Virginia's current governor, Tim Kaine. Their children now sleep in the rooms where the Holton kids made history.

I will always carry with me a special appreciation for having covered the

Holton years. When ABC News assigned me to the White House in 1974, it could very well have been to cover Linwood Holton as president. In 1973, national reporters caught wind of a rumor and flocked to follow Governor Holton to Washington for a ceremony where President Nixon was to announce his new vice president. The *Washington Post* went so far as to set its presses with the headline that Governor Holton was the choice. Ultimately, Congressman Gerald Ford was selected, so when I arrived after the Nixon resignation, he was the first president I covered. But many of us will always believe that the choice had almost been Holton. His devilish sense of humor in this memoir suggests there may even have been another intriguing political explanation.

History rushes ever forward like a river, and at the confluence of two mighty streams, the force of change can be awesome to behold. Virginia is etched with some of the most beautiful rivers on the continent. Virginia is also the headwaters of American democracy, where our early presidents and constitutional thinkers built a nation of ideals. Two centuries later, another Virginian strove to build on those beliefs. What if Linwood Holton had not been standing at that confluence in 1970? Would another governor have stepped forward to change the course for Virginia, the South, and the nation?

Linwood Holton tells why he walked forward with determination at a moment when leadership was needed. His personal story is political memoir at its best: a reaffirmation of idealism recalled with wry humor, a refreshing mix of candor about both himself and others, and a portrait—melded with irrepressible optimism and zest for public service—of a moment that history shows was, indeed, "Opportunity Time."

Ann W. Compton
ABC News White House Correspondent

Opportunity Time

Prologue

"You've got the one!"

Those were some of the sweetest words I've ever heard, sweet to me for a very good reason.

It was early evening, election day, November 1969, and the end of my four-year campaign to be Virginia's governor. My wife, Jinks (never known to anyone by her given name, Virginia), and I, along with three of our four children, had jumped around the state during the day visiting polling places.

We ended the peripatetic day in Roanoke, where we had lived on Avenham Avenue for the last ten years. Making a quick stop at our home, we found that our ten-year-old son, Woody, had been bicycling that afternoon under the tutelage of Roger Hull and Rodger Provo—campaign assistants who had more than earned their campaign nicknames of "Gloom" and "Doom." Woody had encountered an unexpected curb, resulting in a black eye almost as memorable as the rest of the day would prove to be.

The whole family gathered at the Roanoke Republican headquarters about 6:00 p.m., just an hour before the polls would close. Excitement and expectancy filled that storefront room on Church Avenue. The early-arriving crowd sensed victory. The euphoria that comes with intensive campaigning had pushed our hopes to a high.

After I gave a short thumbs-up speech, the family and I made an emotional stop at the home of Jinks's parents, then headed for the Roanoke airport for what we believed would be our transit to a big First for Virginia: Our arrival in Richmond could quite possibly begin the celebration of the first election of a Republican Party nominee to a statewide office since Reconstruction.*

*Gilbert Walker was elected governor of Virginia in 1869; he was nominated for governor by conservative Republicans, but in effect he was elected and governed as a member of the Conservative Party—a party created in 1867 to ward off black supremacy. See Allen Wesley Moger, *Virginia: Bourbonism to Byrd, 1870–1925* (Charlottesville: University Press of Virginia, 1968), 10–14.

Marshall Babb, the pilot who would now make the last of his many trips for us in the Virginia Iron Coal and Coke Queenair, was ready and waiting. Just before we boarded the airplane for our hop to Richmond, someone in the little crowd waving us off told me I had carried the city of Virginia Beach by 1,500 votes. That removed the last scintilla of doubt from my mind because I had lost Virginia Beach four years earlier. To me, the marked improvement over the earlier result more than likely indicated a trend that, statewide, would bring the big victory.

Confirmation came just a few minutes later. On our final approach to the runway in Richmond, I heard over the loudspeaker system of the airplane an inquiry from the FAA operator in the Richmond tower:

"Which one you got?"

I didn't hear Marshall's response, but the next audible transmission was, "YOU'VE GOT THE ONE!" We would soon learn for ourselves that I was "the one." Joe Weeks of radio station WRVA in Richmond declared Linwood Holton the winner of the gubernatorial election at the exact moment of our arrival in front of the John Marshall Hotel. It was then just about 8:30 p.m.

We found the crowd in the John Marshall ballroom nearly delirious. My family and I also were nearly delirious, though I was a little bit rattled because we soon lost Woody in the crowd, and I was concerned about whether his injury was more than a simple black eye. Nonetheless, I managed to get through at least some of the deserved thank-yous, and Woody surfaced, surprised that we were worried.

The next thing I saw I could hardly believe: Bill and Barry Battle, our friends before the race began, were pressing their way through that happy crowd to congratulate me, the Republican nominee, for beating Bill, my Democratic opponent. Losing that race had to be a shock for them, but they both had the courage and the integrity to publicly acknowledge and support the choice just made by the voters of Virginia.

"This is Virginia!" shouted an ebullient Sam Carpenter, Republican state chairman, over and over. And indeed it was Virginia, with southern civility at its finest. It had been a high-level campaign conducted on both sides by friends whose friendship survived the contest. We had stressed issues we considered important to the future of Virginia, but without any semblance of negative campaigning or mudslinging.

Later that evening, a small group gathered in our favorite eleventh-floor corner suite of the John Marshall. During the celebration, President Nixon called with congratulations and the news that Bill Cahill, Republican candidate for governor of New Jersey, had also won that day. Jinks was a little embarrassed when I turned from the telephone conversation with President Nixon and asked—I thought with humor—"Do you have something you can wear to the White House for lunch tomorrow?" She replied with some indignation, "Of course!" I therefore quickly and enthusiastically accepted the president's invitation for a celebratory lunch at the White House on the following day. And what a celebration it was to be.

One of Nixon's ambitions in life, I think, was to create a lasting Republican majority party. Here were two important additions: Virginia, which had never before elected a statewide Republican candidate, and New Jersey, where moderate Bill Cahill was the new Republican governor in a major urban, industrial northeastern state. There was to be much joy in the family dining room at the White House the next day when those principals, plus Vice President and Mrs. Agnew, gathered with their wives at a luncheon hosted by President and Mrs. Nixon to savor those important victories.

Still giddy with excitement but understandably exhausted as the adrenalin faded on election night, we finally slipped away to our hideout in the Howard Johnson Motel at the corner of Franklin and Belvedere. It had been quite a day.

Jinks and I both slept fairly soundly (considering), and as we awoke the next morning, I stretched happily and announced with unabashed delight, "I'd rather be governor of Virginia than president of the United States!" My election as a Republican was, in itself, the culmination of efforts to create two-party democracy in Virginia, but little did I then realize what a wonderful panorama of opportunities would be presented during the next four years: to reform the structure of Virginia's government, to enhance its environment, to develop Hampton Roads, and, at the top of the list, to help Virginia turn its back on its discriminatory past and become a model of race relations.

Big Stone Gap

I can't remember a time when the goal of one day being governor of Virginia wasn't simmering in the back of my mind. At our 1990 Big Stone Gap High School reunion, "Skinhead" Horton, one of my contemporaries, confirmed that that plan had been in my head from very early on. He told Dr. Bill Painter (another Big Stone native, recently retired from medical practice in Fort Defiance, Virginia) that "Linwood Holton was running for governor when he was in the fourth grade."

Skinhead was probably right. The thought could well have been born right about then in 1934 or 1935. That thought grew over the next couple of years, during which a local lawyer named Lewis McCormack was a candidate for Big Stone Gap's town council. I was in the habit of visiting Lewis in his over-the-drugstore office on my way home from school almost every day, and he took time from his not very busy practice to have long chats with me about law and politics. He also fanned the ambition of this would-be lawyer by letting me read the transcripts of evidence taken in the trial of Edith Maxwell.

A local woman, Edith had been charged and tried for the murder of her father by beating him about the head with the heels of her dancing slippers. Press accounts of the trial provided titillation for the entire community, but my insider's view was even better: I could read the actual testimony.

Lewis had been retained by the Commonwealth to assist in the prosecution, and he theorized that she had whacked her daddy with a mine axe. The axe was never found, however, and though she was convicted, intimations of paternal abuse were magnified in the national press, and after appeals and a second trial followed by a gubernatorial pardon, she served only a relatively minor sentence. The prosecutors should have been disappointed at the ultimate outcome five years later, but in the middle of the Depression, I am sure the monetary compensation Lewis received more than offset any great chagrin he may have felt.

At any rate, my first active campaigning arose from my friendship with Lewis. I handed out his campaign material, flying around door-to-door, tirelessly trying to do everything I could to see that my friend was elected to the town council. My parents even gave me permission to stay out later than usual so I could stand outside the room and listen while the election judges counted the ballots. But we lost, and I probably felt worse than Lewis did. I did not know then how many more defeats would become stepping-stones to reach the biggest prize.

Big Stone Gap was a little town of three thousand people when I was growing up. I don't think it's changed much even now. It was a kind of white-collar community for the coal company, the land company, and the railroad company—all corporate cousins. The railroad was owned by the land company, and the coal company operated in the bituminous coal fields of Southwest Virginia, which had a great many high-quality bituminous coal reserves.

I started becoming aware of things going on around me during the middle of the Depression. Dad was then vice president of the railroad company. He had come to Big Stone Gap in 1914 from Knoxville, Tennessee, where he was employed by the Southern Railway. Dad's boss—a yardmaster or holder of some similar post in Knoxville—was named president of the Interstate Railroad, and he brought Dad along to Big Stone Gap to be his secretary. (Male secretaries predominated in the railroad industry in those days.) Dad taught himself a great deal about the very complicated field of freight rates, and his expertise in that field brought him up the corporate ladder at Interstate Railroad.

Mother had come to Big Stone Gap from Middlesboro, Kentucky, with her family at about the same time Dad arrived. Mother's family came to Big Stone Gap because her father, Charles Oscar VanGorder, was superintendent of a plant in Middlesboro, Kentucky, belonging to the Teas Extract Company, which rendered tannin from chestnut wood for use in tanning leather. Apparently he was quite successful, because he was sent up to Big Stone Gap to open a plant there in about 1915 and later sent to open a similar plant in Marlington, West Virginia. So you might say that natural resources brought my parents together.

Dad tells the story that "Uncle" Jack Goodloe—no relation, but a well-known early pioneer in Big Stone Gap—introduced him to one of the attractive young VanGorder twins by taking him out to the Blue Hole, a deep swimming spot in the Powell River, to meet Edith VanGorder. At least, Dad always said that was where he met Mother, though she never confirmed it. But it was a fact that they did meet and that Dad courted her pretty assiduously, over the initial objection of Mr. VanGorder, who was concerned about his young daughter. Though she was almost twenty-seven and getting toward what was then considered old-maid status, Mr. Van, as he was called by his younger friends, was a little dubious about this "old man" hanging around Edith, one of his pretty twin daughters.

Dad overcame that fatherly concern. My parents were married in 1921, and through the years Dad gained Mr. Van's confidence and friendship. Ethel, my mother's twin sister, was married somewhat later, and she and her husband, Philip Libby, ultimately settled and reared three sons in Kingsport, Tennessee.

I was born on September 21, 1923, and my brother, Van, was only two years younger. We did everything together; whatever I did, Van wanted to do too. We had an older half sister, Louisa, whose mother, my father's first wife, had died in 1915. Louisa was twelve or thirteen years older than I. She never really lived with us at home when I was growing up because she was in college, and as soon as she graduated she began teaching school in St. Paul, a little town in Wise County thirty miles away from us. Although she was never a permanent or continuous presence in our household, I was always very fond of her, and she was of me. We spent a lot of time together on vacations when she was home from college and on her visits home on breaks from teaching in St. Paul.

Louisa was married in 1940 to Rolfe Morris, a former student of hers, a great guy, and just the right man for her. They made a wonderful couple, but he died of lung cancer soon after the end of World War II. She has been by herself since then, always with a circle of friends in Wise County.

Louisa never learned to drive. There was something about Dad having tried to teach her that made her averse to driving, so she always depended on public transportation. She continued to live in St. Paul until her retirement; only when public buses stopped serving St. Paul did she move to Abingdon. Louisa now lives in Brandon Oaks, an attractive retirement home in Roanoke, and at the age of ninety-six she was a lively participant in Williamsburg at all of the inaugural festivities when her nephew-in-law, Tim Kaine, took the oath as governor of Virginia in January 2006.

Louisa always had a very strong opinion on things relating to Virginia. For instance, she was in the audience when I made a speech in Abingdon sometime after I was out of office. Bill Wampler, then the congressman from that district, introduced me by saying, "*This* is the governor who knows that Virginia doesn't stop at Roanoke." (It was then the perception of most Southwest Virginians—and perhaps this still holds true—that the attitude of the Richmond establishment is that you've reached the end of the state when you get to Roanoke.) Louisa came up to me after that speech, looking up from her height of five feet, and said, "Lin, Virginia *does* end at Roanoke, *if* you're going east!"

Mother was a little more stern with us kids than Dad, but both of them were imbued with a strict, almost fundamentalist, Protestant ethic. We had to respect Sunday; we could read the funny papers, but we couldn't do much else. We were always present at Sunday school and church, the First Presbyterian Church of Big Stone Gap. Dad was superintendent of the Sunday school; Mother was active in the women's circle of the church, just a block away from our house. Both of my parents had a strong influence on us—particularly on me, I think.

It's interesting to go through some of Dad's correspondence (which my daughter Anne has now) and try to trace whether our ancestors were early in this country. I don't think Dad ever really reached any conclusion about where his family originated. Born in 1879, he left the family farm in Georgia when he was fourteen years old. The panic in 1893 was very serious for plantation owners in the South, and the ensuing depression probably caused Dad to leave the farm that year. He was self-sufficient and self-educated ever after, though he did acquire secretarial skills at the National Business College in Norfolk or Atlanta after he left the farm. Mother, on the other hand, went to high school and on to college for at least a year in Oxford, Ohio. I don't know why she didn't stay longer; she was extremely intelligent, but women in those days didn't very often go to college.

She and I always differed greatly in one major area. She would have to be considered a Bible fundamentalist (not what I would call an extremist, though possibly a literalist). It would have been hard to convince her that the Bible wasn't the final word on everything, and she came from a background where everyone believed that the Bible says that black people were created to hew the wood and draw the water. Black people were to serve, and white people were to be their superiors. I had some very serious discussions with her on this subject over the years, and she had begun to recognize reality a little more by the time she died, but she was still pretty prejudiced even in her last years. As far as I am concerned, it was her one and only blind spot.

I became interested in politics fairly early in life. Dad was a Democrat who supported Hoover's reelection. I found out later—I didn't know it at the time—that he had supported Al Smith in the 1928 election, partially because he resented the discrimination against Catholics that was prevalent in that election (and which was responsible for Virginia's vote for a Republican president in 1928). But also, most businessmen in the South at that time were southern Democrats. So just being a Democrat wasn't anything unusual, except that in 1928 the majority of Virginians were voting Republican against Catholic Al Smith, and Dad didn't do that. Of course, in 1928 I didn't know anything about this; I was only five years old.

I *did* know about the 1932 election, however. The family (including me) supported Hoover and was enormously disappointed at Roosevelt's election. In 1936, I had gotten into the election pretty strenuously for a thirteen-year-old. The *Literary Digest* polls were predicting the election of Alf Landon. I was supporting Landon just because he was a Republican and because my family was supporting him and because the *Literary Digest* was saying he was going to be elected president. I don't remember anything about the merits of Alf Landon, but later on I came to know his daughter Nancy very well. She was a moderate Republican in the U.S. Senate in the 1970s and 1980s.

Bill Rush, who owned and ran the Gulf service station down the street from us, a New Dealer from way back, ridiculed the *Literary Digest* polling device. I remember his getting pretty vehement toward me about my prediction of Landon's election because, as he explained it, "You rich people send in answers to these surveys, but the rest of us send them to the wastebasket." He was going to vote for a Democrat.

The night of the election, I'd gotten my hopes up in spite of the early radio broadcasts forecasting Roosevelt's win. My hopes were renewed when Dad came into my bedroom the next morning and said, "Well, I've got a new president for you!" But then he unfolded the Bristol paper, and there was a picture of Roosevelt. I was one disappointed kid.

My dad was interested in politics but only as a good citizen; he never ran for office himself. He was always fascinated with *my* interest in politics as it developed. He was convinced, I'm sure, before he died in 1968—having witnessed my campaign in 1965 and knowing about my plans to run again in 1969—that I was going to be the next governor of Virginia. I remember an incident at the Lonesome Pine Country Club, probably in 1968, when Dad pointed to me and announced to Dick Flanary (a prominent Democrat), "There's the next governor of Virginia!" Dick wasn't impressed, but he didn't argue with Dad, who was several years his senior.

One of the things that carried over from Big Stone Gap into my time as governor was my friendship with black people. Mary Catherine Cane and her husband, Walter, were among those. She bragged to reporters after I was governor that she had "bounced him on my knee": she probably did, but that was before my memory took hold. Walter was working for the railroad when I first knew him; he and Herbert Taylor were negotiators for their union, and they were both complimentary of what they called my father's "fairness" in their interracial negotiations. Herbert's wife, Athena, an older sister of Carrie Porter (more of her later), worked for several years in our home as a domestic.

All four of these people were intelligent, educated to the extent possible in the public schools available to them, and aware without apparent bitterness that they suffered second-class status as a result of the color of their skin. Mary Catherine and Walter ultimately came to manage the coal company's entertainment house for years. They maintained the property, planned and prepared necessary meals, and acted as hosts for the visiting officials who came often from Philadelphia. All four would have occupied a much superior social and economic status if they had enjoyed opportunities equal to mine.

Carrie Porter was a regular babysitter for my brother, Van, and me before Harriet was born. Carrie was more like an older sister than a babysitter and spent a lot of time with us. She took us to movies, played games with us, and took us on other outings. We were very aware of the fact that when seeing movies with Carrie, we had to climb the steep stairs to sit in the gallery reserved for black people, who weren't permitted into the main auditorium. I minded it, not for myself, but for Carrie. I remember Carrie commenting once about someone who used the word "nigger," letting me know—I don't remember her exact words—that it was an offensive term; because of that early conversation, I have had a passionate lifelong aversion to the word.

Another black friend in Big Stone Gap—a mentor, really—was John Cloud. He was an uncle, I think, of Mary Catherine Cane, and a dear, dear friend of mine. As the head manservant for former congressman Bascom Slemp, John ran that household while his wife, Millie, was the cook in a nearby residence. I would go by after school and visit with him. He had a great sense of humor; once when I took a visiting lady friend by to see him, he, assuming more seriousness than was merited, asked, "Has she got any money?" She enjoyed his humor and described his as a "squirky face." I think it was her recognition that his whole face twinkled when he smiled.

I got into the chicken business in high school, buying day-old chicks and raising them in brooders, then moving them to a chicken house Dad and I built, where they lived until they were two-pound fryers or broilers ready to sell. John helped me both pick the chickens and then dress them to sell. He could dress a chicken like you couldn't believe: dip it in hot water, slap it a couple of times, and it was clean! I got ten cents a pound "on foot" and an additional ten cents for each dressed chicken. John also advised me about my corn when I got into the sweet corn business later on: a little nitrate of soda helps form the grains, and don't eat corn after a frost; that will cause "flux."

A dedicated worker, John Cloud was loyal to all his friends and his employers. The last time I saw him was when I made a short visit back home to Big Stone Gap. Mary Catherine greeted me when I went to his house and said, "Uncle John is up in the garden." I went up there looking for him, but couldn't find him. I came back and reported, "He must be somewhere else." "No, he's up there," she replied, "but he's down on the ground. He can't get up, but he's up there pulling weeds." I went back to find him lying on the ground on his side, weeding the garden despite his crippling arthritis.

I met John through Jack Camblos. Jack Camblos and Harry Meador were two of the white pals I grew up with. We were nearly inseparable and pretty much the terror of the town for a while. Though Jack was my friend, I knew he was something of a bully, bull-headed and insensitive, and he once hurt our friend John's feelings very badly. When John confided to me this hurtful thing Jack had said to him, he introduced the conversation by saying, "Now, I know I'm a nigger . . ." I hardly heard what he said next. It didn't make any difference—the beginning of that sentence gave me pain that I still carry. That experience is one of the many reasons I've been as active as I have in trying to overcome discriminatory practices against black people.

One of my greatest treasures is the last letter that I received from John Cloud, still in its three-cent stamped envelope. It was written in his clear, firm hand on a blue-lined notepad on April 24, 1950. Reading it never fails to move me.

Dear friend:
this leaves me feeling very well to-day. I received your letter to-day. I was happy to hear from you but surprised. I am very glad to know that you are doing fine. I often think about you even though I don't see you. The people are very good to me here, but nothing like Big Stone Gap. I wish you were married I would like to come and stay with you for what I could eat (smile) if you had a farm I would come & stay with you some time any way. Before you get married you had better study about it hard & long because it is so hard to get a good wife now. I miss Millie so much I hate to go home, but I think I am going home this

summer. When you goes to see Mr. Jenks tell him about me, if he doesn't remember me tell him I am the one that was with his wife when Buster Moore killed his daughter tell Mr. Jenks to send me a little donation. I have not worked in two years now. It looks very much like the young men are going to have to go across the pond again I mean to war. I am glad that your mother & father are well & doing fine. I hope to hear from you again & if I don't I will always be thinking about you.

Sincerely yours,
John Cloud
P.O. Box 321
Coretta, W. Va

Besides my deep friendship with John Cloud, Elmer Miller and Kenneth Simpson (black contemporaries of mine) were my good friends and playmates until we were almost in our teens, when they had to be bused to another town if they wanted to go to high school, while I went on to the all-white Big Stone Gap High School. I think they probably dropped out finally, which was pretty typical of the way things went. But both of them were close friends of my youth.

Elmer was still alive when I was elected governor. I learned he was running a parking lot at Washington's National Airport, and I arranged for him to visit me in the Executive Mansion. I tried to persuade him to take a job as a butler while I was still governor, but he probably wouldn't have been very good at it, nor would he have enjoyed it. Fortunately for him, his wife wouldn't hear of moving from Washington into a southern city. She wasn't too sure they would be welcome in Richmond, even in the 1970s. But I did have that one final, very heartwarming visit with him before he died.

And then there was Peace. I expect Peace was a son of slaves, and I don't know how he and Dad ever got connected. During the seven years before Dad built the new house to which we moved in 1930 or 1931, we lived on Wood Avenue in the house where I was born. Behind the Wood Avenue house was a converted garage, which was used at the time as a home for Peace. He was an old man then, certainly from my perspective. Dad was forty-four when I was born, and Peace was considerably older than Dad. He did handyman chores and took care of the furnace; in return, Dad provided him a place to live; my sister Louisa thinks that he "just came with the place" when Dad rented it for our home. I have a great photo of me as a toddler reaching up to hold hands with Peace.

The main thing I remember about Peace is that I adored him. One day an old black man, walking with a cane and shuffling along, came up to our new house on Clinton Avenue on a Sunday morning. I was sitting on the stoop, waiting to go to Sunday school. He bent over the fence, still leaning on his cane, and said two words: "Peace dead."

I dashed into the house to report this awful news to Mother, which turned out to be true. Mother said sadly, "When I was taking care of Peace and he'd have those pains, I'd give him milk of magnesia and he'd get all right. Now that I wasn't there, he died." I think she oversimplified matters, but in any case, my old friend was gone.

My brother, Van, of course wanted to do everything I did, even choosing the U.S. Navy as I had. He spent a little time in Navy Air, one of the navy officers programs that the U.S. Navy ran at Emory and Henry College. When the war ended, he was still in that training program, but they released those trainees from the navy right away. He then went to Georgia Tech in about 1947, but a bit prematurely. Georgia Tech in those days was a little careless about admissions, and they gave him credit for math he had taken at Emory and Henry that didn't qualify him for the engineering course that he wanted to take at Georgia Tech. His grades took a nosedive, and the school was about to ask him to leave at the end of one or two semesters. But he and I talked to the dean and made an arrangement whereby he could go to night school, repeat some courses, and be reinstated. That is how it worked out. He was graduated as a mechanical engineer from Georgia Tech.

Van had a great family. He married Jessie Carpenter, a peppy, attractive little redhead from Delray Beach, Florida, whom he met at Agnes Scott College when he was at Georgia Tech, and they produced five children. After graduation he followed through on his longtime desire to go into the executive training program at Norfolk and Western Railway, after which he was promoted very regularly. I have lost track of the years he spent happily with the Norfolk and Western, but alcohol intervened, and his marriage was terminated by divorce. Van died in a senseless and tragic accident in 1975 unrelated to his career. I lost my only brother when he was only in his early fifties.

My sister Harriet was a latecomer to our little group. About the middle of 1934 there began to be talk from the adults around the house about the need for a little sister. This was long before today's practice of candid disclosure; in those days, the stork brought new babies, and the word "pregnant" was not in the acceptable vocabulary of ten-year-olds, which I was. Nevertheless, Bill

Moore, a twelve-year-old neighbor, and I began to make some surreptitious speculations, and we watched my mother's gradual expansion around the middle with intense interest.

There was more open family discussion of the coming blessed event during the late fall, and I, for some crazy reason, began to insist that this be a baby brother, not the little sister hoped for by all the other members of the family. I even asserted that I would help send her back if the new arrival was female.

Christmas came and went with no new sibling. But a new air of expectancy was prevalent soon after New Year's. I gave Bill Moore daily reports at school, and we were very smug about the fact that we older boys understood what was really going on. The night of January 8, 1935, I awoke when I heard my father making a mysterious phone call from the landing on the stairs near my room, where our only telephone was located. My immediate speculation that "This is it!" was confirmed a few minutes later. Out my front window I watched Doctor Kyle's car back out of the garage behind his residence, located catty-cornered from our house. He drove over and entered our house, but nothing happened that night.

There was obvious excitement at breakfast, and though there was no adult discussion, it was known that Dr. Kyle had come and gone and that Mother was still abed in the back bedroom upstairs. When we came home for lunch— in those days we had our big meal in the middle of the day—Dr. Kyle was in attendance. I remember his walking through our living room during the lunch hour, saying to my father, "We have plenty of time yet." But there was still no adult discussion about it with Van and me. I gave full reports of all of this to Bill Moore during the afternoon school session.

When I got home from school that afternoon, things were very quiet. Mother was asleep, and Dad, or maybe it was the nurse—a Miss Kilgore, who had mysteriously appeared in the meantime—took me up to Mother's room, which we entered quietly in order not to wake her, and there, bundled up in a large laundry basket serving as a crib, was a perfectly beautiful little red-haired doll. I dashed out to broadcast the news to my friends, including Bill Moore, and stayed out long enough that my awakened mother was anxiously inquiring, "Where is Linwood?" I think she was concerned that I might have been disappointed in not having that little brother, but I had retracted my preference and verbally rationalized to the others that it was "all right to keep her, since she's a redhead like me." That was my sister Harriet.

After growing up in Big Stone Gap, graduating from Big Stone Gap High School and Randolph-Macon Woman's College in Lynchburg, and teaching in Wise County public schools, Harriet married Wilmot Jones, who came from Pennsylvania. I don't remember whether Wilmot's family was part of the owners' organization of the three large Big Stone Gap companies—the land company, the coal company, and the railroad company—which were held basically by Pennsylvania interests. In any case, through the owners' group, Wilmot came to Big Stone Gap for orientation to the coal industry. He was a mining engineer by training, and he stayed in the coal business all of his life. The Wilmot Joneses still live in Beckley, West Virginia, and though retired, Wilmot has been a very successful consultant to various coal companies. Both of their two very attractive sons married, and though Bill Bey is now going through a divorce, his marriage produced for Wilmot and Harriet two grandchildren, both well, happy, and sources of joy for the whole family. The other son, David—to whom I refer as the Keeper of Davy Jones's locker—and his wife, Lori, round out that happy family.

Wonderful teachers had an impact on me in my early years. I was a fortunate kid because during the Depression, teaching provided the best careers available in town for the best-trained people. Those were my teachers, and I remember them clearly and with great fondness.

Bertha Mahaffy, my first-grade teacher, recommended that I skip most of the second grade because I could already read when I started the first grade. (I'd been through a couple of kindergartens and had had a lot of training at home.) Miss Matthews had me for a couple of weeks in the second grade, and then Miss Gibson introduced me to arithmetic in the third. Another memorable teacher was Gladys Meador, who taught me in fourth grade. Then there was French Taylor, who was my fifth-grade teacher. She was a strict disciplinarian and kept me after school one day because I didn't spell "Baptist" right on a test. I was to look it up in the dictionary, and after I found it I could go home. But I couldn't find "Baptist" in the dictionary and kept insisting to her that it wasn't there. She stood firm. Finally, when I went down through the alphabet, *a, b, c, d,* and got to "Ba*p*" instead of "Ba*b,*" I finally found "Baptist." Perhaps it was then that I began to learn the merit in persistence.

Miss Emma Duncan in the seventh grade led the transition to high school, and how well I remember Elisabeth Jackson, who taught high school English; Katherine McElroy, who taught math; Hugh Castle, who taught civics; and Roy Horne, the high school principal. All were just outstanding people with important and lasting influence on young people. Nell DiZerega, French Taylor's sister, was my debate coach. Our debate team, comprised of classmates Anne

Painter, Betty Asbury, and me, won the state debate championship under her tutelage when I was a senior in high school. One of the debate subjects I remember was something like "More Power to the Federal Government." I took the affirmative side for some reason, probably because it was assigned. That isn't the position I would take today!

I'm sure a major factor contributing to my eagerness to enter the political arena was something called "Boys State." Sponsored by the American Legion, the program was a mock set-up of the state government. Delegates were chosen from the schools throughout Virginia to attend Boys State at Virginia Polytechnic Institute for a week or two in the summertime and to conduct a model state government. The kids selected to attend were divided into jurisdictions based on the towns and counties in Virginia. They ran a government with an elected governor, lieutenant governor, and attorney general, just like the real thing. They even had a General Assembly and a Supreme Court.

I don't know which Virginia schools were invited to participate, but my school was among them. Two delegates, whom I don't remember, were chosen from my school; I was not one of them. But I was determined to go and convinced the principal, Mr. Horne, to send me when I offered to pay my own expenses. I paid them with profits from my chicken and corn businesses.

I would have liked to run for governor of Boys State, but I realized pretty soon after arrival on the VPI campus that a great deal of preliminary work had already been done on the gubernatorial election by students who knew a lot more about Boys State than I did. It was pretty much a foregone conclusion that the contest would be between only two candidates and nobody else, so I didn't get into the gubernatorial race at that stage. I was appointed to the model Supreme Court along with Dave Thornton, of Salem. Dave later became a Republican member of the Virginia State Senate, elected in the midterm election during my term as governor.

Even at Boys State I was casting far ahead, hoping and dreaming that one day I would be the *real* governor of Virginia.

College, War, and Harvard

There was never any discussion in my family about whether I would go to college. That was understood. And there was very little discussion even about *where* I would go because there was no problem about family tradition. Dad had not gone to college, and Mother had had only one, maybe two years of college at Miami University in Oxford, Ohio. Mother knew that Clifford Smith, one of the officials in the Stonega Coke and Coal Company (a corporate cousin of Dad's Interstate Railroad Company) had gone to Washington and Lee University, and everyone respected Clifford. Mother also knew that Washington and Lee was a small school, and I think that was attractive to all of us. So Washington and Lee is where I ended up. There was no admissions problem. Dean Gilliam *was* the Admissions Committee, priding himself on selecting boys who would be "congenial," but aside from his personal approval, the main requirement appeared to be whether you could pay the tuition fee of three hundred dollars per semester.

There were no extended trips to "look over" other colleges. (The only other colleges I had seen were Sullins, in Bristol, where I had attended a summer church conference, and the University of Virginia, which was the site of our debate championship.) When the time came, Dad drove me to Lexington, paid the registrar, helped lift my trunk out of the car onto the sidewalk outside the freshman dorm, and announced, "Well, I've got to get to Bluefield." Off he went, and there I was, on my own.

My first semester as a freshman went fairly well, and the curriculum was pretty standard. I enjoyed English literature under Professor Lawrence E. Watkin, author of the then-popular novel *On Borrowed Time*. He required some writing from his students, and I recall a few lines of a poem that were part of one of my submissions:

My teacher thinks that I'm a bard
But I must disagree; . . .
Rhyme and meter are not for me . . .
. . . But hope I'll get a C.

Watkin did much better:

I'll read it over and hand it back
And hope that you'll agree
That though full merit it may lack
. . . It's worth at least a B.

Math was a little more troublesome. The superannuated chairman of the English department, Dr. Moffitt, was my freshman advisor. On the basis of my performance in high school with geometry and trigonometry, which was pretty good, Dr. Moffitt put me into Math 151—calculus. Dr. E. K. Paxton was my professor, a very kindly old gentleman, but he and I never could get together on just what calculus was all about—and I still don't know. Dr. Paxton gave me a C, but I think he was responding to my interest, which was high, rather than to my knowledge of the subject.

The real shock, which changed the lives of all of us, came near the end of our first freshman semester. On December 7, 1941, someone came running into our group yelling, "The Japs just bombed Pearl Harbor!" No one knew how to react.

"Pearl Harbor?"

"What's that?"

"Where is it?

"Wow!"

We didn't fully grasp just how much the news of that fateful Sunday morning was going to affect our futures, though excitement did build up during the day. I remember standing in the quadrangle of the Graham-Lees freshman dormitory with a group of classmates when George Junkin Irwin, a World War I veteran who taught in the romance languages department, happened to walk by. He warned us to beware of rumors, which he predicted would become rife, and cautioned that we should be fully aware of the facts before making any significant decisions.

I don't remember whether I talked by telephone with Mother that day, but I do know I could not have talked to Dad. He was away at the time on a duck-hunting trip with Mr. J. D. Rogers, the vice president and officer in charge of the local branch of Stonega Coke and Coal Company. The first communication I had from Dad after Pearl Harbor was a letter dated December 9, 1941.

My Dear Boy, [I never heard that salutation from my father before or ever after; it reflected the emotion that enveloped him as he wrote that letter.]

Your letter and all the bad news came together. Mr. Rogers and I came home Sunday and did not know the "yellow peril" had stuck its teeth into a part of our country, until we arrived home. I thought Japan had more sense than to provoke a war with the U.S. and Brittain and then commit suicide. I think that country is done for.

When the bands come along and play the Star Spangled Banner and march songs it's hard to resist starting out to help and share in the glory. When I was just a little older than you are we had a little baby war with Spain. It didn't last long enough for me to get into it.

If possible try to control your actions and until you are a little older don't do anything rash. It may be that the Government may decide that it must have minors, or boys under 21, in which event there is nothing we can do about it but pray always for you and all of our men in our army, and work also for victory. We don't anticipate a victory without somebody fighting.

Have just heard the President and a later broadcast—it is now 11:15 p.m. and something is now being done to the Japs. . . . Everything will come out all right for the world, in the end but it surely looks somewhat "muddled" tonight. We just have to trust in the Lord and work and hope for the best. Surely will be glad to see you.

Loads of love from
Dad
and the family

As I read that letter almost sixty-five years later, I'm almost overcome with the same emotion that he must have felt when he wrote it.

I did find it "possible to control my actions" and not do anything "rash" until I was a little older, but not much. The leadership of President Roosevelt was inspiring indeed, and with rare exceptions, every citizen completely committed to winning the war. The U.S. Army, the U.S. Navy, and the Army Air Corps quickly developed programs leading to officer status for college "boys" who were close to completing their college careers and for some of the rest of us as well.

My preference was the navy—if you eat, you eat at a table, and if you sleep, you sleep in a bed (hammocks by then were obsolete)—and the navy's college program appealed to me. I enlisted in the navy in Lexington on "Lexington Day," July 4, 1942, a day when hundreds of us took the enlistment oath in towns or cities named Lexington throughout the country. My program, which later came to be called the V-12 program, reflected the navy's desire to obtain maximum college training for members of its officer corps, so those in my category who had completed some college work were pretty well assured that we would not be called to active duty before the end of our sophomore year. Washington and Lee held its first summer school session in 1942, which I attended, taking some math review courses and a fascinating physics course under the department head, Dr. Robert Dickey. He was a strict disciplinarian with very high criteria for performance, and that summer session under his tutelage was certainly as valuable, if not more, than any college course I ever took.

There were lots of smart students in that class, including some who had already graduated but were taking the physics class in anticipation of it being helpful to them in military service. My fraternity big brother, Robert F. Campbell Jr., who had graduated as a Phi Beta Kappa in 1942, was in that category. I competed well with all of them, motivated by the war and my fascination with the subject. I may not have led that class, but I was close to the top of it. My performance there earned me a position as lab instructor during my sophomore year, working with Dr. Dickey and Mr. Lothery, his assistant professor. My compensation was the six-hundred-dollar tuition for my sophomore year. I split that windfall with Dad: he only had to put out three hundred dollars, which I got in cash.

In the spring of 1943, at the conclusion of my sophomore year at Washington and Lee, I was called to active duty in the navy. Because of the navy's policy of "the more college the better," my first assignment was to a V-12 unit at the University of North Carolina in Chapel Hill. Captain W. S. Popham, USN-Ret., had been called back from retirement to be the skipper of that V-12 unit, and he encouraged us to devote our full energy to our college classes. We did have to attend a military orientation course taught by a marine lieutenant, but that didn't require much effort. The only other military requirement was that we muster every morning (so that we were accounted for) and then march to breakfast. Uniforms, tuition, books, and room and board were all paid by Uncle Sam, and we had salaries of fifty dollars per month. All I could think was "Whee!"—fifty dollars each month was a fantastic sum. We were on our own so long as we performed satisfactorily in our college classes. I did okay.

My averages at Washington and Lee had been at the B level; my average performance at Chapel Hill went up to A. I felt pretty smug about that until after the war, when I went back to Washington and Lee for a semester, and my average dropped back to the Washington and Lee B. The two schools just approached the grading business a little differently.

In February 1944, when I had completed two more regular college semesters at Chapel Hill, I was transferred—with a brief stopover at something called a pre-midshipman school in Asbury Park, New Jersey—to real navy duty at the U.S. Naval Reserve Midshipman School in Abbott Hall, Northwestern University, in Chicago. There were several of those schools throughout the country that trained ensigns who would subsequently serve as officers with units of the U.S. Navy almost anywhere in the world. Products of those midshipman schools were originally called "ninety-day wonders," though by the time I got there, the course had been extended to approximately four months. We received some training in seamanship, navigation, and gunnery, but the program's main objective was to indoctrinate us to respond instantly and affirmatively to any orders coming to us at any time through the chain of command. I completed the course and was commissioned an ensign in the U.S. Naval Reserve in June 1944.

A pleasant and romantic interlude began during some of the limited free time that was available to us while we were midshipmen—pleasant, that is, until its end. A Washington and Lee fraternity brother and friend, Lt. j.g. Robert "Buzz" Lee, was on the faculty of the midshipman school, though his assignment was on another campus than mine, and we had no official relationship at the school. Buzz had been stationed in Chicago for several months before I got there. He had become friends of the Evanston, Illinois, family of Mr. and Mrs. Leslie Parker, comprised of mother, dad, and two very attractive daughters who were about my age. Their daughter Lindley was married to a destroyer officer then serving in the Pacific, but the other, Leslie, was not married, though I suspect that their respective families assumed she would one day marry C. Danforth Killips, then on duty with the Army Air Corps in Europe.

But Buzz had other ideas; he had decided that Leslie was *the* girl for me. By his arrangement, I met the Parker family at an outdoor music festival on a beautiful spring evening at Ravinia Park in Illinois, just north of Evanston. Buzz knew what my reaction would be, and he was right. I was smitten. Happily, Leslie's reaction to me was positive as well, and we spent considerable time together during the weeks that remained of my tour in Chicago. But that friendship almost ended when I was transferred to my first duty station in San Diego, because I thoughtlessly did not follow up with any correspondence. I later had some 'splaining to do. I blamed that courtship lapse on several things: one, the excitement of a six-month assignment to an active submarine squadron headquartered in San Diego Bay on the USS *Beaver,* a submarine tender (only five out of a hundred applicants from my class were selected); second, an appendectomy at the naval hospital at San Diego, which, because of complications, was followed by a long convalescence at a hospital annex in Rancho Santa Fe, California; and third, my first transcontinental air flight in December 1944, when I was transferred back to the submarine school at New London, Connecticut, on the Atlantic Coast.

Our submarines were old. They were designated "S Boats," built in the 1920s, and, though they had made some war patrols off the islands of Alaska in the early part of World War II, they had been retired from combat service and were consigned to orientation and training duty for officers and enlisted submarine recruits. But they were submarines! We were diving them in the very deep Pacific Ocean waters off San Diego, making mock attacks on U.S. Navy surface antisubmarine vessels and conducting evasive tactics while those surface vessels made mock attacks on us. We were getting close to the Real Thing.

My first dive was a lulu. We had boarded the boats on a Sunday night, and since we had trainees on board as well as the regular crews, our quarters were less than commodious. My bunk was a canvas fold-down affair in the forward torpedo room. For some reason I don't remember, I was still asleep at the beginning of our first dive. The diving klaxon of course awakened me, but I wasn't even sure what the commotion was all about. It was soon apparent to me that the boat was angled downward and that we were diving, and then an announcement came over the loudspeaker system to the effect that there was a "fire in the forward torpedo room," where I had been sound asleep. It turned out to be not quite as dangerous or exciting as it sounds because the crew soon discovered that it was only an electrical short that had caused some smoke, and they quickly corrected it. That excitement turned out to be the only aberration in my safe experience on submarines, which never included any combat duty or any more fire alarms.

Our ward room (the officers' dining room) was comprised of nothing more than a booth such as those in the drugstores or ice cream parlors of the 1940s, but our very carefully selected crews were completely congenial, everybody knew everybody else's job as well as his own, and, being very young, we adapted soon to the compactness.

We did have one opportunity in San Diego to compare what we were doing on the old boats with what we might someday do on the "fleet boats" that were joining the fleet in the Pacific as soon as they could be built and commissioned. The USS *Trepang,* a brand-new boat built either in New London at the Electric Boat Company or at the Navy Yard in Portsmouth, New Hampshire, stopped by our little operation in San Diego Bay on its way to combat duty in the South Pacific. Compared to what we were on, it was a luxury hotel. It whetted our appetite to get on with our training and really take part in winning the war.

The submarine school at New London—certainly the finest submarine training operation in the world—kept us pretty busy. We learned about diesel engines, electric motors, torpedoes and torpedo tubes, batteries (huge batteries), more navigation, seamanship, fire-control problems, all new ground to most of us. But the programs were excellent, and we were fascinated with all of it, diving periodically in even older submarines in the very shallow waters of Long Island Sound.

Colleges were more than eager to support the war effort; requirements for degrees were interpreted liberally for former students now in the military service. Washington and Lee was no exception, and I was given elective credit toward my degree for completion of both midshipman and submarine schools, as well as transfer credits for the college courses I took at the University of North Carolina. Frank Gilliam, dean of students at Washington and Lee, who considered each of us as his very own, wrote my father after I had transferred to a Pacific submarine squadron in Pearl Harbor. He explained that he had reviewed my record, including the elective credits from the military, and explained, "Lin has enough of the right credits for a bachelor of *science* degree in commerce, but not for the bachelor of *arts* degree in commerce that he was seeking. What shall we do?" Dad, who had never seen a male Holton's name on a college degree, promptly replied, "Why don't you give him whatever you've got!" The diploma for a B.S. in commerce, cum laude, arrived in the mail very shortly.

Even with all the demands of submarine school, I could not get the memory of that pretty girl in Evanston out of my mind. From New London I wrote her a long letter and tried to explain the absence of correspondence by the distractions that I've mentioned, and I very aggressively suggested to her that she and I should give serious consideration to marriage. I had no idea how she would react. Maybe she would laugh at me, or tell me I was crazy, or, worst of all, ignore me completely. None of that happened. She replied promptly, conceding that during our time together in Chicago, we were "racing our motors" over each other, and even suggesting in that first letter or in another soon thereafter that "we meet under the clock" in the Biltmore Hotel in New York—just like the movies—to see where things might go from there.

It didn't take long to work that out. We had a very pleasant weekend together in New York, including being entertained at dinner by friends of her family, and our motors started racing all over again. A whirlwind courtship followed, mostly by mail, and by the time I completed submarine school and enjoyed a couple of weeks of leave immediately thereafter, I had visited her and her family in Chicago, and she had joined me on a train trip for a visit with my family in Big Stone Gap. At the end of my leave, she was wearing an engagement ring.

That love affair continued by mail from the time I left for San Francisco in June 1945, to await transportation to Pearl Harbor, until I returned to the States on about the first of March 1946. Leslie wrote me almost every single day, numbering the envelopes on the outside serially so I would know that I was receiving them in proper sequence. I did my best to respond, though there were many days at sea when mailing letters wasn't feasible.

I thought I detected a slight coolness when Leslie met me at the train station in Chicago upon my return from the Pacific. I thought maybe I was imagining it because I wasn't feeling very well. I had been desperately sick for the entire trip on a submarine tender from Pearl Harbor to San Francisco. The illness was the result of drinking some fresh (probably green) coconut milk offered before dinner by a young, recently freed Filipino, while I was at the Royal Hawaiian in Waikiki the night before we sailed. That stuff had caused an explosion in my gastrointestinal system, and I was still feeling the effects when I arrived in Chicago ten days later.

Within a few days, I received the shock of my life. Les had concluded that I didn't love her. Perhaps this was because of my seeming diffidence when I was just really feeling sick, and also maybe my not-so-great attempts at keeping up my end of the letter writing made her think this was true. At any rate, in the course of the next few minutes, the ring was off and so was the engagement.

It was months before I got over that shock. But it proved to be a blessing for both of us. She soon married Dan Killips, who had returned from Europe to Chicago some months before I returned from the Pacific. They moved to Arizona in the 1970s and had a happy married life until Dan died sometime around 1995. Les and I might have married (even though we hadn't planned a wedding until I completed law school), and the marriage might have been successful. But I doubt it. Leslie had enjoyed a somewhat more protected environment with a little more affluence than my avowed goals might have brought her—and she may not have been prepared to take the risks that a partnership with me would have entailed. For my part, I certainly was not prepared to forego my ambition to become Virginia's governor—despite the uncertainties that pursuit would involve—and take up the staid life of a corporate lawyer in her father's firm in Chicago. I didn't know then that several years later I would meet and marry the love of my life, and for a while I was one dejected lad.

When I graduated from submarine school in May 1945, I was ordered to serve as part of the pre-commissioning crew of a submarine, the USS *Lionfish*, that was being built in Philadelphia. Several months would elapse before the sub would be ready for sea, so with those orders, I could anticipate only non-combatant duty in Philadelphia, probably through the end of the war.

I can't say that I made any real contribution to the war effort as a result of my service on submarines because by the time I completed submarine school, the submarine war was substantially over. Serving on a new construction boat in Philadelphia would really have been just spinning my wheels, so when the executive officer of the submarine school made an energizing speech to us, saying, "You guys ought to recognize that there's still important work out there in the Pacific and you ought to be involved in it," I was galvanized into applying for a transfer from the no-action Philadelphia assignment to the Pacific, where I served with a relief crew in Pearl Harbor beginning in June 1945, awaiting assignment to a fleet submarine for war patrols. We didn't then recognize how close we were to war's end.

When U.S. submarines came back from about two months of patrol, the typical protocol was for the entire crew to be sent to someplace like the Royal Hawaiian Hotel for rest and recreation. A relief crew took over their submarines for needed maintenance and preparation for the next patrol. I was an engineering officer in a squadron of submarines—I think it was Squadron 18—serving in Pearl Harbor on a submarine tender named for a constellation, the *Euryale*. A submarine tender is a mother ship stocked with supplies including food, fuel, and all the supplies for a squadron or division of submarines. The tender was also equipped with elaborate machine shops and skilled artisans to provide whatever maintenance and repairs might be needed by the subs after patrols.

I was in Pearl when the atomic bombs were dropped on Hiroshima and Nagasaki. It was years before the catastrophic significance of those bombs sank into those in my age group. We never questioned the "rightness" of the war. Hitler was universally regarded as an enemy of civilization itself, and the Japs had attacked us, so our reaction to those bombs was immediate and focused: "Home alive in forty-five!"

Those explosions were followed in three days by a false end-of-the-war report that the Japanese had surrendered. That report triggered a huge demonstration of fireworks in Pearl Harbor that I witnessed from the *Euryale*. Every ship in Pearl Harbor (and there were a bunch of them there) fired off all their star shells as a result of that false report. Those shells were loaded with pyrotechnics that provided an incredibly brilliant light when fired. Even the fireworks display I saw from the State Department balcony on July 4, 1976, celebrating the two hundredth anniversary of American independence, failed to equal what I saw in Pearl that summer of 1945.

The *Euryale* and our submarine squadron were transferred to Guam immediately after the real Japanese surrender was announced by President Truman on August 14, 1945. We were transferred to Sasebo, Japan, in late September, and had a short tour there. Our job was to demilitarize the Japanese submarine fleet—what was left of it. Each of us ensigns, very young junior officers, had the responsibility for two or three submarines with Japanese crews still on them. Every morning we inspected the ships to see that they were maintained in the same condition as they were at the time of surrender. We established a very friendly relationship with the Japanese crews, who seemed relieved that the war was over. Certainly they were both submissive and cooperative.

In mid-October, the whole *Euryale* squadron went up to Kure on the Sea of Japan, where we destroyed some two-man submarines found there in a warehouse. Somewhere we acquired possession of three huge Japanese submarines that were basically experimental. These Japanese subs were enormous: two were 5,500 tons, and one was 3,500 tons, contrasted with our standard "fleet boat," which weighed in at about 1,800 tons. All three of the Japanese subs had cylindrical tanks on the top of their main hulls in which one or more aircraft with folded wings could be stored. These subs had catapults designed to launch the aircraft into the air. When the airplane finished its mission, it could return, land on the sea close to its mother sub (equipped with a boom to pick up the plane), and be stuck back into its hangar-cylinder.

That was the concept. Because it was experimental, that Japanese sub created a lot of curiosity in our naval administration, and they wanted some of them back in Pearl Harbor. So my only real underway mission in the war was as chief engineer on the ex-Jap I-401, while transiting it from Sasebo to Pearl Harbor, with stops at Guam and Eniwetok to pick up lubrication oil. That trip took almost thirty days and provided a double New Year's Eve on January 1, 1946, as we crossed the international date line. We were always on the surface; we never dove the Japanese submarines.

We arrived at Pearl and exhibited the Japanese I-401 to visitors for a few days; later the navy used them for target practice out at sea. An AP news article on March 21, 2005, reported that the wreckage of the ex-Jap I-401 had been found by a research diving team on the ocean bottom near the Hawaiian island of Oahu. The Japanese I-400 series of subs didn't really have anything new about them, and the concept of making them aircraft carriers wasn't realistic. It didn't work, and nobody else tried it. After that trip, I was ordered back to the States, and I finished up my military service in an administrative job in Washington, D.C.

After being discharged from active duty in August, I went back to Washington and Lee for one semester. Though my goal was law school, I was in effect turned down for the Harvard class entering in September 1946 and wasn't actually admitted to Harvard until February 1947. At Washington and Lee, I took some courses that I enjoyed: Shakespeare, French conversation, psychology, and one of my favorites—President Gaines's History of Religion. I was getting used to reading and studying again before starting law school, which was supposed to be a very big challenge. When I finally got to Harvard, however, I found it pretty easy; at least I didn't study night and day, and my primary interest—politics—continued unabated.

I barely gained admission to the place. My grades at Washington and Lee were pretty close to a B average, just borderline for Harvard. My application for admission was answered in a polite letter by Warren Seavey, a senior professor of agency and torts and then chairman of the Harvard Admissions Committee. I could read between the lines: Mr. Seavey was really telling this returning veteran (I was still a navy lieutenant, j.g.) that they would be letting him down as easily as possible, and I was absolutely sure the next letter would begin, "We regret to inform you . . ."

But I wasn't going to take no. Preempting a rejection, I shot off a Western

Union telegram requesting an interview. Somewhat to my surprise, Mr. Seavey responded with a quick yes. And one Saturday soon after, I found myself in Cambridge, Massachusetts, seated across the desk from him.

"Have a cigarette?" he offered politely, before carefully selecting one for himself. I joined him. "Keeps you thin," he commented somewhat defensively. "I see that your first name is Abner," he continued, riffling through my application papers. I had an intuition just then, so I sat on the impulse to make a sassy rejoinder about my first name and instead responded very positively to Mr. Warren *A.* Seavey.

"Yes sir. That's an old family name."

My instinct was right. Turned out, *his* name was Abner, too—Warren *Abner* Seavey, which must have clinched the deal, because in spite of my misgivings, I got in. But not immediately; I followed his suggestion to withdraw my September 1946 application and instead successfully sought admission to the somewhat less crowded class that would enter in February 1947.

There was more than a little of the Mount Everest "Because-it's-there" syndrome in my motivation to go to Harvard. I had no family, friends, or alumni connections with the school. The University of Virginia had (and has) an outstanding law school. The law school at the University of Michigan had been recommended to me by a friend, and I was impressed with the photographs of the very attractive quadrangle that housed its law school. In my "negotiations" with Mr. Seavey, he suggested I also consider the University of Pennsylvania and maybe one or two others. But Harvard was, and is, Number One, and I was determined to take it on.

I was right: attending law school at Harvard was a marvelous experience. It was not particularly difficult for me, though there were six hundred very talented, highly competitive fellow students in my class. Many of them struggled to be first in our class, and many others simply struggled. I was somewhere in the middle, and comfortable competition with that crowd built tremendous self-confidence.

My grades reflected my middle status, though I got a 78 in Property I under Professor W. Barton Leach. Of all the faculty egos at Harvard, and there were many, his was the greatest. I remember his imperialistic bearing and his black homburg—none other was ever seen in Cambridge. He drank nothing but Scotch on the rocks, and at one of our get-to-know-the-freshmen parties, he looked pained and insulted when offered a glass of pink punch.

My 78 was comprised of a 45 (an unheard-of high mark on the Harvard grading scale) for the first semester of Property I under Leach, and a 33 for the second semester under Percy Bordwell, a visiting professor from the Midwest who conducted the conveyancing part of Property I. The combined 78 was among the very top scores.

But in the first semester of my freshman year, I got a 55—borderline low—in criminal law under Professor Sheldon Glueck. That was the only grade given during the first two semesters (eight months) of law school, and that near-failing grade startled me enough to make me spend a little more time on the books during the second semester. My ranking at the end of the first year was slightly into the upper half of the class rankings, so I dealt with the last two years with quiet confidence, and stayed all three years, as I remember, just inside that upper half.

Professor Austin Scott was not impressed with my examination paper in his trusts course—I got another borderline 55 in that third-year class. Even now I occasionally look at my diploma (which I can't read—it's in Latin) just to make sure I really made it through.

As a student I was fairly passive, seldom volunteering in class. I was somewhat bored with the tedious questions on elusive points of law raised by the professors or eager classmates, most frequently nerds competing for first place in the class or a position on the *Harvard Law Review*. Their ambitions were for a clerkship with a Supreme Court justice or a prominent spot in academe.

I was once called upon in Judge Calvert MacGruder's torts class to suggest an appropriate remedy for a gentleman who had unknowingly purchased an unsound mule. Judge MacGruder, obviously referring to my southern accent, suggested that I should have an answer: "Mr. Holton sounds like he knows about mules." I now know that I should have suggested, based on the doctrine of *caveat emptor* (let the buyer beware), that the buyer just "hook it off" on somebody else. Unfortunately I wasn't quick enough to make that response in class.

I did, however, enter with a competitive spirit into the Ames Competition, a tournament-style competition among the various clubs at the law school, and a prominent feature of the Harvard Law School program. In the early stages, appellate briefs are followed by oral arguments on hypothetical cases before upperclassmen and then before successively more sophisticated panels (including a Supreme Court justice in the finals) throughout the tournament.

My group formed the Mentchikof Club, naming it for Soya Mentchikof, the first woman instructor at Harvard Law School, and choosing our members solely on the basis of their determination to win the competition. And we almost won. We progressed through each of the six semesters but came out second-best. We lost in the finals to a club whose argument was presented principally by George E. Lee, an African American classmate from Baltimore. My somewhat prejudiced mother was dubious about my protestations that "Mr. Lee really *was* better."

Ernest J. Brown, who conducted the classes I took in constitutional law and federal taxation, came to the law school just before our class did, and more or less adopted our class and we him, a relationship that continued through our fiftieth reunion. Professor Brown was a great person who loved the law, and *only* the law (he never married), and attended all of our five-year reunions through the fiftieth. When he died in 2001, he was something over ninety and was still active as a utility lawyer in the Department of Justice Taxation Section in Washington.

It wasn't all academics for me. I was an addicted fan of the St. Louis Cardinals baseball team at the time, and attended most of the games at Boston Braves Field when the Cardinals were playing there. Those were the days of Terry Moore, Enos Slaughter, Stan Musial, Red Schoendienst, Whitey Kurowski, and Marty Marion—legendary players to a man. Billy Southworth, a recovering alcoholic whom I had first seen when he was a player-manager with the Asheville, North Carolina, Cardinals in the late 1930s, got a big hit as a pinch hitter in a game I attended. He was still the St. Louis Cardinals manager during my days at the law school.

Nicholas Riasonovosky, who roomed in the same house with me during my first semester at law school, often accompanied me to these games. His White Russian family had escaped through China after the 1917 revolution, and he is today a noted scholar in Russian history. Brilliant, blessed with a most pleasant and fascinating personality, he never wasted a second: he read the *New Yorker* between pitches at the ball games but could recite the batting average of every player from memory.

Linda Bowen and Phyllis MacDonald also played a part in the lighter moments of my Cambridge tour. Linda was a legal secretary in Boston whom I met at the bar in McBrides, a well-known watering hole on a prominent corner in the middle of Harvard Square. Bob Campbell, my big brother at the Beta house at Washington and Lee, who was then on a Nieman Fellowship at Harvard, began talking with Linda over a beer. I was taking a break with Bob in my very early days in Cambridge, and I, too, began to chat with Linda. Whenever I felt restless under the constraints of academe, it was great fun and most relaxing to have another beer with Linda.

I met Phyllis when she attended a law school function with my classmate

Jack Hoffman, and later we became quite close friends. It was she who initiated me into skiing, something Jinks and I have enjoyed together throughout all the years of our marriage. Phyllis got me on skis at a country club near Cambridge, but the extent of her instruction was to show me how to snowplow—a method for slowing down that involves pointing the tips of the skis at each other. Today the kids say, "Make a pizza with your skis," meaning, point the skis to a wedge, à la a slice of pizza. My ten-dollar skis were secondhand surplus from the army store and had bear-trap bindings with no safety-release features. I'm lucky not to have broken both legs.

The outstanding political event during my law school tour was the Truman-Dewey election in 1948. Even then I expected, and hoped, that Thurmond's Dixiecrat ticket would go nowhere. Henry Wallace's race brought only ridicule; I attended a rally for him on Harvard's campus when his "My Uncle Joe wants peace" speech just brought laughter.

I was almost a lone supporter of Dewey. Most of my classmates supported Truman—and I felt a great deal of trepidation about "my guy" before that election. We heard Truman on the radio promising everything to everybody from the back end of a campaign train. We heard Thomas Dewey, in many ways not much of a candidate, in Cleveland, Ohio, promising only "good government." My trepidation was not unfounded. With the exception of Vice Dean Livingston Hall (the Dewey manager for Massachusetts that year), everybody else recognized by 11:00 a.m. the day after the election that Truman had upset Dewey. I must confess to having felt relief that Truman's strong civil rights stand had not defeated him. When I saw Dean Hall on the campus that morning, he was still confidently awaiting the returns from the rural precincts. I don't think he ever gave up, and he may still, from his heavenly perch, be awaiting those rural returns.

Erwin Griswold was our dean at the time, and an outstanding figure. I came to know him much better during the late 1970s and 1980s while I was serving as president of the U.S. Supreme Court Historical Society, and through our mutual membership in the Metropolitan Club of Washington, D.C., I had some interesting correspondence with him about civil rights in the South, and he was very complimentary about the positions I had taken as governor with respect to compliance with the requirements of *Brown vs. Board of Education*. He continued, however, to refer to me as one of "Seavey's estoppels." He told me that was the term the law school faculty used for those of us whom Seavey admitted to the law school in spite of minimal admission credentials, simply because of Seavey's admiration and awe for those of us whose applications to

Harvard originated in some part of the war zones of World War II and arrived in Cambridge with a picture of the applicant in uniform. The faculty recognized the borderline nature of some of his acceptances, but out of respect for him, they chose not to reverse his decisions. I remain forever grateful to have been one of Seavey's estoppels.

Roanoke, My GOP Incubator

3

The year was 1949. Now fresh out of Harvard with a law degree tucked under my arm, I was ready to "follow my bliss"—namely, get a job in a law firm and, at the same time, further my strong political ambitions.

It was clear to me that the place to begin working on my long-term political goals was Roanoke. It was a young city without the strong Democratic tradition that had guided politics in Richmond and Lynchburg since plantation days. I was not familiar enough with the Hampton Roads area to appraise the potential there, and "Northern Virginia" in 1949 was, from a population standpoint, comprised mostly of Arlington County, a bedroom suburb where there were lots of federal employees who were not necessarily Virginia voters.

As I explored job possibilities after my second law school year, it turned out that getting a job in Roanoke was not so easy. There were two large firms in Roanoke I had my eye on. Perk Hazlegrove, whom I had met through Norfolk and Western Railway friends of my father, was a senior partner in one of those firms. Perk was friendly, but he pointed out that the office space in his firm was already too full. Joe Smith, the youngest associate, even had to practice law from the office library.

Frank Rogers was head of the other large firm in which I was interested. He was also fairly friendly, but he suggested that my zero chance of a job at his firm could *possibly* have been improved if I had only gone to the right law school—the University of Virginia, of course! (Unknown to either of us at the time, Frank would be my father-in-law in just a few years.) Cliff Woodrum and Alan Staples, senior partners in a smaller firm, had just hired Kossen Gregory and didn't think their practice was large enough to justify a second associate at the time.

So back I went to Harvard's Warren Abner Seavey, who had become my friend and mentor. I told him of my troubles in Roanoke and about the somewhat tempting possibility that Judge Peter Woodbury, of the U.S. Court of Appeals for the First Circuit, might employ me as his clerk for a year at what was then a substantial salary—three thousand dollars a year. I would be located in Vermont or New Hampshire. Seavey would have none of that. "Go back," he said. "Go back to Virginia. The South needs you young people who have been in these Ivy League schools to go back and get into politics."

I considered that not only good advice, but exactly the advice I had been hoping for. I went back to Roanoke to once again see C. E. Hunter of the two-man firm of Hunter and Fox. I had interviewed with them previously but had been turned down because they were not in a position, Mr. Hunter told me, to expand the firm. Following up on a hint from Charles D. Fox Jr., the other partner, who had seemed more agreeable to expanding, I knocked at their door again. This time I won the day by telling Mr. Hunter I was definitely going to settle in Roanoke. Further, my confidence in my ability to "make it" was so strong that I would work for one year for nothing, and prove my value to his firm. No doubt taken aback, he offered me seventy-five dollars a month, and I became an associate of Hunter and Fox in September 1949.

It was a beginning, and though I might starve in the process, I was on my way. Linwood Holton had put out his shingle.

My assurances to Hunter and Fox that I would be a good investment were pretty well redeemed. Following some on-the-job-training conducted by each of the seniors, I soon began to do all of the firm's title work. Those were fairly routine assignments, mostly from financial institutions, which included searches of the official land records to ensure that there were no defects on the title of properties that were to become collateral for loans at the financial institutions. The fees from that work were soon enabling me to earn my keep—the seventy-five-dollar-a-month salary.

A little extra money came to me during my first month at Hunter and Fox, when I was appointed by Dirk Kuyk, judge of the Hustings Court of the City of Roanoke, to defend an indigent defendant charged with malicious wounding. I think the state-allowed fee for that service was twenty-five dollars, which I was allowed to keep. My client, a relatively small but very feisty black man of about thirty, had been involved in an altercation with an acquaintance at a nightspot on High Street in Roanoke. He had used his knife on the stomach of the larger man, resulting in the current charges—not my client's first offense. His record at the courthouse (each offense having been entered on a 3 x 5 index card) was about an inch thick. In a trial that fell on my birthday in

1949, the jury convicted my client. I like to think that sympathy for his inexperienced lawyer affected the jury's decision to sentence my client to only one year in the penitentiary instead of the many years they might have pronounced.

I had another first experience that year. It was with the State Corporation Commission. I prepared and sent to the commission the papers necessary to obtain a charter for the Crelas Corporation. I was surprised and flattered, a few days after sending the papers to Richmond, to receive a call from M. B. Watts, the clerk of the commission—flattered to receive attention from someone I considered a very high official, and surprised that he was attending to so small a detail. He suggested that my draft of the charter be amended to say that the corporation would have power to "have the property surveyed" in lieu of the words in my draft that read "to survey." His position, more prevalent than now, was that corporations were not permitted to perform services that were allowed to be performed only by individuals who were properly certified in their respective professions—in this case, certified engineers.

I was amused, after notice of the issuance of the Crelas Corporation's charter was published in the press, to have an inquiry from J. W. Lindsay, an older lawyer whose office was in the same building as ours and who had befriended me. "Is that an Indian name?" he asked me one day at lunch, evidencing satisfaction with himself for perceiving the origin of the corporation's name. He seemed a little disappointed to learn that he hadn't guessed right when I told him, "No, it's a contraction of the names of the owners of the corporation— Mr. Cress and Mr. Lucas."

I then began to do some property-damage recovery cases for insurance companies, beginning with the Maryland Casualty Company, one of Mr. Hunter's clients. During my three years plus with Hunter and Fox, I also conducted automobile personal injury cases for the Hartford Accident and Indemnity Company as well as the United States Fidelity and Guaranty Company. These became client companies that stayed with me when I left Hunter and Fox.

As a result of my successful beginning with Hunter and Fox, I was made a partner of the firm on January 1, 1950. I don't remember the percentage of the firm income allocated to me, but the minimum drawing account of $120 a month made me almost self-sufficient.

Probably my most significant contribution to the work of that firm was my assistance to Mr. Hunter in the preparation and trial of a case that arose out of the improper assembly of a large batching bin used in the manufacture of concrete blocks at a plant owned by a man named Winter Ferguson. The collapse of the structure resulting from the incomplete assembly killed a worker and caused very substantial property damages. We didn't handle the death case, which was covered by workman's compensation, but we did sue to recover the property damages. We obtained a verdict of $199,000, the largest for property damages ever won in the Roanoke area up to that time. Mr. Hunter conducted the case, but I was with him all the way in the preparation and trial.

A very significant happenstance that ultimately affected my entire future took place in December 1950. I had paused on Luck Avenue beside the Roanoke Book and Stationery Company to chat with Andy Coxe, one of the younger partners at Woods, Rogers, Muse and Walker. Andy and I were fans of the comic strip *Pogo*, and we frequently shared hilarity as we recalled something from a recent strip. As Andy and I were laughing there together, a young lady whirled around the corner from First Street and paused to speak before heading toward her car. Andy thereupon introduced me to Jinks Rogers, daughter of his senior partner, Frank Rogers. I distinctly remember that my first impression was, "That's the most beautiful smile I've ever seen!" But that was the end of that for about a year.

In December 1951, I received a telephone call from Jean Gill (nicknamed "Pill"), a popular member of a group of my contemporaries, inviting me to a Christmas party at her home. I declined on the grounds that I had scheduled a visit to my parents' home in Big Stone Gap on the day of her party. "Oh," she said, "I'm so sorry. I had hoped to arrange a blind date for you with one of my best friends." "Who is that?" I asked. When she responded that it was Jinks Rogers, I—remembering that smile—quickly changed my Big Stone Gap travel plans and accepted her invitation. At the time, Jinks was working for the State Department—actually the CIA in Washington—but she would be at home in Roanoke for the holidays. After our very successful blind date at Pill's party, we began arranging to see each other as frequently as we could, either in Roanoke or in Washington.

Things became progressively more serious during the summer of 1952, even though Jinks declined my invitation to ride with me on the "Eisenhower Special" from Roanoke to Lynchburg when the general's train was going through town on a campaign trip. She was vigorous in her refusal. "To be seen *publicly* with a *Republican*?" was her horrified reaction. In spite of my Republican "handicap," and in spite of an even more serious handicap in her father's eyes—that I sang in the church choir, a not very masculine thing to do—at the end of my ride on that train from Roanoke to Lynchburg I was able to report to Cynthia Newman, a political friend from Fairfax County who boarded the train in Lynchburg, "Jinks said 'yes'!" Jinks did not, however, make an immediate conversion to the Republican Party; that took some time. We were married on January 10, 1953.

Our first year of marriage was more than busy. It included focus on the gubernatorial campaign of Ted Dalton, and at the same time, Purnell Eggleston and I began the negotiations that resulted in the creation on January 1, 1954, of the law firm of Eggleston and Holton. Purnell had come to the firm of Hazelgrove, Shackelford and Carr after graduating from the University of Virginia Law School in 1947. He had left that firm and was working as a sole practitioner by the time we began our talks in 1953. I was not unhappy at Hunter and Fox, but I think Mr. Hunter was a little anxious about my activities outside the law practice, and I was increasingly aware that my future political ambitions would probably be better served with the greater independence I would have in my own firm. Purnell and I therefore joined forces with just a handshake and never a written partnership agreement, in what was to become a most pleasant and successful undertaking. We differed at times, but never seriously, and to this date I have not met anyone with a sense of integrity more sterling than Purnell Eggleston's.

Bob Glenn joined our firm somewhere around 1960, and Caldwell Butler joined us in late 1962. Caldwell also had begun his practice at Hazelgrove, Shackelford and Carr, and was practicing alone when he was elected as a Republican to the Virginia House of Delegates in 1961. The firm practiced as Eggleston Holton Butler and Glenn until I was elected governor in 1969. Caldwell left the firm when he was elected to Congress in 1971. Purnell and Bob Glenn had serious differences later on, which resulted in Purnell's leaving the firm, but that firm still exists under the name of Glenn, Feldman, Darby and Goodlatte, and is a significant part of the legal scene in Roanoke. Bob Glenn, though recently officially retired, is still associated with it.

He never knew it, but Governor Bill Tuck unwittingly whetted and abetted my political ambition. He had won the 1945 Democratic nomination for governor of Virginia (tantamount in those days to winning the election) with a vote that amounted to only 6.2 percent of the adult population of Virginia. I was appalled, and I attributed that paltry participation in an important election to the fact that the political process in Virginia was completely dominated by one party, universally known as the "Byrd Machine." This was the organization headed by Senator Harry Flood Byrd, of Winchester. He served as a (then) fairly progressive governor of Virginia from 1926 to 1930, and he was elected to the U.S. Senate in 1932.

The five officers granted for each county and city by the constitution of Virginia (clerk of the court, treasurer, commissioner of revenue, sheriff, and Commonwealth's attorney) provided the core of support for the "organization," and the "organization" was very careful to see that loyalists were always elected to those offices in each of Virginia's counties. State government was kept small, taxes were inadequate, needs of schools and treatment facilities for the mentally ill and retarded were neglected, and economic development was not encouraged. The poll tax as a prerequisite to vote was a device to keep the basically rural electorate in Virginia small. With minor exceptions, since the election of Governor Jim Price in 1937, the domination of the Byrd organization was almost complete until the 1960s.

In 1946 I was only twenty-three years old, but seeing those election returns when I came home from the Pacific, I vowed right then: "I am going to break this up." Every move I made in politics thereafter was motivated, at least in part, by a determination to make that happen. An inviolate tenet in my evolving strategy to break up the Byrd organization was to create a Republican party in Virginia. Julian Rutherfoord, a Democrat friend who was one of the "Young Turk" faction in the Virginia House of Delegates, advised that joining his progressive group would more quickly produce the substantive reforms in the field of voting rights, treatment of the mentally ill, and enhancement of educational opportunities that we both desired. I rejected his advice because I felt that creating a strong Republican party would bring improvements in governmental services that we all desired and, as well, would produce permanent two-party competition. Even Young Turks who functioned successfully within the one-party structure could be subject to the ultimate abuses produced by a continuing lack of competition.

Beginning in the 1950s, a small group of other like-minded Republicans and I would provide that competition so lacking for so many years in Virginia.

Republican
Confidence Growing

4

The year 1952 was pivotal in the history of the Republican Party in Virginia. Up until then, the interest of those who controlled the GOP apparatus was limited largely to presidential elections. Republicans from some of the western counties and parts of the Shenandoah Valley held a few seats in the Virginia General Assembly from time to time. Rare Republicans held a constitutional office here and there. In Tidewater, a Republican was elected to Congress on the coattails of the anti-Catholic vote in 1928. In the far western "Fightin' Ninth" District, father and son Bascom Slemp held the congressional seat for a number of years, but by any standard, Republican elected officials in Virginia were notable for their scarcity.

Then came 1952. Many Virginians, especially veterans of World War II and generally younger residents, were fed up with the Truman administration. They feared threats to Virginia's popular "right-to-work" laws; there was postwar inflation; there was concern about civil rights proposals. There was also the issue of the seemingly endless Korean War. There was disgust caused by reports of scandal in high places, such as 5 percent kickbacks on government contracts to lobbyists and cronies of the president.

Many of these younger Virginians had great interest in the possibility of electing General Eisenhower as president. His views on issues, and even his party affiliation, were little known, but he was a popular hero and widely considered electable. Having attended a "Mass Meeting" in 1950 where no more than six or eight Republicans elected the officers of the Roanoke Republican organization for the next two years, I was sure it would be a snap to bring a number of these younger people to the 1952 Mass Meeting and get myself elected chairman of the Republican Party in Roanoke. Wrong!

We young lions attended the meeting in significant numbers, but when the Old Guard (who had also turned out in greater numbers than usual because it was a presidential election year) realized that we upstarts had the most votes, they adjourned the meeting without electing a chairman. I got my wrists slapped for my audacity by the outgoing Republican chairman, Otto Whitaker, who was quoted in a *Roanoke Times* article. I should work my way up the leadership ladder, he scolded, and not "try to pole vault to the top" at my first meeting. I got a chuckle out of that. I knew we were winning, and that time would tell.

Our group had not contested the election of the City Committee itself; that committee was comprised of one or more representatives from each voting precinct in the city. We felt it important to elect a new chairman, but we also thought we could strengthen the party by keeping in office members who had served on the City Committee before. There was some ideological difference; most of those incumbent carryovers were supporters of Robert Taft, a very conservative Republican senator from Ohio whom the Old Guard was eager to nominate as the 1952 Republican candidate for president. Taft was a long-time party regular, and the darling of that crowd. Most of our younger crowd preferred to nominate General Eisenhower, but they voted for the slate of the City Committee nominees, comprised mostly of incumbents and a few of our newcomers. But we had no idea that the newly elected City Committee would decline to call a new Mass Meeting to complete the business of the previously adjourned Mass Meeting. They did so decline, and the committee itself purported to elect a new chairman. To our dismay, their choice was Otto Whitaker, the incumbent chairman, who was a nice gentleman but a strong Taft supporter. He symbolized the status quo and was not likely to lead an effort to build the Republican Party into a strong and competitive force in Virginia politics.

Our group protested the failure to elect a chairman at a Mass Meeting, and the refusal of the new committee to call another Mass Meeting for the purpose of electing a chairman. Our appeal to the Sixth District Republican committee was sustained on those grounds. Bentley Hite, then district chairman and a Christiansburg lawyer who had been, or was then, serving in the Virginia House of Delegates (one of the rare ones), and Richard H. Poff, newly elected chairman of the Radford City Republican Party, were influential in having the District Committee order that a new Mass Meeting be held to elect a new chairman of the Roanoke City Republican Committee.

No one had ever seen such a vigorous campaign on behalf of Republican candidates for any office, even offices in the party apparatus, as that which ensued. Whitaker dropped out, and C. M. "Butterbeans" Ellis became the candidate of the Old Guard; I remained the candidate of the younger interlopers. People who never before thought of attending a Republican meeting crowded the Patrick Henry Hotel ballroom the night of the election. The mavericks won—I beat Ellis by a vote of 92 to 87, the first time I was ever elected to any political position.

The Roanoke press had given considerable attention to our contest. It boiled down to a contest between those who wanted to broaden participation in the Republican Party as part of a true two-party system, and those who were content with the status quo—that is, don't rock the state's one-party domination and thus continue to enjoy patronage from Republican presidents. Our group wanted to run candidates at all levels of elective office, and most of us believed the nomination of General Eisenhower would be the best move for the party to make in 1952. The fact that we won on these issues in a highly publicized contest created a very positive impression of us in the Roanoke community.

Our first effort to put a Republican in an elected public office came in June 1952. We convinced John B. Waldrop, a popular hardware store owner, and Hughes T. "Jubal" Angell, an independent insurance and real estate broker, to run with our endorsement for the Roanoke City Council. John won, but Jubal garnered a respectable vote.

Buoyed by that success, we insisted—over the sometimes pretty vigorous opposition of some of the Old Guard—on nominating a candidate for Congress in the Sixth District of Virginia. During the open meeting of the Sixth District convention, the intensity of the opposition was tempered somewhat when Pete Hilton, Roanoke County chairman and one of the Old Guard, screamed at Brack Stovall, an insurgent new Republican from Lynchburg, "Where were you in 1948? Where were you in 1944?" He was intemperately suggesting we were Johnny-come-latelies trying to push aside the longtime loyalist Republicans Pete represented. Pete realized he had overstepped when Brack extended his arm and hand with two missing fingers and responded, "Fighting a war!" He had left those two fingers on the battlefields of Europe during World War II.

That convention did nominate Richard Poff for Congress. Ted Dalton, one of the three Republican state senators, and our New Guard party sage and mentor, had made a vain attempt to persuade some better-known Republicans (such as H. L. "Lefty" Lawson, a prominent and respected Roanoke businessman, or Greene Lawson, Lefty's brother, or possibly Ted himself) to accept the nomination. Dalton had thereafter announced at a meeting of a small group in his office in Radford before the district convention, "Well, if the others won't run, I'm going to let Richard run." "Richard" was Richard Poff, a brand-new associate in Ted's law office, and a very enthusiastic Republican, but very few people in the Sixth District in Virginia had ever heard of him.

Dick Poff was a native of Christiansburg, in Montgomery County, Virginia, who had been chief pilot on B-24 Liberator bombers on several bombing runs over Europe during World War II. He attended the University of Virginia Law School, and as a married student, he lived in temporary housing for married students generally known as "Copley Hill." There Dick acquired the title (by consensus, I think) "Mayor of Copley Hill." That was his only political experience prior to joining Ted Dalton's law office in 1949, when he was about twenty-six years old.

Clarence Burton, the incumbent Democratic congressman whom Poff would challenge, cracked, "Yes, I will campaign, but I will not ride around the district with little horns on top of my car." He was referring to Richard's station wagon with loudspeakers mounted on its roof. Richard made campaign speeches blared through those horns in every hamlet in the Sixth District of Virginia. His campaign message was, "I'm going to Washington to help Eisenhower, as I helped him when I flew bombers over Europe during the War." "Ike and Poff" appeared everywhere on bumper stickers and posters. One unfortunate but funny gaffe on Eisenhower's part occurred when he referred to "My friend *Poss*" in his speech from the back of a campaign train parked in South Roanoke Park. The gaffe resulted in a little more publicity, and the teasing by the press did not detract from the message of "Ike and Poff."

During other preliminaries of that 1952 campaign, state senator Floyd Landreth of Galax was elected chairman of the state Republican Party in a spirited contest against Bob Wood of Pearisburg, which took place at the state Republican convention in the old American Legion auditorium in Roanoke. State senator Ted Dalton was elected national committeeman at the 1952 Republican National Convention. There was big national excitement caused by a bitter contest over the issue of a "fair play" amendment,* the outcome of

*There were contested delegations to the national convention from Texas and Georgia. These came about when the Taft forces, who were in control of the local party machinery, excluded newly interested Republicans who were favorable to Eisenhower from the votes for delegates in contested delegations to be seated at the national convention. Under existing rules, such contests were to be decided by the Republican National Committee, a group firmly committed to Taft. The "fair play" amendment allowed such contests to be decided by the convention itself, and its adoption, by a vote of 658 to 548, resulted in seating the delegations favorable to Ike and was the key to his victory over Taft for the presidential nomination.

which—in a spirited contest for the presidential nomination between Robert Taft, U.S. senator from Ohio, and Dwight D. Eisenhower—gave the victory to Ike. The Republicans had also nominated Bill Wampler in the "Fightin' Ninth" District and Joel T. Broyhill in the newly created Tenth District of Virginia, located on the outskirts of Washington, as candidates for Congress for those respective districts. All three of our congressional candidates won, and Eisenhower carried Virginia resoundingly.

Our new chairman, Floyd Landreth, wrote a letter dated the day after the 1952 election to me, Ted Dalton, Dick Poff, Lefty Lawson, Greene Lawson, and perhaps to some others, omitting the salutation of "Dear Anybody." He just started it, "Well, boys, we come out all right all over." And we had. The campaign to create a true two-party democracy in Virginia was just beginning, but it was an auspicious beginning.

Confidence growing, many Republicans—including me, of course—were eager to build on the local and state victories of 1952. Heartened by our new leadership with lovable state senator Floyd Landreth as state chairman and widely known Senator Ted Dalton as national committeeman, we young Republicans were most euphoric about the future.

A gubernatorial year was coming up in 1953. The stature of Ted Dalton as "Mr. Republican" in Radford and Southwest Virginia was growing. He had gained statewide and national attention as he skillfully navigated the rocks and shoals (i.e., Taft delegates) in the Virginia delegation to the national convention. He not only got himself elected as national committeeman from Virginia, but he was quietly instrumental in having the majority of the Virginia delegation vote for the Eisenhower side of the "fair play" amendment. And despite being a Republican, he had been a popular member of the Virginia Senate for several years.

We were encouraged by the fact that the likely Democratic candidate for governor was Thomas B. Stanley of Stanleytown. Though a highly successful businessman and Speaker of the House of Delegates, Stanley did not appear to us as an imposing candidate, nor as a particularly effective campaigner. As it turned out, the Republicans would be blessed with a superb set of candidates for the three statewide offices—governor, lieutenant governor, and attorney general. They didn't win, but their positive campaign and near-win result were important positive steps toward eventual Republican victories—including mine.

Even from the very beginning, I believe Ted Dalton wanted to run for governor. He was a very cautious person, however, so along with several others, I spent many hours trying to overcome his stated reservations about throwing his hat in the ring. Money, he thought, would be a problem. How could we raise $100,000? A minuscule amount to us these days, in 1952 it seemed like a million dollars. He also thought the ticket would be a problem. How could we attract candidates for lieutenant governor and attorney general with the stature and name recognition needed to win the support of the voting public? How could we overcome the traditionally huge majorities the Democrats always racked up? Ted cited Lunenberg and Mecklenburg counties particularly, noting that Byrd Machine victory margins were sometimes eight- or ten-to-one in those Southside counties.

We ignored the money problem, all of us probably thinking subconsciously that Ted would supply it himself. (In the end, he did put up a lot.) Actually, Ted hoped that Democrat Bob Whitehead would be able to raise the $100,000 he had set as a condition of his running in the Democratic primary against Stanley. Although I don't remember Ted's ever saying it, I am confident he believed there was a good chance that Whitehead would defeat Stanley in the Democratic primary. Bob was a liberal member of the Virginia Senate— a true rarity. He was congenial, articulate, and an outstanding orator. But Ted, I think, felt that a Republican victory in the general election was more probable against a known liberal than against Stanley, a Byrd Machine conservative. He envisioned a coalition of conservative Democrats and regular Republicans forming an electoral majority for himself over the liberal candidacy of Bob Whitehead.

We argued that the independent Virginians who had voted in the cities and Northern Virginia for Eisenhower, plus the normally Republican vote (though small) in the Shenandoah Valley and Southwest Virginia, plus the African American vote and the vote of organized labor, could offset those Byrd majorities for Stanley, which were largely in the less populous rural areas.

As the time for our state convention drew nearer, Steve Timberlake, a successful businessman well known in the southern Shenandoah Valley, began to intimate that he might be willing to be a candidate for lieutenant governor if Ted Dalton were at the top of the ticket.

Walter Hoffman, a top lawyer in Norfolk and a well-known Republican, was the choice of Ted and his immediate supporters to run for attorney general. But Walter, also known as "Beef" from his football days at Washington and Lee, was adamantly opposed to running. He knew he could help the ticket both with his legal reputation, which was outstanding as to integrity, ability, and success, and with the geography of his home base. But he also knew he was in line for appointment by President Eisenhower to the U.S. District Court in the Eastern District of Virginia. He wanted to make no move that would in any way dampen his chances for that appointment. After much discussion, culminating in late-night hours at the state convention during which he was given the assurance from Ted and all of us that he could resign from the race if the judicial appointment came through, Beef agreed to run.

Ted Dalton was obviously very enthusiastic about having Beef Hoffman become a candidate for attorney general. It was therefore almost automatic that, if Beef agreed to run, Dalton would likewise agree, and he did. Our statewide ticket of Dalton for governor, Timberlake for lieutenant governor, and Hoffman for attorney general was indeed impressive. This slate would oppose the Democratic slate headed by Thomas B. Stanley. It turned out Bob Whitehead was not able to raise the $100,000 commitment for campaign expenses he had set as a condition of becoming a candidate in the Democratic primary, so Stanley became the Democratic candidate without opposition for the nomination.

Dalton was an enthusiastic, ebullient campaigner whose happy personality and infectious grin attracted interest and support from voters all over the state. He espoused issues that were stock-in-trade for progressive Republicans: Repeal the poll tax as a prerequisite to voting; strengthen the absentee ballot law to prevent voting in state elections by former residents of Virginia who had long ago moved out of the state; lower the voting age to eighteen; reduce the appointive powers of circuit judges; elect members of school boards; increase the income of public school teachers; and improve the treatment of retarded or mentally ill patients in mental hospitals.

As a candidate, Stanley was colorless and noncommittal, with one major exception: he repeatedly promised that there would be "no increase in taxes" during a Stanley administration. His commitment against any new taxes and the bad condition of Virginia's highway system seemed to Dalton; to Joe Parsons, his campaign manager; and to others, including me, to create an opportunity for Ted, if he could devise a plan to pay for new roads without increasing taxes. To the best of my memory, editors of *all* the state dailies were urging the candidates to confront this need. It was logical to assume that some support from these editors would flow to the candidate who could propose a reasonable solution.

Ted and Joe Parsons devised such a plan. They proposed issuing $100 million in road construction bonds, to be amortized over a period of years with revenues anticipated from the existing state motor vehicles fuel tax. It has been a device subsequently used in Virginia for many purposes in recent years, and it did receive substantial editorial support from some of the major daily newspapers in Virginia.

But the words "bond" and "state borrowing" were anathema to Senator Harry Flood Byrd. Ted's proposal brought Byrd out of Winchester like a bee out of a smoking hive. He landed on every radio station in Virginia, almost screaming over the airwaves that Dalton's plan would abandon "pay as you go" and reverse the fiscal policy of the Byrd organization, which considered state borrowing strictly taboo. He ignored Ted's accurate assertion that the counties were head over heels in debt because of the state's penurious failure to support municipal needs, principally public education; he ignored the editorials. Stanley, who wasn't much in the race anyway, all but disappeared, and it became a contest of Dalton against Byrd.

Byrd's emotional outcries reached all levels of voters. I remember the story about one old man, a known Republican who couldn't have been much above poverty level, who was met on his way to the polls by Ethel Chrisman, his longtime friend and the GOP precinct chairman in northwest Roanoke. She urged him to vote for Dalton. He shook his head "no" and explained tersely with one word: "Bonds!"

Byrd won, but not by much. Stanley got 54.8 percent of the vote against Dalton, substantially less than the Byrd Machine candidates were accustomed to receiving. Ted got the remaining 44.2 percent, a showing that spelled the beginning of the end of one-party domination in Virginia. The end of the end would have come sooner than it did were it not for Massive Resistance, a story to which I'll turn later.

As more than a footnote to the 1953 campaign and maddeningly to those of us who had put our hearts and souls into that gubernatorial run, Stanley, in his inaugural address, advocated a one-cent increase in the gas tax to build roads in Virginia. We were amazed at the gall of reneging on his own campaign promise, but his friends in the legislature were even more astounded and promptly defeated the proposal.

Years later, members of his family commended him to me for his "courage to change his position." I continue to condemn such a lack of candor during a campaign, and I maintain that it was one-party arrogance that emboldened Governor Stanley to ignore his antitax campaign promise, which had been made for political expedience.

5 Building the Party

The Ted Dalton race for governor in 1953 went far toward building the Republican Party into an effective and permanent part of a competitive two-party system in Virginia. We didn't win that race, but we certainly did surprise a lot of people by coming so close. The result of that race encouraged those of us who sought to build a two-party system and became a base for subsequent successes.

In the Roanoke area, our first-term congressman, Richard Poff, had the good luck to be opposed for reelection in 1954 by Ernest "Pig" Robertson, a member of the Virginia House of Delegates who didn't have the backing of the Democratic establishment in the Sixth District. Poff won that race handily. His comfortable majority came from a combination of having a weak opponent and his own extremely focused attention to the needs of his constituency—he served them consistently almost as an ombudsman. Poff's performance and reelection did much to add stature to the Republican Party in the Roanoke area.

Republican Joel Broyhill was also reelected as congressman from the Tenth District of Virginia (the Northern Virginia suburbs of Washington), which gave real encouragement to a lot of hardworking Republicans in that area. Congressman Bill Wampler, a Republican elected to Congress in 1952 from Southwest Virginia's Ninth District, was defeated in 1954. Newly married during his term, it is certainly possible that his attention was distracted from his constituency. It was a sad personal loss, but losing that seat did not have any major impact on the development of the Republican Party throughout the rest of Virginia.

I had my first try at running for public office in 1955. Ted Dalton, by then a good friend and mentor, urged me to run for the state Senate against Earl Fitzpatrick, a member of the same church I attended in Roanoke, and a veteran member of the Virginia Senate. But I was very uneasy about reaching for the Senate my first time out as a candidate. Taking on Kossen Gregory or Julian Rutherfoord, the incumbent members of the Virginia House of Delegates from Roanoke, seemed more appropriate. But Kossen was a friend, and we were in the same social and business set. Not only that, he was very popular, and I didn't think he could be defeated.

Julian Rutherfoord, although a competent general insurance agent, was less charismatic than Kossen, and perhaps more vulnerable. Hazel Barger, living in the Williamson Road area of Roanoke, believed she and I could beat them both. Other party members thought the combination of support from her area of the city and my South Roanoke–Raleigh Court area would carry us, so we became the first candidates ever nominated for the Virginia House of Delegates by the Roanoke City Republican Party.

It was a heady time, and a busy one. We were two candidates in a four-person race. The victories would go to the two candidates who garnered the most votes. Hazel Barger and I ran a very aggressive race, emphasizing the need for an effective two-party system. We didn't win, but we did demonstrate to the public and to ourselves that candidates running under the Republican label now had the potential of winning in our Democrat-controlled state. Though I came in third among the four, with over 49 percent of the vote, I was more than ever convinced that we could build a real party. Kossen won with a comfortable margin. Julian eked out a victory, but only with just over 50 percent of the vote. When I told Hazel we should phone Kossen and Julian to congratulate them for their victories, she declined the honor, so I was the one to speak to both of them. It was kind of fun to have Julian (barely ahead of me in the results) ask me about the returns from a certain precinct. He wasn't sure he'd definitely won until I gave him the final vote from that precinct, which put him over me by a very small margin.

Eisenhower's popularity as president and the fact that he had carried Virginia in 1952 were of course helpful to all our efforts to build a Republican Party, so we had a scare when he had a heart attack in 1955. My brother-in-law, Ed Vaden, a pediatrician in Lynchburg, was sure that after the heart attack Eisenhower wouldn't be able to run again in 1956. That was the conventional thinking among the members of the medical profession at the time, but with treatment and advice from Paul Dudley White, the nationally prominent cardiologist from Boston, Eisenhower did recover and ran successfully again in 1956. We were more than delighted. Congressman Poff was reelected a second time in 1956 and again in 1958, over a very strong campaign waged by William

B. Hopkins, a Roanoke lawyer who would later become majority leader in the Virginia Senate. Poff was always reelected comfortably thereafter until I appointed him to the Virginia Supreme Court of Appeals in 1971.

During those Eisenhower years I continued to help with party-building activities at the local and state levels, but out of necessity, I did give some attention to the law practice Purnell Eggleston and I were building after we formed the law partnership in January 1954. Our practice grew well, and over the next few years I developed some significant skills as a trial lawyer. Between 1954 and 1964, I had the good fortune to be involved in some rather important cases. In one, I was invited to be junior counsel by Penn Sandridge, a prominent member of the Winston-Salem, North Carolina, bar, to represent the Stroup Mirror Company. Our clients were indicted and charged with having participated in a criminal conspiracy with Pittsburgh Plate Glass and other mirror manufacturers in Virginia and North Carolina to illegally fix the prices of mirrors—a serious federal felony.

The government had a solid case. The evidence showed that a group of mirror manufacturers, including representatives of our client, had held a meeting at the deserted Grandfather Mountain Lodge on the Blue Ridge Parkway in the middle of December, reaching an agreement to fix the prices—so ultimately all the defendants were convicted. It was a trial that drew a lot of attention, and Mr. Sandridge generously allowed me to conduct the case for our clients.

Accolades came my way from many lawyers who were in the courtroom representing various defendants, after an exchange I had with Judge Paul during my summation. Judge Paul, known for impatience and irascibility, was manifestly convinced that all of our clients in this case were guilty. When I came to the point of saying, "Now what the government usually does in these cases is . . . ," Judge Paul interrupted with a snarl, "Mr. Holton, how many of 'these cases' have you tried?" The accolades resulted because I snapped right back, "This is the first one, Judge, but I have read the reports of every one I could find in the library," and, unflustered, continued immediately with my summation.

That antitrust trial enhanced my reputation. Along with Billy Dixon, a member of the Norfolk, Virginia, bar and a former president of the Virginia Bar Association, I was retained in 1964 to represent a group of Minnesota architect-engineers in a civil suit in which they were accused of faulty design for the foundation of a paper mill in Big Island, Virginia, owned by Owens

Illinois Corporation. That case involved mostly discovery depositions; both we and the plaintiffs hired and deposed expert engineers from all over the United States during a good portion of 1964. We settled the case—under the prodding of then–U.S. district judge Ted Dalton—on the day after the presidential election of 1964. It was the day Republican Barry Goldwater was soundly defeated by Democrat Lyndon Johnson.

A third litigation occupying me through that ten-year period involved the Jewel Ridge Coal Company, which owned valuable metallurgical coal reserves in Tazewell County, Virginia. I was retained by a fellow Washington and Lee alumnus, Robert Moore of Bluefield, Virginia. He and members of his family owned a minority interest in Jewel Ridge. John S. Battle Jr., a contemporary of mine and a prominent Richmond lawyer, was one of the attorneys on the other side of the case, as were Eppa Hunton and John Ritchie, of the prominent Richmond law firm now practicing under the name of Hunton and Williams.

As a result of my getting to know him during that litigation, John Ritchie first became my campaign manager and later my executive assistant in the governor's office. John Battle became a good friend, and I used to tease him, saying that the contingent fee I received in that case was large enough for me to take time off to run for governor against his brother, Bill Battle.

Though my law practice kept me hopping during these years, I was still very active in backstage work, building our Virginia GOP. At first we didn't realize just how expertly the developing resistance to the Supreme Court's orders to eliminate "separate but equal" school systems was being whipped into an emotional frenzy before and during the gubernatorial elections in 1957. Meanwhile, the Republican Party of Virginia was able to mount what appeared to be a very impressive slate for the gubernatorial campaign that year. Ted Dalton was the repeat nominee for governor; Horace Henderson (whose wife, Jane, had inherited part of the Corning Glass fortune) eagerly sought the nomination for lieutenant governor; and Livingston Dillow, a successful plaintiffs' and trial lawyer from Pearisburg, Virginia, was a willing candidate for attorney general.

On the Democratic side, J. Lindsay Almond, the incumbent attorney general of Virginia, outmaneuvered Senator Byrd and preempted the nomination for governor. Senator Byrd's preference was Senator Garland Gray of Sussex, but Byrd finally acquiesced to Almond's nomination. Senator Byrd hadn't been sure that Lindsay Almond was "reliable" and gave only vague responses when Almond called on him, seeking a nod of approval and asking his support. With Byrd's approval not forthcoming, Almond (who had been waiting his turn for at least four years) simply went ahead and announced his candidacy. Enough friends responded affirmatively so that Senator Gray soon took his name out of the running. A. E. S. "Gi" Stephens, the incumbent lieutenant governor, agreed to run again for that post. Howard Gilmer, a prominent lawyer from Pulaski and former U.S. attorney for the Western District of Virginia, was slated for the attorney general's slot. He had to withdraw when it was discovered he had committed some ethical errors in connection with a life insurance promotion. The powers that be (i.e., Senator Byrd) arranged for Albertis Harrison of Brunswick County to be substituted as the candidate for attorney general.

All the pieces were in place for a great competitive race. Two good sets of candidates faced each other, each with a chance to win. In the past, Republicans would not have had much hope, but the closeness of the race in 1953, the deception that Governor Stanley had committed with his gas tax proposal, the black mark left on the organization by Howard Gilmer's ethical lapse, and the growing interest of the public in the more progressive programs the Republicans were espousing made it appear that this could be a close race.

At the local level, Hazel Barger and I were nominated as candidates for the House of Delegates again, and in view of Ted Dalton's great popularity in the Roanoke area, we fully expected to catch his coattails and win. Don't count your chickens before they hatch!

In its *Brown vs. Board of Education* decision, the U.S. Supreme Court had decreed that separate-but-equal segregation was unconstitutional. Open defiance of that decree by the governor of Arkansas made it necessary for President Eisenhower to order federal troops to Little Rock to protect African American children seeking admission to a previously all-white high school. The demagogues had a field day.

Candidate Lindsay Almond led the way: "I would rather lose my right arm than see the first nigra child admitted to the white schools of Virginia during my term as governor." That is an exact excerpt from one of his campaign speeches made in the Jefferson High School in Roanoke, and it was typical of his exhortations throughout the campaign all over Virginia. The more moderate positions taken by the Republicans, urging gradualism but acknowledging the necessity to comply with the decrees of the courts, were simply not heard above the emotional furor of the demagogues.

Ted Dalton had gained 43 percent of the vote in 1953, but in 1957 his totals fell to 36 percent. Hazel and I did not even come close to winning, but we went down with flags flying: In defiance of the massive resistance laws mandating the closing of any all-white school that admitted a Negro child, we had run a full-page ad in the *Roanoke Times* on the Sunday before election. The headline of two-inch-high letters printed in red ink across the page proclaimed, "KEEP OUR SCHOOLS OPEN."

In the end, we lost to trashy rhetoric, but we were right. That ad, by the way, was very convincing when I asked for support from President Eisenhower during my first gubernatorial campaign in 1965 and when I exhibited it to the Richmond Crusade for Voters in my 1969 campaign. Of this, more later.

Frank Angell, a Republican candidate in Roanoke County for the House of Delegates that fateful year of 1957, tried to combat the Little Rock syndrome with his signature humor. He went around the county saying he was more concerned about Hanging Rock—a well-known landmark in the northwest corner of Roanoke County—than Little Rock. But humor was drowned out by the emotional harangues of the demagogues. The Democrats won easily all through the state, and Lindsay Almond would be the next governor. Had it not been for Little Rock, I truly believe I would have been elected to the House of Delegates in 1957, and quite likely Hazel Barger as well. We lost four years in the building of a viable two-party system in Virginia as a result of the Little Rock incident.

I was one of the Virginia delegates to the Republican National Convention in the year 1960, when a possible contest for the presidential nomination developed between Nixon and Nelson Rockefeller, governor of New York. After Nixon called on Rockefeller in New York to discuss proposals for the campaign, particularly issues concerning civil rights, some southern Republicans, including the state Republican chairman from North Carolina, were critical of the meeting and critical of Nixon's perceived pandering to Rockefeller. I was pleased at the outcome of the meeting, however, and particularly pleased with Nixon's report of his commitment to encourage minority participation in federal contracts; he summarized his position with the words, "It's the people's money; all the people should have a shot at it."

I have to admit that the Nixon defeat in 1960 was a surprise to me. Nixon was very popular in Virginia, especially so in our western areas, and he carried our state. But he was sick during the campaign; he had some sort of infection in one of his knees, and he plainly was not up to par when he made a campaign appearance in South Roanoke Park. It was on that occasion that I first met Nixon, and I felt sorry for him, having to maintain a heavy campaign schedule when he was so visibly in pain.

I also had my first exposure that year to candidate Jack Kennedy when he made an airport stop in Roanoke. Though I was a well-known Republican in that area, out of curiosity I sneaked out to Woodrum Field, my rationale being that it was a historic occasion and that my two young daughters should see a presidential candidate. Tayloe and Anne were then four and two respectively, and they got a glimpse of Senator Kennedy while each was perched on one of my shoulders. Mrs. Lyndon Johnson, who was on the campaign plane with Senator Kennedy, saw me standing in the crowd with the two girls peering over the crowd on my shoulders. Lady Bird exclaimed, "There's a brave man!" She had no idea who I was, and certainly not that I was a Republican. I doubt that in the noisy and enthusiastic crowd, anyone but me noted her comment.

At the beginning of 1961, it looked as though the Republicans in Virginia might be able to stage some kind of a comeback. Horace Henderson, then of Newport News, was eager to gain the nomination for governor, and through his wife was able to garner enough financial resources to stage a reasonable campaign. But it was not to be. Henderson was regarded by some of our traditional Republicans as something of a carpetbagger. He had been the First District Republican chairman and was well known in Tidewater, but not elsewhere. H. Clyde Pearson of tiny Lee County at the far southwest corner of Virginia beat Horace in the nomination contest at the state convention. Clyde was and is a wonderful person, with the right ideas about the governmental services Virginia should provide; he had been in the House of Delegates for several terms and was pretty well known throughout the state. However, he had no resources other than his long-standing loyalty as a Republican, and his campaign went nowhere. I served as his state campaign manager because of our friendship, but I wasn't able to be of much help.

Albertis Harrison and his teammates, Mills Godwin for lieutenant governor and Robert Y. Button for attorney general, had survived a serious challenge in the Democratic primary from the moderate ticket of A. E. S. "Gi" Stephens, Armistead Booth for lieutenant governor, and T. Munford Boyd—a law professor at the University of Virginia—for attorney general. After nomination, however, the Harrison slate was elected handily in the general election.

Albertis Harrison's leadership provided a turning point for Virginia's political history. I summarize his inaugural address by saying that he exhorted Virginians to "stop looking over their shoulders to the past," and recommended instead, "Let's see if we can't make some money." Thus began a serious effort for economic and industrial development in Virginia, perhaps the most significant portion of which was to create a study commission that recommended and ultimately resulted in the creation of our community college system. That system has been an important vehicle for economic development in Virginia from its inception. The first school opened its doors during the administration of Governor Godwin, but the idea came from the exploratory commission created during the term of Governor Harrison.

The one bright spot for Republicans during the 1961 election cycle was the election in Roanoke to the House of Delegates of my future law partner, M. Caldwell Butler. His first try for public office was for a Roanoke City Council seat in 1958. He lost by thirteen votes. "Lucky thirteen," I said, for it freed him to run for and win one of Roanoke's two House of Delegates seats in 1961. That election put us back on a positive path to becoming a two-party state, after our progress toward that goal had been interrupted in 1957 by the Massive Resistance fiasco. Caldwell was a valuable incumbent in the House of Delegates. Smart, quick on his feet, and an excellent campaigner, he had very sound ideas that were invariably presented with a wonderful sense of humor. He became the leader of a growing group of Republicans in the House of Delegates, and, fortunately for me, was still serving in that role when I was elected governor in 1969.

Caldwell Butler's skill with the verbal needle once produced a slight embarrassment for the Harrison administration and the dominant Democratic Party in the General Assembly. The establishment had decided that a reapportionment bill should take effect immediately rather than on the usual date of July 1. An immediate effect required a two-thirds vote—and the declaration of an "emergency." On the floor of the House of Delegates, Minority Leader Butler inquired, "What is the emergency?" No one in the Assembly could provide the answer. Caldwell was therefore allowed to pose the question to Governor Harrison, who likewise could not clearly identify the "emergency." The effort to obtain the two-thirds vote was allowed to die, quietly. This incident provided just the first public evidence that the growing Republican Party was something the Democratic establishment could no longer overlook.

GOP Loss Spawns
Holton Strategy

6

The Republican Party got clobbered all over the country in 1964. Going into that election, though, hopes were high. The conservative wing of the party was gleeful. They had nominated their hero, Barry Goldwater, a U.S. senator from Arizona and the "Mister Conservative" of his time, and had unabashedly thrown down the gauntlet to Nelson Rockefeller's moderate faction: "Extremism in defense of freedom is no vice!" echoed across the country.

New faces appeared at functions sponsored by "Virginians for Goldwater" organizations, and even outright Republican functions were crowded with newcomers—many of them Democrats (and many of them supporters of Senator Harry Byrd). Much of the movement to Goldwater was based on an aversion to the racial attitudes supported by leading Democrats, including President Johnson, which called for laws favoring equal employment opportunities, voting rights, and integration of public facilities, as well as by court decisions outlawing traditional racial discrimination.

One Virginia Democrat refused to be swayed by the momentum building among Democrats swinging to Goldwater: Mills Godwin, who rode the "Lady Bird Special" with Mrs. Johnson on a campaign train through Virginia on behalf of her husband. That ride helped Godwin retain the support of the Democratic Party in Virginia, but it was among the causes for the racial conservatives in the state to support the third-party candidacy of Bill Story in the 1965 governor's race.

Linwood Holton was busy during the Goldwater campaign, but not with politics. Billy Dixon, a lawyer friend from Norfolk, and I spent a great deal of time in 1964 preparing the defense of the lawsuit brought against the Minnesota architect-engineers I describe in detail in chapter 5. We had taken discovery depositions in Wisconsin on election day, and my only connection with the election that year was to wait in Chicago, on our way home, for the bars—which by Illinois law were closed during the hours of voting—to re-open so we could get a drink. It had been a busy and stressful day in our law-suit; when the sun went down, it was time for a little libation.

The Republicans lost—big time. We even lost Virginia. There was a total vacuum, and no one made any suggestion for a future course. No one, that is, except Hazel Barger, my close friend and political ally in Roanoke, who then held the position of national committeewoman from Virginia.

Soon after the first meeting of the Republican National Committee follow-ing the Goldwater defeat, I got a call from Raymond V. Humphries, a mem-ber of the staff of the National Committee, whose title was something like "director of education and training." Raymond had heard about me and my previous political record as a builder of the Republican Party in Roanoke from Hazel Barger.

Raymond was a superb promoter. He came to visit me in Roanoke early in 1965 and drew beautiful pictures of how he and Ray Bliss (who had been elected Republican national chairman at that resurrection meeting of the National Committee) and others in the Republican leadership were eager to invest sub-stantial resources of the Republican Party in some "bright young person" who could win an important race and put the Republican Party on the road to recovery. Raymond told me of how eager Pennsylvania's Governor Scranton (then chairman of the Republican Governors Association) was to enlist the other Republican governors to help wage a winning effort. They believed Vir-ginia, which was to hold a gubernatorial election that year, had a chance for a Republican win. I think Raymond sincerely believed everything he told me. I didn't, but his grand ideas and willingness to try convinced me that now was the time to begin implementing my long-held plans to become governor of Virginia.

I responded positively enough to Raymond's overtures so that he did in-deed invest some small amounts of National Committee money from his Mobilize Republican Enterprise (MORE) program in Virginia. I appeared at several of the MORE meetings throughout Virginia, urging first small and then larger audiences to participate in the political process *as Republicans.*

Dortch Warriner, a conservative Democrat lawyer from Emporia, Virginia, was an early convert. He turned around a then-current cigarette ad, "I'd rather fight than switch," to describe his plan to "switch and then fight," that is, to turn Republican and then seek elective office. It was obvious that Dortch would be a willing candidate for attorney general if we could put a statewide ticket together.

There was no chance for a Republican to win a Virginia gubernatorial race in 1965. Then–lieutenant governor Mills Godwin had touched every base. He had been a strong Massive Resister, which pleased most of the right-wing element in the state; he had ridden the "Lady Bird Special" across Virginia to support Johnson's presidential campaign in 1964, a move pleasing to Democratic liberals. He had been part of the establishment ticket of Albertis Harrison, Mills Godwin, and Bob Button for the three statewide offices in 1961. Their handy defeat that year of the major Democratic primary effort by "Gi" Stephens, Armistead Boothe, and "Munny" Boyd was a serious disappointment for the moderate voters of Virginia, and no one was sufficiently energized to oppose Mills Godwin when he sought the nomination for governor in 1965. There were no obstacles in his path; he was going to be elected the next governor of Virginia.

Although there was no chance to elect a Republican governor in 1965, I saw that it was, nonetheless, "Opportunity Time." After giving it a lot of thought, one evening I sat in the green leather chair we had inherited indirectly from Bishop Jett, Jinks's Episcopalian grandfather. From this inherited seat of comfort, I outlined for Jinks what I was envisioning for our future: I could get the Virginia Republican nomination for governor, I told her, because in the post-Goldwater vacuum, no one else was interested. The Republican National Committee might provide some resources. Not enough—but some of the things they could and possibly *might* do would be helpful. I saw enough vote sources from the regular Republicans, members of the African American community, members of labor unions, moderate voters who had been turned off by Godwin's support for Massive Resistance, and others who recognized the merits of establishing a two-party system, to make me believe that I, as a Republican candidate for governor, could get as much as 35–40 percent of the vote in the general election, even against the apparently invincible Mills Godwin.

My thinking, which was evolving into a plan, was that producing a vote of that magnitude against Godwin in 1965 would, first, establish Linwood Holton's name identification throughout Virginia; second, usurp the inside track for the Republican nomination for governor in 1969; and third, give me a reasonable opportunity to win in 1969. After more than a few discussions, Jinks—who usually thought things through pretty carefully—became a believer in this risky proposition, and we decided to give it try.

We first had to line up a slate. My instincts about Dortch Warriner were correct. He was willing to "switch and then fight" as our Republican candidate for attorney general. There were some uncertain moments as we approached the state convention date without a candidate for lieutenant governor. But one night at supper time (again at our Avenham Avenue home, but this time in the breakfast room), I got a call from Vince Callahan of McLean, who assured me that he would indeed be willing to be the lieutenant governor candidate. I think he may even have admitted right then that a statewide candidacy would, at a minimum, give him sufficient identity and credibility to enable him to win a Fairfax County House of Delegates race in 1967.

The 1965 campaign worked out just that way, and as I write this, Vince is the incumbent chairman of the Appropriations Committee of the House of Delegates, which has had a Republican majority since 1999. Dortch was appointed by Richard Nixon to the District Court of the Eastern District of Virginia, fulfilling for him a lifetime ambition. And I was elected governor in 1969. But that's ahead of the story.

Neither Raymond Humphries nor the Republican National Committee produced any significant financial resources for the 1965 campaign. Nevertheless, Raymond Humphries really did his part. He produced in other ways. He produced Governor Henry Bellmon, Republican governor of Oklahoma, to make the keynote address at the state Republican convention, which would nominate the Holton-Callahan-Warriner slate in Norfolk in June 1965. Governor Bellmon had also sought to build a Republican party in a one-party state long dominated by the Democratic Party. He gave a down-to-earth, practical address that told how he had won against great odds in Oklahoma, and it inspired our delegates to undertake a real try to emulate that success in Virginia.

Raymond Humphries also produced Roger Hull. Roger had just graduated from Dartmouth and volunteered his services to the Republican National Committee for the summer of 1965. Raymond immersed Roger in Virginia politics, first by having him delve into back issues of Virginia newspapers, and then by sending him to Virginia to act as my chauffeur, aide, and advance man—in a word, to be an indispensable factotum. Roger drove the Ford automobile loaned for the duration of the campaign by Charles Fox III, son of my first boss in Roanoke. (This was a great example of "bread on the waters" being returned. I had helped Charlie learn to drive when he was still a kid.)

While Roger drove, I slept or studied in the back seat. We tried to visit every radio disc jockey in Virginia, and the editor of every weekly newspaper. We got to most of them. When we couldn't get a reporter or a radio announcer, we shook hands in shopping malls.

Late one Saturday afternoon in Cape Charles, Virginia, I shook hands in a drugstore with a gentleman who responded to my entreaty by saying, "Yes, I'm going to vote for you."

"That's great," I replied. "Would you mind telling me why? It might help me with my campaign."

"I sell stuff to drugstores," he replied. "You have shaken my hand in five drugstores across Southside Virginia just this week. Anybody who works that hard gets my vote."

On another occasion, I whirled around a corner in a department store in Tyson's Corner and made my pitch to a mannequin, who remained quite unmoved by my eloquence. We also encountered our share of crazies and extremists during the campaign. Once, in the T. C. Williams High School in Alexandria, our meeting was invaded by a white supremacy group wearing Nazi uniforms. When one of them attempted to jump up onto the stage, former marine Vince Callahan caught him in midjump and pushed him backward. His head hit the linoleum floor with a thump so loud you could have heard it in Big Stone Gap. I was sure he'd be dead, but he shook himself, got up, and staggered out. We heard no more from the Nazis.

Ray Humphries went on to produce a meeting for me with Governor Scranton of Pennsylvania. The governor was not successful in arranging for the Republican Governors Association to fund any part of my campaign, but he did contribute enough of his personal funds to pay for a statewide telecast on which I appeared, answering questions called in by telephone from potential Virginia voters.

Toward the end of my visit with Governor Scranton, rather out of the blue, he asked me, "Have you seen Ike?" My negative response corresponded with an inner comment to myself: "Have I seen *Ike*?? Boy, I'm getting into the high cotton now!" (I was only forty-two years old and a first-time statewide candidate.)

Governor Scranton buzzed his secretary and asked her to "get General Schultz on the phone." I was so uninformed at that point that I thought "Schultz" must be some kind of a code word they used in the governor's office to refer to General Eisenhower. I was also a little surprised that Governor Scranton seemed to feel that all he had to do to talk to President Eisenhower was to phone him up.

It turned out that Schultz was real. General Bob Schultz was President Eisenhower's personal aide, who, along with Mrs. Ann Whitman, the president's secretary, comprised the sole members of President Eisenhower's staff in retirement. At any rate, I was soon listening to one end of a telephone conversation in which Governor Scranton was proposing that I visit President Eisenhower to inform him of the plans for my gubernatorial campaign. It was an appointment easily arranged, and it was made for the very next day in Gettysburg. This I reported to Jinks by telephone with undisguised elation.

General Schultz met me at the Gettysburg farm and sat me down in President Eisenhower's outer office, where I could see him pacing back and forth as he finished some dictation. Very warm greetings came from him and Mrs. Whitman after just a few minutes. The president was relaxed, seemed to be in no hurry, and by his manner and questions seemed genuinely interested in my description of efforts to build a Republican party in Virginia. We covered a lot of conversational ground; among other things, he reminisced about having developed his proposal for the interstate highway system from his observation of the autobahn network in Germany.

I reminded him of his campaign appearance in South Roanoke Park when I was the Roanoke City Republican chairman in 1952, noting that in that year we had elected Richard Poff to Congress on his Eisenhower coattails. I told him of our effort in 1955, a first for Roanoke Republicans, to elect Republicans to the Virginia House of Delegates, and that I had received over 49 percent of the vote in that election. He was listening pretty intently by then, hearing that I had again been a candidate for the House of Delegates in 1957, and that we had expected a pretty strong favorable vote for our gubernatorial candidate, Ted Dalton.

"General," I then reminded him, "you did what you *had* to do that September in Little Rock, Arkansas, and I supported you because, manifestly, you were right. I even ran a full-page advertisement in the *Roanoke Times* on the Sunday before the election, with huge letters in red ink across the middle of the page reading, 'KEEP OUR SCHOOLS OPEN.' I would likely have been elected except for the backlash from Little Rock, but I was proud to support you because I knew you were doing the right thing."

Parenthetically, I well remember the television newscasts reporting federal troops escorting black kids to the Little Rock High School in 1957. I commented to Jinks as we watched that broadcast together, "Thank goodness he sent the 101st." I was referring to his use of massive force (the 101st Airborne Division of the U.S. Army) to protect those kids, and I recounted those thoughts to the president. Now my 1957 reaction was rewarded by the president's warm 1965 response to me in Gettysburg. He had been criticized for using so much force, he told me, "But nobody got hurt. When others tried using U.S. marshals on another occasion, somebody got killed."

Throughout my conversation with President Eisenhower, I expressed my enthusiasm for the possibility of his making a visit to Virginia in support of my campaign. His initial responses indicated reluctance, along the lines of his "not doing much campaigning anymore." He said he had about gotten to the state where, if he *did* appear, someone else would have to do the principal part of the speaking, and "I would just do a little benediction." But as I was leaving, in an obvious reference to the connection between my lost House of Delegates race in 1957 and his actions in Little Rock, he said, "I will consider your invitation to campaign for you very seriously; I expect I owe you one."

Again, Raymond Humphries made a major contribution. He arranged for me to meet Bryce Harlow, a prominent lobbyist in Washington who had been a very close confidant of Eisenhower's during his two terms as president. Bryce encouraged Eisenhower's visit to Virginia and agreed to escort him on the trip. I was hopeful but never certain until it actually happened that such a trip would materialize. What I thought would be an insurmountable problem came when General Schultz advised us that Eisenhower would travel only in jet airplanes.

"Where would we ever get a jet airplane?" I thought. But David Canfield, who was acting as campaign manager, messenger boy, and factotum, brazenly telephoned the Lockheed folks somewhere in Georgia and offered them the opportunity to take the former president for a ride on one of their new jet airplanes. To my great surprise, gratification, and relief, they agreed.

Bryce and I showed up early one morning in September in Gettysburg in Lockheed's new jet airplane and met Generals Eisenhower and Schultz. We had an uneventful flight to Richmond on a beautiful day, and were met at the Richmond airport by George Olmstead, a banker from Washington who had served in Eisenhower's administration; by Republican Winifred "Pete" Mundle, an African American member of the Richmond City Council; and by Jinks and our four children. (The as yet unnamed Dwight was very dependent upon his mother at the time, and did not put in a visible presence until December 18 of that year.)

A prized memento of that Eisenhower arrival is a picture of our three older children with Olmstead and Mundle greeting the former president at the airport; each of the older Holton children today has a picture of that occasion individually autographed by the former president. I did an end run around General Schultz by having our three older children stand in front of us in the back seat of the red Mercury convertible where Eisenhower, Jinks, and I were sitting on the ride from the airport to downtown Richmond. They were just behind the front seat where the driver and General Schultz were sitting. (Schultz had objected to my suggestion of having the kids there, and it was admittedly a little crowded, but I was determined that the children would have maximum exposure to the president and that spectators have maximum exposure to my great family.)

Schools were let out for the occasion, and a reasonable number of people lined the streets on our way into town from the airport with lots of loud "I like Ike!" shouts and "Welcome Ike" signs visible. At one point, Eisenhower turned to Jinks and said, "It makes you feel a little self-conscious, but it would be a helluva lot worse if they didn't 'like Ike.'" He responded to many of the spectators with a cheerful, "I like you, too!"

There was only a modest crowd for Ike's appearance at the Capitol, and there was a minor calamity when one part of the platform fell down, but no one was hurt. Nor was anything significant said in any of the speeches. When a twenty-one-gun salute began as we approached the Capitol, I was amused to hear the president ask with a little irritation, "Where's my hat, Bob?" General Schultz quickly supplied the president's homburg so he could hold it over his heart appropriately during the salute. He obviously didn't want to risk a photo of an improper response to the salute.

The Capitol appearance was followed by a luncheon at the John Marshall Hotel, and Jinks reported afterward that the president, seated next to her at the head table, ate a hearty lunch, which had been preceded by his short visit to one of the John Marshall bedrooms. (General Schultz confided that during that brief visit upstairs General Eisenhower had phoned Mamie, undressed, donned pajamas, slept for fifteen minutes, redressed, and come down to lunch, all in less than thirty minutes.)

On the return trip to the airport, Jinks commended Eisenhower for the response he gave a lady who requested his autograph. He told the woman that if she would send the program to him in Gettysburg, he would be glad to sign it and return it to her. He explained to Jinks that this ploy usually kept a long line of autograph seekers from forming. This was better, he said, than simply refusing, because refusing would cause a reaction of "Well, what kind of a son of a bitch is that?"

My friend Robert Buford, then chairman of the Third District Republican Committee, was chairman of the event in Richmond, and in that role had asked Governor Harrison's approval for use of the Capitol steps for Eisenhower's appearance. Bobby told me he said to his friend, the governor, that he had a special request to make and added, "This is a request you will have to approve!" After hearing that the request was for a very popular former president to appear on the Capitol steps, Democratic governor Harrison responded wryly, "You're right—it's approved."

We didn't make any money on the event (which was intended only to cover expenses, which it did), and we didn't draw hordes of people, but we *did* get a lot of good press, and I expect that event and the Nixon appearances had as much to do with what I considered to be a successful campaign as any other factor. One regret: Bobby had brass medallions made for all those who attended the luncheon, with a bust of General Eisenhower on one side and a description of the event on the other. Two were cast in sterling silver—one for General Eisenhower and one for me. The regret is that when our home in McLean was burglarized several years later, my sterling silver medallion was stolen. Another regret is that General Eisenhower did not live to see the happy end of my successful four-year campaign. He did have a visit in the hospital from President-elect Nixon and Vice President–elect Agnew in 1968, but he died in 1969 before my election.

Our older children made their own political contribution: they convinced their mother that, "if our new baby is a boy, may we name him for that nice man instead of naming him for a great-grandfather we never knew?" We compromised, and today Dwight Carter Holton bears the names of two icons: President Eisenhower and Bishop Jett (Robert Carter Jett, the first Episcopal bishop of Southwest Virginia).

Raymond Humphries also twice produced Richard Nixon for my campaign in Virginia. To the best of my memory, Nixon's trip to make an address at Washington and Lee for Omicron Delta Kappa (a leadership fraternity founded at Washington and Lee) was probably the result of Humphries' efforts. In any event, Nixon came to Washington and Lee with John Whitaker, a young volunteer assistant who later became secretary of Nixon's cabinet. I gained a little stature by arranging the details of that visit and accompanying Nixon while he was in Virginia for that occasion.

I know that an out-and-out Nixon campaign trip for Holton was arranged by Humphries. Nixon was just at the beginning of his comeback after his 1960 presidential defeat and subsequent defeat in 1962, when he ran for governor of California. He was becoming the "new Nixon" under the tutelage of John Sears—a twenty-seven-year-old political consultant who, in my judgment, was and is one of the best in the business; Sears may have been along on the trip Nixon made for me. Nixon was relaxed, comfortable with the press, without any apparent bitterness, and quite an attractive candidate. There were big crowds everywhere, and Nixon saw enthusiastic responses that likely enhanced his inner conviction that he would yet have a chance to gain the presidency.

The presence of the new Nixon in Virginia in 1965 did help both him and me, and I believe all but one or two of the congressional candidates that he campaigned for in 1966 were successful. It is my opinion that his campaigning in Virginia in 1965 marked the beginning of the momentum that built into the nomination and election of Richard Nixon in 1968. It is sad that the "new Nixon," having by then achieved a broad appeal across a wide spectrum of voter ideology, succumbed to the narrow and racist-based "Southern Strategy" during his 1968 campaign.

The results of the election in 1965 of the governor of Virginia held no surprises for me. It turned out to be a three-way race: the segregationists (read, "white supremacists"), who couldn't abide either Godwin or me, formed the Conservative Party and nominated a man named Bill Story. He got about 14 percent of the total vote; I got just under 38 percent; and Godwin won with a plurality of just 48 percent. Of the 481,000 votes cast for Godwin and me (leaving out the third-party candidate), I got 44 percent, and Godwin got 56 percent.

My objective had been reached. I got 38 percent of the total vote—exactly halfway between my 35–40 percent prediction. Mills Godwin won, but not by a majority, receiving only 48 percent of the total vote. The press described my 1965 campaign as unsuccessful, but I regarded it as just the first year of a four-year campaign to be successfully completed in 1969. And I was right.

Campaign '69

The euphoria generated by Nixon's 1968 election, in which he carried Virginia handily, provided fuel for our 1969 gubernatorial campaign. All over the state, Republicans were optimistic. Some of the more conservative Republicans were, I think, a little suspicious that I was not conservative enough, but because of the impressive results of my 1965 campaign and my activities on behalf of Nixon's nomination and election, I would be unopposed for nomination as the Republican candidate for governor.

The State Central Committee went along unanimously with my recommendation that an early nominating convention be held in Roanoke on March 1, 1969. The early convention date put some pressure on me to put together a campaign staff. It was also essential that willing and capable candidates for lieutenant governor and attorney general be available when the nominating convention convened.

John Ritchie, a lawyer who impressed me when I first met him during his appearance as an associate counsel in the Jewel Ridge Coal litigation, was my first brick in building a campaign staff. He had written me soon after Nixon's election in the fall of 1968, saying that if the Nixon personnel people were serious about their publicly announced intention to acquire the very best talent for the new administration, he, John Ritchie, would like to be considered. Would I, Linwood Holton, help him? My response to John: "Don't bury yourself in that great big federal bureaucracy. I'm going to be elected governor in 1969; join me now at the very beginning of my campaign, and help me to put it all together."

To my great delight, he accepted that challenge with some alacrity. It was one of the best moves I ever made; John became and remained my closest confidant throughout my entire term. Four years later, during an official visit John and I made as part of a Virginia delegation to Sweden, Pierre Gillenheimer (chairman and CEO of the Volvo organization in Sweden) asked me what John's title of "executive assistant" meant. I told him, "John Ritchie hears everything I hear; he hears everything I say; he has a vocabulary of two words, and when he says, 'But, Governor . . . ,' I know I'd better rethink whatever it was I was getting ready to do." He did a great many more things than serve as my conscience, but highest on his list of contributions to the success of my administration was his wisdom.

Acquiring running mates was considerably more involved. I was eager to have Senator H. D. "Buzz" Dawbarn as the candidate for lieutenant governor. Buzz had been elected to the Virginia Senate in 1967, upsetting incumbent Senator George Cochran, one of the stars of the younger generation of Democratic officeholders—the Young Turks. Buzz lived in Waynesboro, part of the Shenandoah Valley, and his presence on the ticket would give us representation in an area where the potential for Republican majorities was great. Buzz, whose first wife had died after a long bout with cancer a few years earlier, had remarried only a few weeks before the convention and was in no mood to undertake a full-time statewide political campaign.

His new wife, Mary Cam, was a great sport and very patient with those of us, including me, who persisted in our solicitation of Buzz to run. Our importunate calls to his room in the Hotel Roanoke came even up to midnight the night before the convention. When he finally capitulated, he joined wholeheartedly and enthusiastically in the campaign, as did Mary Cam. The presence of the newlyweds was a very valuable and attractive addition to our ticket.

Dick Obenshain was not quite so reluctant as Buzz, but he was one of those who expressed concern about whether I was conservative enough. I tried to reassure him, pointing out that my dedication to fiscal responsibility was equal to that of anyone, though I made it abundantly clear that my campaign would give major emphasis to much-needed enhancements of opportunities for the minorities in our state, then almost exclusively African American.

Dick was also somewhat concerned that I, the more moderate of the two, would be elected, and he would be defeated. "In that event," I told him, "I will ask you to serve as an important member in my administration." Dick was a successful young lawyer practicing in Richmond, so his presence would add not only a more conservative viewpoint, but also geographical balance to our ticket. He ultimately agreed to join the ticket as our candidate for attorney general.

With a great deal of enthusiasm, the ticket of Holton, Dawbarn, and Obenshain was nominated unanimously at the state Republican convention held at the Hotel Roanoke in my hometown. California governor Ronald Reagan made the keynote address, and his rousing speech magnified the excitement of the entire delegation. With a huge display of unity, our ardent supporters were raring to go.

The Democratic Opposition

On the other hand, the Democrats were not united in 1969 as to who should be anointed to run for governor. Their primary would find three hats in the ring.

Henry Howell was a Democratic state senator from Norfolk. A gregarious fellow with a lot of appeal to rank-and-file workers—a Virginia-style populist—he was anathema to the Democratic Party establishment, having successfully challenged some important rulings of the State Corporation Commission, which favored the big utilities.

Howell had a good sense of humor. Case in point: He published a bumper sticker guaranteed to garner wrath from the establishment, which blared "Welcome to Virginia—owned and operated by VEPCO." (VEPCO was the acronym for the Virginia Electric Power Company serving consumers throughout the greater part of Virginia.) Other slogans such as "Keep the Big Boys Honest" and "There's More Running Around in the Dark Besides Santa Claus" made the managements of major Virginia utilities, and indeed, the entire business community, very nervous. Important political figures, including Governor Godwin and Commissioner Ralph Catterall of the Virginia State Corporation Commission, were also bristling about Mr. Howell. Henry, however, was determined to be governor, and he made public very early his intention to seek the nomination for governor in the Democratic primary in 1969.

Lieutenant Governor Fred G. Pollard was in line to be the gubernatorial candidate as the tacit choice of the remnant of the Byrd organization. Fred was smart, he had long represented Richmond in the Virginia State Senate, and he had the reputation of being something of a financial genius. He probably would have made a good governor, but he was as close, I guess, as anything we had in Virginia to a "Boston Brahmin." His personality simply did not radiate charisma, but he too entered the 1969 Democratic primary for governor.

Ambassador William Corwin Battle had served during World War II with John F. Kennedy in a squadron of U.S. Navy PT boats in the Pacific theater of operations. That association, along with his subsequent support for Kennedy's presidential campaign, brought Bill Battle an appointment as the U.S. ambassador to Australia. Bill and his wife, Barry, enjoyed that experience and served there happily without notable incident. That smooth-running service constituted his only governmental experience; nevertheless, he became the darling of the younger and more moderate members of the Democratic Party in 1969. Support from those groups encouraged Bill to enter the Democratic primary for governor, and I suspect that most of the supporters, including Bill himself, believed that attaining nomination in the Democratic primary would, as usual, be tantamount to election as governor.

At the time, Bill and Barry were casual acquaintances, for we had met them at annual meetings of the Virginia State Bar Association at either the Homestead Hotel in Bath County or at the Greenbrier Hotel in West Virginia. Bill was an attractive, competent lawyer practicing then in Charlottesville as a member of a well-known and highly regarded small law firm. As a couple they would have made a governor and first lady of whom Virginians would have been very proud.

A state senator, J. Sargeant Reynolds of the Reynolds Metals family, was the Democratic nominee for lieutenant governor; he polled a majority vote in the primary against three other candidates, so no runoff was necessary. Sarge was great, a political natural with just the right touch, appealing to all groups. As it turned out, our Republican Buzz Dawbarn gave him a pretty good race, but Sarge won the general election and looked forward to a great political future. It was not to be. About fifteen months into his term, he was diagnosed with an inoperable brain tumor and died at the age of thirty-three. Henry Howell was elected in a special election to fill out his unexpired term.

For attorney general, Andrew P. Miller was the Democratic nominee, but he had three opponents: Guy Farley, a Northern Virginia lawyer who was a member of the House of Delegates; Bernie Levin, a Norfolk lawyer and also a member of the House; and C. Flippo Hicks, a common-sense lawyer who had strong rural support and extensive experience as an assistant attorney general. Farley and Miller led the race in the first primary, and Miller won the runoff. Andy was the son of Francis Pickens Miller, who had bucked the "organization" by giving John Battle Sr. (Bill Battle's father) vigorous opposition in the Democratic primary for governor in 1949 and had run against Senator Byrd a year or two after that. Andy was a Princeton graduate, smart as hell, perceived as arrogant, and was practicing law with the established law firm of Penn Stuart in Abingdon. We thought Dick Obenshain would have a better chance against Miller than Dawbarn would have against Reynolds. But Miller and Reynolds won their respective races in the general election.

My would-be opponent for the gubernatorial slot had a little tougher time getting the nomination. The rules at that time required that the nominee have a majority of the votes, but none of the three candidates—Howell, Pollard, and Battle—won the majority in the first primary. Fred Pollard came in last among the three, so the first primary was followed by a very vigorous campaign between Henry Howell and Bill Battle for the nomination in the runoff primary.

Bill therefore had to campaign practically all summer of 1969, but ultimately he was nominated to face me in the general election. Earlier I described Bill and Barry's courage and integrity about their loss, which had to be a shock to them. I repeat here my admiration for them. I am proud that we were casual friends before the race and have become closer friends through the years since the election.

The Democratic finalists we were to face in November 1969 would have to be categorized as worthy opponents. Very worthy.

The Campaign

I think a lot of the participants—both the candidates and our supporters—felt we were going to win. I certainly did. John Hanes, John Warner, Cynthia Newman, and George Olmstead, sharing that optimism, became the nucleus of a campaign finance committee. John Warner, then undersecretary of the navy, convinced Stetts Coleman, a wealthy retired marine from The Plains, Virginia, to be finance chairman. That group, with the later addition of the "New Republicans" (formerly Byrd Democrats), bore the brunt of raising approximately $800,000—the sum total of what would be spent on our entire campaign.

An interesting little sidelight on the finance effort occurred when Stetts Coleman learned I had endorsed an invitation from a group of Roanoke doctors to have Secretary of Health, Education, and Welfare Bob Finch appear at a hospital dedication in the Roanoke area. Finch had been recently elected as the lieutenant governor of California when Nixon appointed him as his first secretary of health, education, and welfare. The doctors felt that my past Republican relationship with Nixon would help get an affirmative response to their invitation. But Stetts was furious. He saw Finch as nothing less than a "Communist" (though he was actually a middle-of-the-road Republican), and, because I had urged the liberal Finch to come to Virginia, he went through the motions of resigning as my finance chairman.

Unfortunately for Stetts and fortunately for me, he had just arranged a

$100,000 loan to me, probably from George Olmstead's bank, to cover the early expenses of my campaign. Along with Cynthia Newman, John Hanes, and possibly others, Stetts Coleman was one of the endorsers on that note. His "resignation" turned out to be just a little bit of grandstanding, and he continued to raise money (at least until that note was paid and his contingent liability was over).

It became known in the Republican establishment in Washington that President Nixon was supportive of my campaign. Several political consultants came from Washington to review our organization and campaign; they made some helpful suggestions, but most significantly, they arranged for me to interview Marvin Collins, a political consultant who had managed campaigns for George H. W. Bush when he ran for Congress and again for the U.S. Senate from Texas. The Washington consultants believed we needed more experienced management. I was satisfied that John Ritchie and I could do the job, but we were impressed with Marvin, and John and I agreed that the Washington crowd would be happier and more supportive if we went along with their suggestion. Marvin was therefore brought in as the overall campaign manager, and he did a superb job. He fit right in; he and John worked beautifully together, and kept the diverse elements in a statewide campaign focused on winning.

The constellations were aligned right in 1969. I just *knew* we would win. The mantra I had begun in 1965—"Let's have a two-party competitive democracy"—was received with approbation and applause everywhere I spoke. I repeated it in campaign speeches throughout Virginia; my little story about two-drugstore towns brought smiles and assenting nods from every audience: "If you live in a one-drugstore town, you'll get your prescription filled when the druggist gets ready to fill it; if you live in a two-drugstore town, you'll get your prescription filled when you need it." It worked, because it was presented against a history of one-party domination of the political scene in Virginia for more than two generations, and people were well aware of that history.

Over and above that basic theme, there were several key elements that helped add up to victory. For instance, the "Ladies for Lin" entourage was a major inspiration of Cynthia Newman, our Republican national committeewoman. She arranged for a constituent in Northern Virginia to lend us a Dodge motor home that she and her enthusiastic volunteers decorated in our blue, white, and green campaign colors. They filled it up with the three attractive wives of the three candidates and sent it bounding about the Commonwealth every Tuesday through Thursday of the last two months of the campaign, encouraging the women of Virginia to join them as "Ladies for Lin."

Jinks, Mary Cam Dawbarn, and Helen Obenshain had a ball in their traveling motor home dubbed the *Hi Jinks,* as did Cynthia Newman, who arranged the itinerary, and Martha Cook of Berryville, who drove the huge vehicle. The trio of candidates' wives appeared before every Republican women's organization in the state, as well as countless civic and other nonpartisan groups that were delighted to host the visiting campaigners. Cumulatively, the three wives downed at least ten thousand blue and green cookies at morning coffees and literally gallons of green tea in the afternoon; they were rewarded with gallons of free ink that poured from all the weekly newspapers and some dailies too. The peripatetic ladies also generated news reports from every disc jockey at every radio station in Virginia.

Cynthia would turn on the loudspeakers upon entering a town; the music provided by Bob Goodman, our television and advertising specialist, would broadcast tunefully, "Lin Holton has what it takes to lead Virginia . . ." Crowds, some small and some larger, would gather; even those residents who didn't stop to meet the group were intrigued by what was going on.

The "girls," as I somewhat chauvinistically referred to them, had one almost-crisis. They were invited to Grundy, a town in Buchanan County, way out in the mountainous western corner of Virginia, but they couldn't work that stop into their Tuesday-through-Thursday schedule. The ladies of Grundy rejected the invitation of the *Hi Jinks* "girls" to attend their Tuesday appearance in nearby Tazewell County instead. "If you want us," they said, "then come to Grundy."

The crisis was averted when the girls made an exception to their normal schedule and added a Monday-in-Grundy visit. But it meant that Cynthia and Martha had to drive the *Hi Jinks* out there, while the overbooked candidates' wives flew in to the mountaintop airport with one-eyed George Wayne Anderson piloting them in his private airplane. They all gulped when, over the mountains, George Wayne looked down and asked, "Do y'all see a wind sock down there?" One of the three spotted it, and they landed in time for the visit to Grundy on a Monday. We carried Buchanan County.

The New Republicans became part of our campaign toward the end of September. They came in at a crucial time: we were running out of funds, and I had instructed Marvin Collins to cut the payroll if we didn't receive substantial contributions before the next payday. They had money, and they immediately began making large donations. The instigator of the move to join us was

Lawrence Lewis Jr., a wealthy and civic-minded philanthropist, aided substantially by Landon Trigg, a friend of Lawrence's who was a prominent insurance executive in Richmond. Lawrence and I had worked together in the Nixon campaign the prior year, and he had alerted me to his inclination to make the switch from Byrd Democrat who voted generally for Republican presidents to outright Republican. He and Landon sold that idea to several important financial and business leaders centered in Richmond, who signed an ad advising citizens of their intention to support the Republican candidates in the statewide election and urging their friends to do the same. They signed the ad as a group of "New Republicans."

The move to Republican support by the New Republicans was probably aided by my having answered in writing some policy questions put to me early in the campaign by Tom Boushall, retired CEO of the Bank of Virginia and one of the early supporters of the New Republicans. I had been a little concerned about those questions because I was a dedicated liberal on the race issue, and my answers to the questions confirmed that. But my answers to other questions, more in line with conservative positions on fiscal issues, Virginia's right-to-work law, and general attitudes about state-federal relations, may have saved the day. It is my understanding that my opponent, Bill Battle, declined to give written answers to similar questions presented to him. It is a fact that my answers to the questions regarding race issues did not deter the move of the New Republicans to our support.

The contribution we received from the then very influential Crusade for Voters was also extremely important. I had been talking to black leaders throughout the four years following my campaign for governor in 1965, when the endorsement of the Crusade for Voters went to my opponent, Mills Godwin, and made the difference in his election. I'm told that the leadership of the Crusade reasoned in 1965 that Lieutenant Governor Godwin was going to win anyway and it would be better for them to have voted for the winning side. However, the leaders of the Crusade were disappointed with Godwin's response to their entreaties during his 1965–69 term, and that left fertile ground for me to plow as we approached 1969.

Also helpful in winning over the Crusade was showing those leaders a copy of the newspaper advertisement that we had run in our 1957 campaign for the House of Delegates. We had stated our opposition to Massive Resistance by proclaiming in a full-page ad in the *Roanoke Times* in large red letters, "KEEP OUR SCHOOLS OPEN." There was the tangible proof that I was not a newcomer to opposing racial discrimination and promoting equal treatment of blacks. That ad voiced my true sentiments, and it rang true to them.

I knew that the votes of the citizens in African American communities would be very important to the outcome of our campaign, and I had good discussions with many black leaders—including especially Senator Henry Marsh, of Richmond, and Bill Thornton, president of the Richmond Crusade for Voters—frequently between 1965 and 1969 and during the 1969 campaign. One interesting exchange took place, probably in September, in the Hampton–Newport News area. Byron Puryear, a plastering contractor on the peninsula, asked me pointedly after a public meeting: "How do we know you're different? Every four years we hear promises of 'equal treatment,' and every four years we are disappointed. How do we know you are any different?" he repeated.

My response was, "I cannot guarantee for you the future; however, I hope that four years from now I will be able to say to you, 'I told you so.'" Just two years later, after I was elected (with strong support in black communities) and during an appearance before the state conference of the NAACP—the first time a sitting governor of Virginia had ever attended that conference—Byron Puryear introduced me. He told of that exchange on the peninsula during the campaign and said as he introduced me: "I present to you our blue-eyed brother. He can now say, 'I told you so!'"

Indirectly, Mills Godwin contributed to my victory (not that he meant to, because he had strongly supported Bill Battle). His help to me came about because he simply could not stand Henry Howell. At Godwin's insistence, Henry was refused a seat at the head table when the Democrats had their "unity" luncheon after the primaries were over and Bill Battle was finally their nominee for governor. It was therefore not surprising that when Henry Howell made his all-too-obviously unenthusiastic endorsement of the Democratic ticket, he gave a comment to the press that his constituents were "free spirits" and that he didn't know how they would vote in the general election. Those words were taken as a signal from Henry that it was all right to vote for Holton in the general election, and many of them did.

Rounding out the list of various elements that accumulated for a Holton victory was the endorsement of the AFL-CIO. Without doubt that endorsement would have gone to Henry Howell if he had beaten Bill Battle in the primary. Henry was the darling of the leadership of organized labor and of many of its members. The endorsement came to me almost automatically after

Howell's defeat. Consistent with their record in Virginia at least back to World War II, labor took advantage of every opportunity, however slight, to get "out of the Byrd cage!" Battle was no Byrd-ite, but he was closer to being one than I was, and he had the support of Mills Godwin, a former Massive Resister and stalwart of the Byrd organization.

On the positive side, I had had a pleasant relationship with folks from the AFL-CIO ever since I had been endorsed by them dating back to when I ran for the House of Delegates in 1955. Julian Carper and Brewster Snow, AFL-CIO president and treasurer, respectively, were friends with whom I had continued to have a good association and communication. In an earlier time in Virginia political history, a labor endorsement would have had a net negative effect, but in 1969 it was helpful and contributed votes to the victory margin.

It was fun sometime after taking office to have a visit from Julian and Brewster in my little private quarters on the third floor of the Capitol. We socialized and reminisced, and they were very complimentary of my gubernatorial performance. I thanked them for their kind words but expressed some regret that I hadn't been able to do much of anything specific for them or their members. "That's all right, Governor," they said, looking at me and then around at the interior of the inner sanctum: "You do enough by just inviting us in. We've never been here before!"

A two-day break from campaigning that I took in mid-October added renewed energy to the campaign and, I think, was one of the elements that contributed to victory. When the schedules were made up in the summer, I had insisted that there be a one-week moratorium on campaigning in the middle of October. I knew from prior experience that candidates are simply worn out after five or six weeks on the campaign trail, and I thought the rest would be helpful. The hiatus turned out to be only a couple of days of tennis and relaxation, but it was ultimately important.

For example, Bill Battle and I had appeared before a real estate group in Roanoke for an informal campaign debate. We both bombed. We were completely exhausted, he perhaps more than I as a result of his difficult primary campaign. It had been the day before my two-day tennis visit to the Homestead. After checking into the hotel, Roger Hull, my advance man on that trip, gave me unshirted hell for my poor performance in Roanoke earlier that day. He was right, but I already knew I needed to catch my breath, and managed not to wilt under his understandable diatribe.

I got the needed rest, and in our next appearance together, I scored important points over Bill in the Tidewater area. The issue for discussion was consolidation of Virginia's ports. I don't know whether my opponent was prepared on this issue, but I had studied it for several years. I was convinced that the separate efforts of the municipalities involved—Portsmouth, Norfolk, and Newport News—for the development of the port of Hampton Roads needed to be consolidated under a state-sponsored organization that could coordinate the development and marketing activities of that port. As a kid in primary school I'd learned how uniquely valuable the natural port of Hampton Roads was, and as an adult I hated seeing the failure to take advantage of the potential of that natural resource.

When the question was presented on the WAVY television debate between Battle and me, I came out vigorously in support of consolidation. Bill opposed it: "That would make the whole ball of wax come unglued" was his response to the concept of consolidation. Unfortunately for him and fortunately for me in an important vote area, the report of the Breeden Commission, a legislative commission chaired by the popular Norfolk senator Eddie Breeden, supported consolidation of the Hampton Roads ports. The Breeden Commission report was in the *Norfolk Virginian-Pilot* headlines the next day. My support and Battle's opposition were noted in equally significant headlines on the opposite side of the front page of the metro section. Fortuitous? Maybe. In any case, it proved very helpful to my cause.

Support also came from some major figures in the Republican establishment. Vice President Agnew appeared on my behalf at a rally in a Staunton high school and in late September at a dinner meeting in Richmond. Governor Reagan attended an enthusiastic campaign breakfast in Norfolk on October 23; and Governor Louis Nunn, the Republican in Kentucky who had been elected the year before, campaigned with me in Southwest Virginia. I have always remembered his comment to me: "I believe you're going to win, Lin, and I have a piece of advice for you: Get young people on your staff. They don't know it can't be done." I took his advice: the average age of the key members of my staff was not quite thirty.

President Nixon kept more than a finger on the pulse of the campaign. I was able pretty much to adhere to my rule of not campaigning on Sunday, and during those last weeks I was pretty certain to receive a call at home from him on each of those Sundays. He was receiving reports from others as well, and he shared my increasing optimism about the outcome. I'm sure those reports from me and others helped the president decide to make a campaign appearance on my behalf. His support was another of the tangible contributions to my election.

Soon after my nomination in the spring of 1969, a Texas political photographer who had been recommended to us by the Washington Republican establishment went with me to the White House for a picture-taking session with the president. I was first invited into the Oval Office to be alone with Nixon, without the photographer, so I was more than a little surprised to find Henry Kissinger, the national security advisor to the president, just finishing a conversation with him. The president introduced us, and after pleasantries were exchanged, Mr. Kissinger left.

The president then told me that he and Kissinger had been discussing how to respond to the hostile act of North Korea in seizing the USS *Pueblo*. That ship was a fairly small, lightly armed communications vessel that had been eavesdropping in international waters outside North Korea. It had been seized by several small North Korean gunboats and taken to a North Korean port. The president told me that he and Kissinger had been considering several options, of which two seemed the most feasible.

"We could bomb one of their ports for retaliation, or we could seize one of their ships," the president said. He then looked directly at me and asked, "What would *you* do?" In my just-appointed role as a temporary national security advisor, I didn't hesitate: "I would seize one of their ships, but I would not start dropping bombs." Nixon nodded. He and Kissinger felt the same way, he said. To drop bombs would probably invite a similar retaliation from the North Koreans, and the outcome of such an exchange would be unpredictable. He agreed that seizing one of their ships would be preferable, but added ruefully, "We just can't find one."

The photographer was called in, and a picture session followed. Some shots were taken with the president at his desk, some in the living room section of the Oval Office near the fireplace, and some in the Rose Garden just outside the Oval Office. The president seemed in no hurry, and we not only got the pictures we'd hoped for, but I also had a very pleasant and somewhat extended visit. The photographer's comment after we left the White House was, "Boy, you really are friends with the president, aren't you?"

The resulting pictures were used in a variety of our campaign ads, and were helpful in convincing voters that I was close enough to President Nixon that Virginia would indeed benefit from the relationship if I were elected governor. I had already demonstrated the value of that relationship by taking a

Richmond business delegation to importune the secretary of transportation to grant funds to construct Highway I-195 to connect I-95 and I-64 to the new Richmond toll road. Secretary John Volpe granted that request, and I-195 was built as part of the interstate system, with substantial funding from the federal government.

As the campaign developed, there were increasing signals that we were doing well. There was no polling as such; neither Marvin Collins nor I put much stock in what was then only a fad but has since become a political staple—that is, take a poll every morning to see not only how you rank but also what public policy you should favor and what you should oppose. The signals we relied on were the amount of headline coverage, the size of crowds, the reactions of potential voters in question-and-answer sessions, the reactions of audiences to candidate debates, and the results of school and college mock elections. (I won all of the college mock elections except one.) These factors gave us increasing confidence, and in early fall President Nixon committed to a campaign appearance on our behalf.

We selected the Roanoke area as the place, and the Roanoke County Convention Center in Salem for the event to be held, following one of the basic guidelines for political rallies: pick a small hall to ensure that you have a standing-room-only crowd. We did, and then some. When the president's motorcade arrived at the Center, after its short trip from the Roanoke airport, where big, beautiful Air Force One had landed, folks were all but hanging from the rafters.

As the pre-presidential appearance hoopla grew in the press, about the only negative thing the Democrats had been able to come up with was that they were "not going to have any outside agitators" in *their* campaign. Boy, did the president ever lay that one low! After he was presented and when the enthusiastic cheers died down, his first words were, "That's quite a welcome for an 'outside agitator'!" Cheers came, loud and long, and then Nixon's zinger: "I do not think the president of the United States is an outsider in any state of the nation, but especially not here in Virginia where we have lived longer than any state except California. So I speak to you as a former Virginian, speaking for the next governor of Virginia."

Norfolk's *Virginian-Pilot* concluded its description of those introductory remarks with the sentence: "The crowd rose in a final frenzy." It was the best political rally I have ever attended, before or since, and it came just one week before election day. It ensured that our campaign for governor would peak at exactly the right time.

The president was on the phone again before eleven o'clock on election night. Everything had gone well for him in his first year—the honeymoon year—of his administration, and he was thrilled with the progress this election day had produced for his ambition to create a majority Republican Party. Not only had Virginia elected a Republican governor for the first time, but New Jersey, an important industrial state with a naturally heavy Democratic constituency, had also elected a Republican, Bill Cahill. It was a night never to be forgotten.

8 The Nixon Story

Richard Nixon was a man of many personalities. I saw more than a few of them in the years between 1960 and 1974. He was gritting his teeth on our first meeting just before an appearance in Victory Stadium in Roanoke when I was the city Republican chairman and he a 1960 presidential candidate. He was in great pain from a serious knee infection but somehow got through the evening with admirable aplomb and, it seemed to me, with courage. Until very late in his presidency, I admired him for his courage, among many other positive qualities, even though I took passionate exception to his embracing the Southern Strategy.

Only on rare occasions did I see flare-ups of his renowned paranoia. I recall one humorous exchange when he said to me with what I detected as a tinge of hostility: "You're Ivy League, aren't you?" "Mr. President," I protested, "I'm not one of them—I just went to the Harvard *Law School!*" One thing I never personally heard was his reputed salty language. I don't think I ever heard as much as a "hell" or "damn" from the presidential lips, and for fourteen years I certainly had plenty of opportunities to hear some swearing.

I watched the development of the "new" Nixon, a phrase used by the press as Nixon began his comeback, maybe beginning when he campaigned for me in 1965 and certainly during the congressional elections in 1966. You could tell that Nixon was thinking about coming back. This time he did not emerge as the mean Nixon the press had enjoyed focusing on, with the "you won't get the chance to kick Nixon around anymore" attitude. That Nixon had disappeared. He was personable, attractive, candid—and available to a press that welcomed the change. The resulting enhancement of his public image was marked.

His close and possibly only political confidant in those days was John Sears, who had a great relationship with the press and had a great deal to do with molding the new Nixon. I don't remember exactly when I met John. It may have been during the Nixon visit to Virginia in 1965, when I had helped make the arrangements for him to speak to a scholastic fraternity at Washington and Lee. Sears was coaching Nixon in 1965–66 and maintaining a liaison between Nixon and the press, so we likely met then. The new Nixon was an attractive candidate who could appeal to all groups of society, and I was very encouraged by that. He was extremely popular in Virginia, and I asked him to campaign for me. When he came back to help me later in 1965, I was grateful. Our campaign hadn't had a lot going for us, financially. We had spent only $80,000 in that first campaign, with little in the budget for advertising. The only things we really had going for us in any way significant were the campaign visits of General Eisenhower and of Nixon.

The twenty-eight-hour whirlwind Nixon tour of Virginia in a little four-passenger airplane started with a dinner in Arlington. After Norfolk, Harrisonburg, and Lynchburg events the next day, I told Nixon we were about two hours behind schedule. I pointed out that we could cancel our leg to rural Wise County in Southwest Virginia, where I had grown up. I added that the folks there would be mightily disappointed, but admitted that going there would make us quite late for the banquet in Roanoke that evening.

"Will there be whiskey at the banquet?" he inquired, and when I said, "Yes, of course," he said immediately, "Then let's go to Wise." He rightly figured cocktails would keep the Roanoke group waiting patiently. So we flew all the way out to Wise County and landed at the little Lonesome Pine airport on a bitterly cold day. That frozen crowd, which included my parents and my sister Louisa, just loved him; they had waited almost three hours to give him a very warm reception. We came back to a big banquet in Roanoke. Though we were late, he got a similarly warm reception from a big crowd that included my nephew Van Holton, who in his Boy Scout uniform led in the Pledge of Allegiance to the flag. I think that Virginia visit certainly helped build his confidence about a political comeback and maybe getting the nomination for president again.

In February or March 1967, while Jinks and I were on a three-week ski trip to Austria, we received a message to return a telephone call to the States. That created some anxiety in both Jinks and me. We had four young children at home; what did an international call imply? When I returned the call, the operator told me it was somebody named Peter Flanigan. With much relief I turned to Jinks, who was hovering impatiently just outside the phone booth, and said, "Oh, it's just political."

Peter Flanigan chatted lightly about where I was skiing—he had skied there himself, and we talked a little about that before he got to the point. The point was to ask me to join a six-person Nixon for President Committee, one of those pre-campaign committees that are part of the process of building up to a national campaign for the nomination. I've forgotten who all was on that committee, but there was a doctor from California and somebody named Hill who had been an ambassador to Mexico; Maurice Stans was one of the group, and they wanted me to be on it as a representative of the South.

That call may have been precipitated by a luncheon visit I had had with Nixon in his Central Park apartment in early 1967. I had asked for the meeting, my purpose being to ask him to run again for president. I had felt that the gods were on my side when, after several fortuitous coincidences and despite all the odds—including seventeen inches of snow and the 10-degree temperature in Manhattan, closed airports, canceled commercial flights, and a hitch hiked private plane ride—I arrived at his New York apartment at 12:55 p.m. for a 1:00 p.m. appointment!

Nixon admitted candidly he was interested in making the race again, and I think both of us, with our fairly accurate political instincts, suspected that Michigan governor George Romney, although then pretty well ahead in the polls of those seeking the Republican nomination, would stumble. Neither of us was surprised when Romney effectively took himself out of the race by admitting that upon his return from the war zone in Vietnam, he had been "brainwashed." That admission doesn't look too significant now, but admitting that he hadn't seen through the faked reports from the military turned out to be fatal for George Romney's campaign.

Of course I agreed to serve on the six-man Nixon for President Committee, and subsequently was selected to manage the nomination and election campaigns in the middle border states of Virginia, West Virginia, Kentucky, Tennessee, and North Carolina. I selected Harry Flemming, one of our more liberal Republicans from Alexandria, and Dortch Warriner, one of our more conservative Republicans from Greensville County, to cochair the Nixon for President effort in Virginia. At the Republican National Convention, we were successful in obtaining for Nixon the votes of the entire Virginia delegation— all except for those of Cynthia Newman and Wayne Lustig, chair of the Second District Republican Committee (which included Norfolk), both of whom preferred Nelson Rockefeller.

A crisis nearly developed at the Republican convention in Miami Beach when word got out that Nixon, the new nominee, was going to select Spiro Agnew, the little-known governor of Maryland, for the vice-presidential slot. Our delegation agreed to go along with Nixon's selection in spite of serious reservations, but Dortch Warriner was extremely disappointed and disturbed. He was still voicing his misgivings to me as we sat in the convention hall just prior to the convening of the session at which Agnew was to be nominated. I said very quietly to Dortch, "You have performed superbly; you have done everything I have asked you to do in this campaign; it has turned out well so far, our candidate is the nominee; now don't f—— it up!"

Dortch looked as though he would like to bite my head off, but he hesitated long enough for me to point to the stage and say, "Look who's at the podium to nominate Agnew!" He turned to see John Lindsay, the liberal mayor of New York, preparing to make that nomination. That may not have ended Dortch's consternation, but it squelched any intent he might have had to express his dismay publicly.

The ensuing presidential campaign substantially abandoned the more moderate course that I thought Nixon was following and began the active implementation of the Southern Strategy so strongly advocated by South Carolina's Senator Strom Thurmond, his aide Harry Dent, and some political consultants, among whom may have been Kevin Phillips. I thought then it was a mistake, and though I did not protest loudly at that time, Harry Flemming, a Virginia friend who was then a White House personnel officer, and I had an hour-long meeting with U.S. attorney general John Mitchell in 1972. John, a Nixon confidant, was shortly to resign in order to head the Committee to Re-elect the President (CREEP). We tried our best to convince John to urge Nixon to pursue a more moderate course in the coming campaign. Dour John puffed his pipe, *looked* like he was trying to listen, never said a word, and I could tell from his body language that I might as well be speaking to a statue in a nearby park.

Active solicitation of notorious segregationists such as Senators Jim Eastland and John Stennis of Mississippi and Strom Thurmond of South Carolina would, in my judgment, nullify efforts to gain support in the black communities and alienate middle-of-the-road voters who would disapprove of the segregationist appeal. I still think it was a mistake. The Southern Strategy not only almost lost the 1968 election, but it aligned the Republican Party with a group of segregationists from the South that would produce some victories in the near term, but that, I believed, would also doom the Republican Party to minority status in the long run. Results of midterm elections in 2006 furnished more evidence of increasing isolation and minority status for a southern Republican Party.

With political consultants like Lee Atwater, who sponsored the infamous, racist Willy Horton ad in George H. W. Bush's presidential campaign in 1988, and with the arrogance of Tom DeLay, whose base in Texas obviously is of the same ilk as the old-time segregationists, you don't need enemies to ensure your destruction. Fiscal irresponsibility almost lost Virginia its Triple-A bond rating under the leadership of Virginia's Republican governor Jim Gilmore in 2001, whose base is the same group of conservative extremists. Their positions are consistent with Reagan's "I believe in states' rights" speech in Philadelphia, Mississippi—a coded appeal to white supremacists—which opened his 1980 campaign, and with George W. Bush's blatant appearance at racially discriminatory Bob Jones University as part of his campaign for president in the year 2000.

Governor Mark Warner's election as a Democrat in 2001, followed by Democrat Tim Kaine's election in 2005, may well signal the beginning of a return to moderation in the South—at least in Virginia. I write more fully of this in chapter 13.

In the Waldorf Tower on election night, it was interesting to watch some of the principals. John Mitchell, Nixon's campaign manager, was really sweating as we lost New York, Pennsylvania, and Ohio. Murray Chotiner, a close Nixon confidant from the beginning of his political career in California, was nervously making telephone calls over in the corner of the room. But John Sears, who sat next to Jinks and me on the floor in that hotel room, was confident of victory even after we lost some of those big states. And win we did—barely!

Jinks and I were in a hallway in the Waldorf as a happy Nixon walked toward us from the opposite direction at about midmorning the day after the 1968 election. He stopped when he saw us, and immediately gleefully ticked off on his hand the border states of Kentucky, Virginia, North Carolina, and Tennessee (the area my crew and I had been responsible for in the campaign), all of which had gone for him in the election and had made the difference for victory. These were states that Nixon won in spite of his Southern Strategy; more moderate appeal would have made him even stronger there, except possibly in North Carolina.

Later that morning when we were in a room together just before his press conference, Nixon and I had a brief talk. He said, "I'm tired, and I'm going to

Florida for a rest. When I get back, I want to talk to you about an appointment in the administration." My response was, "Mr. President, of course I will do anything you want me to, but what I would like most is for you to help me next year become the first Republican governor of Virginia." He did exactly that.

Reflecting today on the fall and rise and fall again of Richard Nixon, three images come to mind, perhaps somewhat blurred by the passage of time.

The first is of a happy Richard Nixon rejoicing at an informal press conference soon after being elected president of the United States in 1968, where he recalled that during the campaign a very young member of an audience at a campaign stop in Ohio had displayed a banner on which were written the words "Bring Us Together." He then displayed to the press conference some embroidered crewelwork (which I believe he attributed to his daughter Julie) quoting the words "Bring Us Together." I don't remember the specific words he used then about what his administration would do, but clearly his implicit promise was that he would do his utmost to "bring us together."

Following the four years of Nixon's first term, a confluence of forces in 1972—including the campaign of Democratic candidate George McGovern, who ran on the extremely liberal side of the ideological spectrum—resulted in an overwhelming reelection victory for Richard Nixon. He was jubilant. I was in his office shortly after that reelection, where he and everyone at the White House took great delight in displaying two wooden cutouts sent to him by a supporter after the election. One was in the shape of Massachusetts, and the other of the District of Columbia—the only two places Nixon had failed to carry in the 1972 Electoral College vote. He was at the absolute pinnacle of success. Watergate was beginning to materialize on the horizon, but only faintly.

The second image is more distinct because it is taken from an oral history of Elliot Richardson in *Portraits of American Presidents,* produced by the Miller Center at the University of Virginia. In volume 6 of that oral history, Mr. Richardson described his own feelings and a meeting with the president:

> He somehow could not bring himself to overcome the perception of opponents as enemies. I had never had a really close personal relationship with him, but when he asked me to become the attorney general, there was a moment when I thought that his need for me had created a bond of a kind that had never existed before then. In a conversation at Camp David on April 1, 1973,

after agreeing to do it, I said, "Mr. President, there's one thing I've been wanting to say to you for a long time, and it is that I wish somehow deep down inside yourself you could come to believe that you have really won. You won not only the election of 1968 but re-election in 1972 by an overwhelming margin. The American people are rooting for you to succeed. Even your former opponents have a deeper feeling toward the well-being of the United States than a sense of resentment or enmity arising out of past political conflict. If you could only bring yourself to reach out with magnanimity towards your former opponents, you would thereby establish a foundation of support that nothing could overcome." He looked at me, but he said nothing, nothing that I can remember. I don't think he really got it. (p. 54)

The third image is substantively correct but possibly hazy because my only source for it is memory. A future publication by the Miller Center of more Nixon tapes may bring greater clarity. It was at a formal dinner in the State Dining Room at the White House in early 1973, probably February. The occasion was the annual meeting of the National Governors Association, always held in Washington. As chairman of the Republican Governors Association, I was one of the three or four governors asked to make short speeches at the dinner. I used the Ohio plea "bring us together" as my theme and urged that it be the theme of the second term of the Nixon administration. I suggested strongly that even southerners were ready to follow leadership that would leave racial prejudice behind and "bring us together." I gave as evidence that, though Jinks and I had very visibly supported the extremely unpopular busing laws by sending our children to integrated public schools, we received *not one single written protest* from any of our constituents, despite enormous publicity about it.

My statement at that dinner was a not-very-well-disguised plea to abandon the divisiveness of the Southern Strategy. But Richard Nixon didn't get it. He passed close by me on our way out of the dining room, and merely nodded coolly. I had the distinct impression that he was not pleased with what I'd said. I had a sudden feeling of pity for him. He was at the peak of his popularity; he would have retained public support if he had exercised leadership to "bring us together." I think he really wanted to reach out, but he simply did not know how. And that inability was his tragic flaw.

The events leading to and beyond Watergate reflected a deep-seated paranoia that kept him from reaching out. "They" (political opponents, liberal press, whoever) were always the cause of his troubles. If ever he had been able to take Elliot Richardson's wise advice, to reach out "with magnanimity towards [his] former opponents," the ensuing (almost universal) support would surely have generated self-confidence that he had never known. A candid and sincere apology for the "third-rate burglary" that began the sad Watergate saga could possibly have reduced even those major mistakes in judgment to a bump in the road, and perhaps he and the country could have gotten on with the tasks at hand.

Since I have here so confidently psychoanalyzed Nixon, it would be fair to ask me, as my daughter Tayloe once did in response to my frequent assertion that I had known from the beginning that Nixon had an inferiority complex: "If you knew that about him, then why did you support and vote for him?" The reasons I gave her then still hold true: First, I believed he could be elected. This was important because the anxiety and frustration over the Vietnam War under Johnson's leadership was tearing the country apart. Second, I believed he could stop a war that desperately needed to be stopped; and third, I thought that being elected president of the United States would cure anybody's inferiority complex. Tragically for him and for this country, his just grew worse.

Help for Keeping
9 Those Promises

Though I had had no prior serious executive or administrative responsibilities, I was well aware that the success of my term depended on my finding, selecting, appointing, or retaining competent individuals to run the various agencies that comprise the state government. I was fortunate that John W. Hanes Jr., a friend, supporter, and partner in a prominent New York investment firm, was available to chair a secret executive search committee to aid this effort. Two other good friends agreed to serve on the committee: Herman Pevler, then CEO of the Norfolk and Western Railway in Roanoke (which later merged with Southern to become the present Norfolk Southern Railroad), and James W. Wheat Jr., CEO of Wheat First Securities, a prominent investment firm in the East, headquartered in Richmond. They recruited Rodger Provo, a former reporter on the *Norfolk Virginian-Pilot* and a member of my campaign staff, to serve as informal executive director of the secret search committee. Each of these four was a top-notch selection; the search committee either found outstanding potential governmental leaders or, in some cases, retained them, for they reviewed performance of incumbents as well.

Caldwell Butler had intended to drop out of the House of Delegates at the end of his term in 1969. He had very good reasons. His wife was afflicted with severe chronic migraine headaches, and they had four rambunctious teenage sons who needed at least *some* paternal supervision. He said he really needed to spend more time at home in Roanoke.

I understood; nevertheless, I had begged him—literally, *begged* him—to run again for reelection in 1969 and to stay in the House of Delegates for two more years. There was no doubt that he would be reelected, as he was enormously popular with his constituents. He resisted, and I knew he wasn't as convinced as I was that my race for governor would be successful this time. I insisted that I would be elected, and that it was *critical* to have him in the House of Delegates for the first two years of my term. With reluctance, he had agreed. As I had known would be the case, he was of inestimable assistance to me during those first two years. For example, he set up a pre-inauguration meeting between me and Roy Smith, the powerful Democratic chairman of the powerful Appropriations Committee. It was a breakfast meeting for two where we learned that we shared many important views and agreed that neither of us would permit our party differences to interfere with our mutual cooperation. It was an enormously important entente that boded well for Virginia's progress during the next few years.

In the beginning, Caldwell both assisted me in the preparation of my inaugural address and did yeoman's service as a liaison, not only between me and the Republican cadre but also with some of the senior Democratic leaders of the House of Delegates. And I could trust his advice. For instance, when I told him I was considering the appointment of Oliver W. Hill, a highly respected African American Democrat and longtime civil rights leader, to fill a vacancy on the Richmond Circuit Court, he cautioned, "Linwood, when the first Republican governor makes his first judicial appointment, he must appoint a Republican." He was right. Though my inclination was to make appointments on a nonpartisan basis, the appointment of a Democrat to the *first* judicial vacancy would have made it very difficult to expect any party loyalty to me from Republicans in the future.

Caldwell did leave the House of Delegates at the end of his term in 1971, but without much of a time lag, he simply transferred his service to the U.S. House of Representatives. That came about because Richard Poff, who had served as the Sixth District's congressman for almost twenty years since his dramatic win in 1952, had reached the point of battle fatigue. Weary of campaigning, endless chicken dinners, and constituents who looked to him for help well beyond the capacity of any Washington lawmaker, and almost paranoid about any criticism from the press, he no longer had the heart and drive for the political scene.

When Justice Tommy Gordon of the Virginia Supreme Court of Appeals resigned from his post in 1971, Richard Poff promptly accepted my offer to appoint him to fill that vacancy. Richard's comment to me later was, "Linwood, you saved my life when you put me on that court." As recently as 2005, Richard was still serving as a senior judge, hearing arguments supporting requests for that court to hear cases on appeal.

Caldwell was elected to the U.S. House of Representatives with little trouble and served there nobly for ten years. He was a member of the House Judiciary Committee, and his most painful decision while in Congress was voting to impeach Richard Nixon as president of the United States in 1974. He had made a thorough investigation of all the facts available concerning the president's conduct, including careful and extensive attention to the tapes of the conversations in the Oval Office. Caldwell knew in his mind and heart that the president had committed impeachable offenses, and he did not hesitate to vote for impeachment, but it was for him an enormously painful decision.

During the remainder of his years in Congress, Caldwell was instrumental in writing the legislation to reform the bankruptcy laws of the United States. In spite of his minority status as a Republican, with the acquiescence of Peter Rodino, the Democratic chairman of the House Judiciary Committee, Caldwell, as ranking Republican on the appropriate subcommittee, had a leading responsibility for drafting that legislation.

I regret that he never felt he was in a position to run for governor of Virginia, but again, family concerns stood in the way. It is my conviction that he would have been elected handily if he had declared as a candidate in 1973. It might also well be that with Caldwell in the race, Mills Godwin would not have run again for governor. Had Caldwell Butler been my successor rather than Godwin, his leadership would have kept the Republican Party of Virginia (for the time at least) on the more moderate course I tried to set during my term.

John Ritchie, who had been my top campaign confidant, of course continued to supply his wisdom as my executive assistant. He had able assistance from his secretary, Maria Barrow, as I did from Lois Firesheets (later, by marriage, Lois Shaw), my executive secretary. John's principal professional assistant was Alexander ("Sandy") Gilliam. Sandy was the office operations manager; he handled all of the office correspondence and drafted replies to letters requiring my personal attention and signature. He did whatever was necessary and rendered especially valuable service to me when he served as one of my aides on a trip to Israel in 1973. His previous experience as a foreign service officer was invaluable to me on that trip. He had been one of the secretaries to our embassy in Tel Aviv, and he was therefore able to give a more balanced viewpoint than the version we received from some of our enthusiastic Israeli guides.

There's a background story about how Bill Robertson became a very significant special assistant in my administration, paving the way toward some of my longtime goals. Sometime between 1965 and 1967, I learned from news reports that Bill had sold more apple jelly than any other member of the Virginia State Junior Chamber of Commerce. The state Jaycees wanted to establish a summer camp for mentally retarded youngsters in Bedford County, Virginia, and the proceeds of the apple jelly sales were to be used to support that project. There was a lot of hoopla in the press about Bill's sales success, and he was recognized for that outstanding achievement by an award with an appropriate ceremony at a state meeting of the Virginia Jaycees.

Bill Robertson was a black educator, the principal of a small elementary school in Roanoke in which all of the students were black. I made a point of meeting him and was impressed immediately. If memory serves, I discussed as early as that first meeting my activity on behalf of the Republican Party in Virginia, and outlined my plan to run for governor in 1969. Afterward, I told Caldwell Butler—then my law partner and minority leader of the Republicans in the Virginia House of Delegates—that I would like to urge Bill to establish some Republican credentials by running for the House of Delegates from Roanoke in the elections to be held in 1967. I knew his winning would be a long shot, but my rationale was that if I made him part of the management team in the governor's office when I became governor two years later, the fact of his having been a Republican candidate would make it more acceptable to other Republicans. Caldwell wasn't really excited about my idea, though he went along with it.

But Bill Robertson *was* excited about it, even though he understood that it was a gamble. I cautioned him that winning the House of Delegates seat would be difficult. I further cautioned him that there was no certainty in anybody's mind (except mine) that I would be elected governor in 1969. But I assured him that if I *did* become governor, I had in mind a prominent role for an African American on the governor's staff. Bill liked the entire idea, and we made it work. He was nominated for the House of Delegates with my support; he did lose, but when I became governor, he was appointed special assistant to the governor with responsibility for general liaison to the black community and for promoting a program to enhance equal employment opportunities.

In the early part of my administration, Bill Robertson proposed that we sponsor legislation that would have had the effect of putting some degree of coercion on Virginia employers to hire more black people. I overruled that summarily. "Bill," I said, "we have more laws along that line now than we know what to do with. We need now to lead by persuasion and example." Bill understood that, and he began a series of meetings with various agency heads to

convey the governor's serious desire that there be more black people in responsible positions in the state government. He charmed most of those agency
heads, though he met with a degree of reluctance and/or inertia on the part
of some. The superintendent of the State Police moved very slowly, taking the
position that he would not admit any applicant who was "not qualified." Bill
spent a considerable amount of his own personal time recruiting a number of
black preachers to "assist" the superintendent to find qualified black applicants. First, black toll takers were hired; then black secretaries began to appear
around the Capitol; and gradually, more blacks began to occupy midlevel
management positions in various places throughout the state government.

Most importantly, Bill organized four Governor's Conferences on Equal
Employment Opportunities, held in four different regions of the state. He invited, in the governor's name, the top employment officers of Virginia corporations, large and small, to attend conferences that would encourage the hiring of more black people in the private sector. Our theme: Accept them for
jobs that utilize *all* of their talents, and pay them accordingly. Each of those
conferences was attended by standing-room-only audiences, and Bill made the
sale with many of those managers who were responsible for hiring in the private sector. Results were extremely positive; by the time my term was over,
there was a noticeable increase in the "salt and pepper" appearance of employees in financial institutions and other major employers in Virginia.

An aspect of the Bill Robertson story still moves me today. At some point
I learned from Bill that his mother was one of the corps of women who cleaned
the professional offices in the Shenandoah Building, where my law office in
Roanoke was located. I still remember that lady, and how she often had been
accompanied by a young child. I had actually "known" Bill for many more
years than I originally knew. He was a real missionary throughout Virginia and
contributed mightily to the positive environment for racial harmony that I
had outlined as a goal in my inaugural address.

Another important opportunity to advance my goal of improved racial
harmony in Virginia was in the appointment of the state director of Selective
Service. Young Virginians were being drafted daily and sent to participate in
the increasingly unpopular war in Vietnam. Two-thirds of those Virginia
draftees were black. But the entire retinue of the Selective Service system—
from secretaries of the local boards to the state director—was white and con-
sisted mostly of old men. I wanted to appoint someone who had the stature,
capacity, and ability to integrate that system. I believed that if we were to continue to draft Virginians, it would minimize racial frictions if the potential

draftees could see that the draft system was staffed in part by persons who had both experience and understanding of the perspective of black people.

Rodger Provo, director of my secret personnel selection committee, discovered the right candidate. His name was Ernie Fears. Ernie was the athletic director and basketball coach at what was then Norfolk State College, a four-year institution with virtually all-black enrollment. He had produced several championship basketball teams, he was at ease in any setting, he had a great personality, including a fine sense of humor, he was smart, and he was a highly respected citizen. Without question, he was the right person for the job.

But Ernie's appointment was not to be a routine matter. When approached by Rodger about the job, he hesitated on the basis of the negative suspicion in the black community of anything Republican. "The Party of Abe Lincoln" was becoming "the Party of Southern Strategy," code words that the black community recognized as a lure for support from southern white supremacists. How could anyone with a background in rural Virginia (namely me) not be tainted with at least some "good ol' boy" white supremacy? He phrased it later, "I thought anybody who came from Big Stone Gap was bound to have some red on his neck." The upshot was that when I asked him to come up to my office for a talk, *he* interviewed *me.*

"Why are there no black toll takers on the Petersburg Turnpike?"

"Why are there no black state troopers?"

"Why are there so few black secretaries in the state bureaucracy?"

Years later Ernie reported to a public audience that my response to each question was, "Get 'em!" and he decided right then to risk participation in my administration.

In the two years that followed, Ernie implemented every item of the job description that I discussed with him before his appointment. At the end of that time, almost all of the local and appeal boards of the Selective Service system in Virginia included representatives of both the white and the black communities. Though this fairly revolutionary change was effected by Ernie without friction or criticism, there was one rather amusing exception.

Cecil Taylor was chairman of the Selective Service Appeals Board in the jurisdiction that included Lynchburg. Cecil Taylor, a contemporary of mine at Washington and Lee University, was a traditionalist on racial matters, and was moving very slowly toward the goals of integration that I sought. He wrote me that he was in accord with my desire to place the "best qualified" candidates in appointive positions in the state government, and he pointed out that obviously, from among those available for appointment to vacancies on the Lynchburg Appeals Board, "a college graduate is more qualified than a Pullman porter." My responding letter was short. I told Cecil that in some circumstances, the "Pullman porter" might have better qualifications than the college graduate.

Ernie told me later that Cecil's response to his suggestion that the black "Pullman porter" might become the eventual appointee was: "The governor is a friend of mine; I know he is not going to integrate *this* board. If he does, the incumbent board members will resign." Ernie simply smiled at Cecil, knowing that I would appoint the black "Pullman porter," which I did.

In late 1972 or early 1973, Ernie came to my office to report that radio station WMAL in Washington, D.C., had offered him the post of personnel director at a salary of $30,000. He made it appear that he was asking for my advice as to whether he should accept the job. As state director of Selective Service, he had accomplished substantially what I desired, and knowing that Ernie's present salary was about $18,000, I said, "My God, Ernie, why haven't you already accepted it?" With a big grin he said, "Well, I have—but I thought I'd better come up here and go through the formalities."

As we talked a little more about his successes and about how sorry I was to see him go, I asked, "Ernie, whatever happened to Cecil Taylor? I never did hear that he resigned when we put that black man on his appeals board." "No" replied Ernie. "Cecil said, 'If we resign, that son-of-a-bitch in Richmond will put all N———s on this board!'" Ernie and I had a good laugh.

During the next thirty years, Ernie was a prominent fixture in the Washington, D.C., radio-television community. Among other things, he made the music affiliate of WMAL in Washington number one in ratings, and in his later years he taught classes at Catholic and Howard universities. We occasionally had lunch together during those years, always at the Palm Restaurant in Washington, and I never had to identify myself when I called to arrange those lunch dates. When he heard my voice, he always exclaimed, "My main man!" He died in 2003 after a discouraging and lingering illness. His last words to me on the telephone in the week before his death were, "I'm so tired of being sick." It was a sad day for me when he died several days later.

His funeral was a celebration. I, along with several of his friends and professional associates, including Andy Ockershousen, a mutual friend who often joined Ernie and me for lunch, all gave eulogies laced with the kind of humor Ernie displayed throughout his life. Most impressive were the testimonials given by eight immaculately dressed huge black men, former team members who had gathered from all over the country to celebrate the life of the coach for whom they had played championship basketball at Norfolk State College.

An incumbent member of the State Board of Education when I took office, Tom Boushall was the creator of the Bank of Virginia. When he came to our state from North Carolina as a part of the Morris Plan Bank, he was a progressive member of the banking community acquiring pretty early a reputation as something of an upstart. He revolutionized retail banking in Virginia, and did such unconventional things as trying to create a branch banking system throughout the state. That upset the myriad of small, independent banks that were solidly part of the Byrd organization. A law was passed that I called, as early as my 1955 race for the House of Delegates, the "Bank of Virginia Law." It outlawed branch banks, and that not only stopped the expansion of the Bank of Virginia, but encouraged the North Carolina efforts to create statewide banks, which became nationwide banks and ultimately absorbed and controlled the entire banking system of Virginia.

By 1970, Tom had overcome his maverick reputation and was a highly respected member of the Richmond financial and social community. He was also a good friend and supporter of mine; for years I stopped to visit at his "retirement" desk in the Bank of Virginia at Eighth and Main Streets in Richmond and to discuss political developments with him. Promptly upon my taking office, Tom, then well into his eighties, paid me a visit and tendered his resignation from the State Board of Education. "I want you to put younger members on that board." My instant response was, "Tom, you are about the youngest man I know. I want you to remain on that board." He *was* young in his thinking, and he stayed.

Bob Huntley, the president of Washington and Lee University and the former dean of its law school, was also an incumbent member of the State Board of Education when I took office. These two were highly educated, sophisticated, knowledgeable, and wise men. I wanted both of them to understand why I was appointing Billy Frazier to their board.

Before announcing Billy's appointment, I called Bob and filled him in on Billy's background. Billy had grown up during the Depression in Scott County, one of the most rural counties in Virginia. He put himself through high school by pumping gas at the local Shell service station. His only formal education was in the public schools of Scott County; he had served on the Scott County Board of Supervisors, at one time as chairman; he had been a leader on the regional district commission known as Leniwisco—an acronym formed from the letters of Lee, Wise, and Scott counties and the city of Norton. Billy had also served on the school board of Scott County and been its chairman. He was an outstanding leader in efforts to have the counties in the region work cooperatively on governmental services, and his district commission during his tenure as chairman led the state in creating a regional system to dispose of solid waste. He was active in the Republican Party, being chairman of his local and district committees and a representative to the State Central Committee. Importantly, he was a local chairman of my campaign committee when I was elected governor.

"Bob," I said to Huntley, "Billy is going on the state Board of Education because he recognizes the value of a public education, but he uses the most atrocious grammar you ever heard, and I wanted you and Tom Boushall to be forewarned about that." Without a second's hesitation, the president of Washington and Lee University shot back at me, "Governor, in view of what you done told me, hit don't matter none to me." The three became fast friends and formed a leadership cadre that made important contributions to public education in Virginia during my term.

Cynthia Newman and I had worked on building the Republican Party in Virginia since 1950—she in Fairfax County and Falls Church, and I in Roanoke—and had become fast friends. Warren French, of Edinburg in Shenandoah County, was elected state chairman of the Republican Party of Virginia shortly after my election. I appointed Cynthia as secretary of the Commonwealth, whose duties she performed on a half-time basis for a half-time salary while still running her Waters Travel Service in Washington, D.C. I ultimately appointed Warren French to the Board of Visitors of the University of Virginia. Their respective responsibilities included assistance to me by recommending capable Republicans for appointments to positions in the active state government and to the various boards and commissions through which Virginia citizens contributed voluntarily to the operation of its government.

I'm sure Cynthia and Warren both agreed with my philosophical approach to appoint the "best-qualified" persons to these various jobs without regard to political affiliation, but I am also sure they were both somewhat disappointed when I wasn't more aggressive in rewarding loyal Republicans. In spite of their disappointment, however, I think they concurred with the appointments of Ed Temple as chief of staff, Vern Hill as director of the Division of Motor Vehicles, and Bill Forst as commissioner of taxation.

Ed Temple was discovered by John Ritchie and me. We had been urged by some of our conservative and former Byrd organization supporters to appoint Carter Lowance as chief of staff. Carter had been a close confidant of governors of Virginia going all the way back to Bill Tuck in 1946. He was an extremely knowledgeable and capable public servant, but I was concerned that appointing him would inhibit implementation of some of my ideas, such as my proposal for a management study without General Assembly participation. I was therefore much relieved when he made it plain he would not accept appointment to that position if it were offered to him.

Ed Temple became chief of staff. He was a public servant of the first order: He had had a successful tour as city manager of Danville, a Southside city that had had more than its share of racial disturbances. He had served four years under Mills Godwin as director of the Division of Planning and Community Affairs in the governor's office. He knew and understood well the state bureaucracy. He had an uncanny ability to pour oil on troubled waters. He enjoyed the ultimate respect of the more than a hundred agency heads forming the hierarchy of Virginia's government. He was the perfect liaison between me, the new Republican governor, and the various incumbents among whom there was great trepidation about how the transition from the traditional Democratic heritage would affect them and their departments.

Though he had a brief episode of chest pains that hospitalized him for a few days in the middle of my term, he stayed throughout most of my four years and then was appointed by its Board of Visitors as president of Virginia Commonwealth University. He was well fitted for leadership of that institution, which was created in 1968 by the merger of the former Richmond Professional Institute and the Medical College of Virginia. The school was suffering the pangs of change generated by that merger. His family and I were of course saddened when he died prematurely while in office, but it was also unfortunate for that institution; his gentle approach would have accelerated the true integration of those two rather diverse institutions.

As it had turned out in the 1969 election, a popular Democrat, Andy Miller, won the race for attorney general instead of our Republican candidate, Dick Obenshain. The question of what major position Dick would hold in my administration thus became an issue. It was unfortunate that Dick and I disagreed about what my pre-election promise of an important position should be, in the event he should lose. He first requested that I appoint him as my chief of staff. That would have made him a participant in the daily consideration of all important policy decisions. I recognized that our philosophical approaches, with mine more moderate than his, were sufficiently different that such an appointment would have caused a needless waste of time in discussion and possibly would have created acrimony.

He then sought appointment as the commissioner of the Division of Motor Vehicles. That division was then in the worst organizational disarray of any agency in the state government. People stood in long lines to renew driver's licenses; annual registrations were distressingly prolonged; and automobile dealers waited for weeks to obtain certificates of title on which their liens were recorded. Without the certificates, the dealers could not obtain advances from their financing institutions for new cars sold. The situation cried out for experienced expertise and working knowledge of the new information technology then becoming available through the use of computers. That post would have provided Dick a wonderful opportunity to travel about the state cutting ribbons and making speeches, which he was eager to do (possibly a campaign for the U.S. Senate was already in his mind), but he simply did not have the computer experience and technical background that were essential to getting the division up to speed.

Instead, I offered to name Dick as one of the three commissioners of the Alcohol Beverage Control system (the "ABC"). The compensation for that job was comparable to that of the other agency heads, and it was a system that really needed a lawyer. That commission had responsibility for many semijudicial decisions involving licensing of establishments to serve alcoholic beverages and enforcement of all the regulations dealing with the sale, possession, and distribution of alcohol. Dick did not buy my argument that it was a position that needed his legal abilities, and he declined the appointment. I am still sorry that we never got together on a suitable appointment for him.

Since I believed that Dick Obenshain was not the right person for the post at the Division of Motor Vehicles, Vern Hill was an important discovery, both for me and for the Commonwealth of Virginia. I had known when I took office that the Division of Motor Vehicles was in a mess. Vern Hill was discovered by Rodger Provo and the personnel committee, of which Rodger was the working director. Vern had been the director of the Division of Motor Vehicles of the State of Oregon, with responsibilities that were basically the same as those he would have in that position in Virginia. He had left Oregon to accept a position with the Hertz Corporation in New York City, where he was to direct the system that kept up with the status of all of the vehicles in that rent-a-car operation. Fortunately for us, he had realized in 1970 that he couldn't stand living in New York City. With alacrity he accepted my offer to serve as the commissioner of the Division of Motor Vehicles in Virginia, and the transition in the performance of that division was miraculous. The long lines disappeared, the computers began doing their expected jobs, the morale of the employees skyrocketed, and the change gave my administration a public relations boost that was unsurpassed. On a tour of the agency not too long after Vern's appointment, one of his employees got my attention and whispered to me, "Thank you for giving us a boss who makes us smile!"

Bill Forst effected a similar transition in the Department of Taxation. That department had long been the personal empire of Judge E. H. Morrisette. "The Judge," as he was always known by everybody, had all the rules of the department in his head. There were no written regulations, and policy decisions were his own. His projections of future revenues were famous; he could always be counted on, when the "organization" got in a pinch, to "find" some money from somewhere. One of his gimmicks was to shift payment due-dates on taxes so that the same taxes were collected twice in one fiscal year, resulting in a one-time windfall. Forst had been commissioner of taxation in both Kentucky and Iowa, but he was ready to move to Richmond, and he succeeded Judge Morrisette shortly after the beginning of my term. He organized the department along functional lines and soon began publishing a set of regulations that provided stable guidance for citizens and tax practitioners throughout the state.

Part of my campaign platform included a promise to have a comprehensive study of the government of Virginia made by business executives of Virginia. The idea came to me from a similar study made by then governor Ronald Reagan of California; he had boasted widely of the success of his study in promoting the efficiency and savings in the operation of California's government.

For that concept to succeed in Virginia, it was important to obtain the right leadership for the study. It was particularly so when I decided—against Carter Lowance's advice in informal discussions of the idea—to bypass the General Assembly with the whole project. I wanted it to be financed and conducted by outside experts as a function of the executive branch of the government. I was soon convinced that Billy Zimmer—then president of the A. H. Robins pharmaceutical company, headquartered in Richmond—was the right person to do the job. When I asked Billy's boss, Claiborne Robins (then chairman of the A. H. Robins Company), to come to see me, he dropped any conflict in his schedule and appeared in my office on very short notice. Further confirmation of the power and prestige of the governor's office came from Claiborne's response to my request that he lend me the services of Billy Zimmer for a period of about six months. He told me he had looked forward to some degree of retirement when Billy was scheduled to take over his (Claiborne's) responsibilities as CEO of the Robins Company on January 1, 1970, but, "Governor, if you want him, you can have him."

Billy took on the responsibilities of that job with enthusiasm. He recruited executive volunteers who raised the money to finance the study, and within the six-month schedule, his group did a complete study of Virginia's government and produced a bound copy of a report with recommendations that, when implemented, avoided expenditures or effected savings by the Commonwealth that ran into the millions of dollars.

There was no instrument of the state government that comprehensively dealt with the environment when I took office. I created one. With impetus from John Hanes, a close friend and financial supporter, and with the assistance of Ed Temple in his new role as chief of staff, and by executive order, I "volunteered" resources from related agencies to constitute a "council on the environment." John Hanes became chairman, and he found Jerry McCarthy amid the bureaucracy. Jerry became the informal executive director of the informal council on the environment, and in periodic meetings that organization sought to discover instances deleterious to Virginia's environment and opportunities that would enhance Virginia's environment. The new emphasis on the environment was recognized with approbation by the General Assembly when it legislatively created the Department of Environmental Quality some years later.

Trained as a nuclear physicist, Jerry McCarthy became an environmental specialist and for over thirty years has served as the executive director of the Virginia Environmental Endowment (VEE). That organization was created by U.S. district judge Robert H. Mehrige when he cajoled the chemical company that had polluted the James River with a very sophisticated rat poison into endowing the VEE with a substantial monetary contribution. It may be presumed that this action by the chemical company mitigated the fine imposed for the very serious violation of federal pollution laws, but the details of any "deal" are not known. In any event, the VEE and Jerry McCarthy have played a prominent role in stimulating projects, principally by research grants, to improve the quality of Virginia's air and water; to encourage environmental education at all levels, beginning with kindergarten; and to articulate concerns about possible detrimental aspects of proposals that might be made by governments or business entities from time to time.

Important environmental accomplishments also included the acquisition of two substantial additions to our system of state parks—the first additions since most of our existing state parks came into being through the activities of the Depression-born Civilian Conservation Corps (CCC) in the 1930s. Following the enthusiastic recommendation of state parks commissioner Ben Bohlen—a truly outstanding public servant—the state bought five thousand acres of rugged mountain land near Ben's birthplace in Carroll County, which became the Grayson Highlands State Park. Maybe Ben felt a little guilty about preserving land so close to his home place because he also recommended that we buy five thousand acres of what were essentially wetlands on the Atlantic Coast just south of Virginia Beach. A critic of the purchase reached me by telephone and summed up his objections to what he considered a waste of money by saying, "Why, you can't even get to it!" I summed up my reaction to his comment by saying, "I know." We bought it, and it is now the False Cape State Park.

An opportunity for symbolic support of environmental enhancement came on April 22, 1970. A group of mostly students at Virginia Commonwealth University sponsored participation in the first Earth Day. They were thrilled to have me stop by for a brief appearance on their program, and I was thrilled to publicly support their goal to preserve and improve our environment. It was essentially a "first." I believe no other governor to that date had endorsed the Earth Day movement publicly.

All in all, one of the major satisfactions from serving as governor came from being able to reach out, through the capable hands of so many men and women, to meet Virginia's needs in a wide spectrum of human experience. It was for me "Opportunity Time" in the first degree.

Me, around age two, with Peace, behind the house on Wood Avenue in Big Stone Gap in which I was born

Around 1930, with my dad and my brother, Van (*right*), at Cracker's Neck, near Big Stone Gap

My parents and I
at the wedding of
my brother, Van,
in 1951

With General Dwight
Eisenhower on the "Eisen-
hower Special" campaign
train from Roanoke to
Lynchburg in 1952

Jinks and I on
our wedding day,
January 10, 1953

President Eisenhower making a campaign appearance with me and my children Anne, Tayloe, and Woody, during my 1965 gubernatorial run

Catching a quick nap during my first gubernatorial run in 1965

With Ronald
Reagan during his
visit to the Roanoke
Valley on behalf of
my 1969 campaign

With Jinks at the inaugural
ball at the Jefferson Hotel in
Richmond, January 17, 1970

Our first family portrait in the Executive Mansion, soon after inauguration: Anne, Tayloe, me, Jinks, and Woody, with Dwight in the center, 1970

Accompanying Tayloe to school on August 31, 1970, her first day at the previously all-black Kennedy High School. (Librado Romero / The New York Times / Redux)

With President Nixon in Williamsburg at the National Conference on the Judiciary, 1971

With John Warner in 1972, when he was secretary of the navy and I was governor

Woody with me and others from Virginia (view of the back of Norman Sisisky's head) at an audience with Prime Minister Golda Meir in Jerusalem, 1973

My official portrait, painted by Bud MacNelly, which hangs in the Capitol

My family gathered outside the Executive Mansion in January 1974, as I prepare to hand the reins back to Mills Godwin

Being sworn in as assistant secretary of state by the chief of protocol, with Bill Casey, under secretary of state for economic affairs (and later, under Reagan, director of the CIA), looking on, February 2, 1974

On a visit with Jinks to the Oval Office, August 1993, during Dwight's two-year stint as special assistant in President Clinton's West Wing

With Doug Wilder, governor from 1990 to 1994, now Richmond mayor

With President
Jimmy Carter
and presidential
scholar Dr. James
Young at the
rededication of the
Miller Center at
the University of
Virginia in Sep-
tember 2002

With my son-in-law Tim Kaine, during his campaign for governor in 2005.
(Reprinted by permission of Aaron Mahler)

Jinks and I, enjoying our retirement

10   Leading by Example

U.S. Senator Harry Flood Byrd Sr. created the so-called "Massive Resistance" movement as Virginia's response to the U.S. Supreme Court decision in *Brown vs. Board of Education* to require integration of the public schools. In a speech in Richmond in February 1956, Byrd may have advocated "passive" resistance, but between him and the press, the word morphed into "massive." Massive Resistance became the byword of Virginia's strenuous opposition to the decision until elements of it were held unconstitutional by Virginia's highest court and by a separate federal district court in 1959. Governors Faubus of Arkansas, Maddox of Georgia, Wallace of Alabama, and Barnett of Mississippi, among others, symbolized the Massive Resistance movement throughout the world by open defiance of the federal courts and the U.S. Constitution in the name of "states' rights."

It was nurtured by James Kilpatrick, editor of the *Richmond News Leader*, under the banner of "interposition." Many Virginia opinion leaders supported Massive Resistance because they, by long ingrained habit, regarded any word from Harry Byrd as sacred gospel. The senator was blissfully ignorant of a missed opportunity: they would have loyally followed advice from him to comply with the Court's articulation of the law of the land.

Wishful thinkers were still clinging to the concept of Massive Resistance on the early morning of August 31, 1970, but in front of Kennedy High School in Richmond, I—as the newly elected governor of Virginia—administered the final, fatal blow. There had been two earlier blows to the Byrd leadership following futile efforts to thwart the decision: Plans for tuition grants to private segregated schools intended to avoid integration and other similar devices had failed constitutional muster. And there had been a Gray Commission proposal to actually close schools to avoid integration, which also had not passed constitutional authority. A vote to keep schools open had squeaked by the Virginia Senate, but only by a hair: 20 to 19.

On the first day of school in August 1970, our thirteen-year-old daughter, Tayloe, and I, at Kennedy High School—and Jinks with Anne and Woody, aged twelve and ten, at Mosby Middle School—voluntarily carried out the orders of the U.S. District Court that had been affirmed earlier that month on appeal to the U.S. Supreme Court. The orders required cross-town busing to eliminate the effects of racial discrimination prohibited by the U.S. Constitution.

I was exuberant that morning. Supported by a believing family, and confident that most Virginians and certainly posterity would agree, I proclaimed by one simple act that "Virginia is a part of this Republic, and Virginia will comply with its laws." In other words, we were putting our actions and our children where my mouth was. This commitment of Virginia's first family implemented, through very visible *deeds,* the *words* of my inaugural address: "The era of defiance is behind us," and "Let our goal in Virginia be an aristocracy of ability, regardless of race, color or creed."

There was an expectant press awaiting us that fateful August day, sure that some kind of an incident was going to develop. They were aware that our kids would be going to these schools, but I had sent out word that I hoped they would let this be a private matter. The press and TV cameras were there anyway. It was a big enough story that representatives of the *New York Times* were on hand, and a picture taken of Tayloe and me as we approached the high school appeared the next day on the front page of the *New York Times.* That photograph became an icon of my administration.

Except for North Carolina's Terry Sanford, southern governors had all assumed an attitude of defiance toward the Supreme Court's *Brown* decision and its interpretation of the federal Constitution. (In the 1960 North Carolina Democratic primary for governor, on a moderate platform, Terry had beaten Beverly Lake, who had strenuously advocated continued segregation in North Carolina's public schools.) Orville Faubus in Arkansas, George Wallace in Alabama, Ross Barnett in Mississippi, and Georgia's Lester Maddox—pictured nationally brandishing a defiant pistol and his signature ax-handle bat—had all taken the position that they weren't going to let any integration take place in their schools, and in effect, "The U.S. Supreme Court be damned." But in Virginia there was a governor saying to the world, "We understand the requirements of the Constitution of the United States as interpreted by the Supreme Court, and we will comply with those requirements in a symbolic way to encourage others to comply."

Colgate Darden, Virginia governor from 1942 to 1946, was a recognized elder statesman in Virginia by the time I was governor. A close friend and confidant of mine, he was somebody to whom I could go whenever I had a serious problem to discuss and be sure of getting sound advice. Several years later he asked for a copy of that picture that appeared on the front page of the *New York Times*. When I sent it to him, he wrote back in acknowledgment, "Your Excellency: I am much obliged to you for the photograph. It represents the most significant happening in this Commonwealth in my lifetime." That was exactly what I felt walking to school that morning: that it was a significant happening, and I was doing exactly what I wanted to do, putting into action the words of my inaugural address.

It's interesting to note that even as of this writing, I haven't heard favorably from any Nixon people except for George Schultz. Schultz was the former secretary of labor, and in 1970 he was serving as the first director of the Office of Management and Budget, where he remained until his appointment as the secretary of the treasury in 1972. He had become my friend while we were both campaigning for Nixon. He phoned me that momentous day and said, "This is what we're all about. This is why we're in government." He had seen the picture in the *New York Times* and called to give words of encouragement for taking the stand the historic photo depicted.

The principal of Kennedy High School met Tayloe and me at the door on that morning. With him was the student commander of the ROTC, who saluted and greeted us with the words, "Good morning, Governor. We're glad to see you and we're glad to have your daughter in this school, and we want you to know you don't have to worry about her." I thought, "Well, that ends my concerns about any violence or unmanageable reaction. Everything's going to be all right." I recognized that what I was doing was very significant from a historical standpoint, and I was thrilled, knowing that what I had wanted to do for improvement of racial harmony and racial relations in Virginia was going to be significantly enhanced by the symbol that this would become.

Jinks drew similar satisfaction from escorting Anne and Woody into Mosby Middle School. One shining memory of hers is of a *Los Angeles Times* reporter standing outside the building who told her that several white parents were waiting for her to come out, and they entered with their children only after seeing the example that Jinks had set. Tayloe was starting her first year in high school, and she happily finished all four years at Kennedy High. She was very calm and sophisticated that first morning, and I think the fact that I was with her helped. We had agreed that it was the right thing to do, and she was willing to take it on. Within a few days, she had formed a friendship with a girl named Kathy.

The family laughed about the fact that Richmond papers were trying to play every incident as a major violent eruption. Our kids knew the true picture, because they were there. For example, one day Anne, responding to my expressed concern about a news report of a "gang fight," reported, "Well, Daddy, what they described as a gang fight was a couple of boys fighting and a gang standing around watching them. What's so unusual about that?" That was the type of reaction our kids had to the newspapers' trying to make it sound as bad as they could.

Once Tayloe had a tale to tell. She said, "Daddy, we had an incident today at Kennedy." I gulped, thinking, "Oh my, what's this going to mean?" She said, "Kathy and I were walking down a long hall, and we realized that a big boy was following us. When we speeded up, he speeded up. When we slowed down, he slowed down. We were really nervous about what was going to happen. When we got up to the classroom where we were headed, we ducked quickly into the classroom and shut the door." She began to giggle as she finished the story: "He was *white!*"

Later on Tayloe became a cheerleader, and at the football games we could look down from the bleachers to see eight or ten cheerleaders there on the sidelines in the stadium. There were eight little black dots and two little white dots. One of the white dots was mine. When the rest of the family left Richmond at the end of my tenure in the middle of her senior year, Tayloe arranged to stay with a friend in Richmond in order to finish with her class. There were several valedictorians in that class, and she was one of them.

Anne also took entering an integrated school in stride. Anne could handle anything and made a lot of fun of the way the newspapers were treating it. Woody was also fine with deciding to take the big step. But in the afternoon of the first day, my secretary called me on my intercom and said, "There's a call coming in from someone who says he's Linwood Holton, and I think you'd better talk to him." I picked up the phone warily, and eleven-year-old Woody said, "Dad, this is Woody. You asked me to try that school. I tried it. I don't like it. I'm not going back."

I said, "Okay, Woody, that's fine. You did what I asked you to do, but is that the end of the story, or can we talk about it?"

"We can talk about it, but I'm not going to be a tourist attraction. All afternoon it was, 'Are you the governor's son? Are you the governor's son?' I'm just *not* going to be a tourist attraction."

So I said, "Well, let's talk about it." But I had to go to Charlottesville to make a speech, so I didn't see him that night. When I got home after the speech, Jinks reported a sad telephone conversation she'd had that day with Mary Ballou Reynolds, wife of our lieutenant governor, J. Sargeant Reynolds, and an idol of Woody's. Woody had overheard Jinks's end of the conversation, and knew Sarge had just been diagnosed with terminal brain cancer. As soon as Jinks hung up the phone, Woody was very critical of Jinks for laughing and joking with Mary Ballou on the phone with Sarge in such a tragic situation. Jinks explained to him that when faced with tragedy, you have to use all your resources to cope with it, including a sense of humor.

Though Woody had had a lot to handle emotionally that day, he went on to bed and seemed to be calm. The next morning, with everybody having slept on the day's events, I went into Woody's room and sat on the edge of the bed. I said, "Would you like to come down and have breakfast with me?" Well, yeah, he would come and have breakfast with me. He got downstairs before me and was sitting at that huge table in the State Dining Room, his slight figure making it seem even larger.

"Woody," I said, "I'm not going to make you go back to that school if you don't want to go. But from what you described to me yesterday about being a tourist attraction, it seems to me all you have to do is stick your hand out and say, 'Yes, I'm Woody Holton, and I'm glad to be in school with you.'" He said, "Yeah. I've thought about it a lot too. Have you got a pen? Can I have a pen to write with?"

"Sure. Here's a pen."

"I'm going to tell them they can have my autograph for a dime." He went back, with no problems from there on. Woody is probably the most avid integrationist in our family now. Gatherings in his home are invariably diverse. All participate comfortably as equal members of the group.

All four of our children recognize and appreciate the leadership opportunity they had when the schools opened that August day in 1970. Years later, in 2000, Tayloe flew down from her home in Syracuse, New York, to attend a Black History Month celebration at the Linwood Holton Elementary School in Richmond. The Titans, Alexandria's famous well-integrated football team, and its coaches were the honorees of the event. Players from formerly all-white and all-black schools integrated successfully and—under a coaching staff that included members from both races (with a black head coach in the formerly all-white T. C. Williams High School)—won the state championship in 1971; it was an almost miraculous demonstration of successful integration.

Tayloe stood with me and looked out over the thoroughly integrated black and white audience gathered to celebrate that success and said, "Daddy, I can't tell you how proud it makes me feel to realize that I had a part in bringing something like this about."

With similar sentiments, Anne, at a large gathering of mostly black citizens on Martin Luther King Day during Black History Month in 2004, expressed public appreciation to Jinks and me for "having asked us to do something outside of ourselves." Dwight had been a little young to do very much profound thinking that historic year of 1970, but as time went by, he too recognized and latched on to similar opportunities. While a senior at Brown University, he wrote a paper on integration of the public schools in Richmond. He interviewed Oliver W. Hill as part of his research for that paper and became devoted to the venerable man, who with good reason is now one of Dwight's idols. For those either too young, too old, or too forgetful to remember, I will add that Oliver W. Hill, an African American born in Richmond in 1907, spent his life as a civil rights attorney in Virginia. He represented the students of Prince Edward County in the historic Supreme Court *Brown* case that was decided favorably to his clients in 1954. In 1999, President Clinton presented Oliver Hill with the Presidential Medal of Freedom.

Dwight telephoned us in July 2004 from Portland, Oregon, letting us know about the arrival of the first *Holton* grandchild, born a few minutes earlier. (There were six other grandchildren: three Loftuses and three Kaines.) Dwight told us that the new baby would be named *Terence* (in honor of his mother's brother); *Oliver* (in honor of Oliver W. Hill); and *Linwood* (after me) Holton. Terence Oliver Linwood Holton has quite a heritage in those names. I am one proud and flattered grandfather to be included among his namesakes.

Oliver Hill and I had long been good friends. He had attended the dedication of the Linwood Holton Elementary School and there teased me with, "I want you to know they have already named a building after *me!*" So I took great delight in visiting him in his home on Noble Avenue in Richmond to tell him of the arrival of his namesake: "I know 'they' have named a building for you, and a street for you, but this is the first time that 'they' have named a white grandchild for you." He was pleased, of course, and wrote the parents to advise that he would "watch that baby's progress with great interest." Mr. Hill was then a very young ninety-seven years old.

Contributions,
Benchmarks,
and Anecdotes

Emerging as the 1969 gubernatorial choice of the Virginia Republican Party paved the way for implementing the major goal of all my earlier years in politics: the creation of a permanent two-party system in Virginia to replace the one-party political domination that had existed for generations before my time. My election that fall as the official candidate of the previously minority (even token) Republican Party signaled the birth of a viable two-party system in Virginia that promises to be permanent.

My four years as governor provided, in addition to my overriding goal of enhancing racial harmony, many other important opportunities to initiate changes for the good of the Commonwealth. There were also occasions for humor. I look back with gratitude for both.

The Virginia Port Authority

I think I first heard about the natural port of Hampton Roads in a required Virginia history course while I was in the fifth grade, where Hampton Roads was accurately presented as one of the world's greatest natural ports. The more I learned about it through the years, the more I realized the Commonwealth had not taken advantage of the opportunity to develop its full potential. During preparation for my 1969 gubernatorial campaign, I learned that the cities of Portsmouth, Norfolk, and Newport News were making efforts to equip their municipal port facilities to handle waterborne shipments in containers—containerization—a relatively new development promising great potential for expansion. But even the combined efforts of those three cities were feeble when measured against the need for full development. Bobby Bray was then a lawyer in the general counsel's office of the Virginia Port Authority, a relatively skeletal organization. It probably contributed some public relations value to port development, but it had no real substantive responsibility. Bobby confirmed my suspicion that those three munici-palities, acting separately and basically in competition with each other, could neither devote sufficient financial resources to acquire the modern equipment nor pay for the marketing to support a coordinated push to take advantage of the expansion opportunities offered by containerization. Bobby also gave me confidence that my idea of developing the port on a coordinated basis through a statewide organization, the Virginia Port Authority, was sound.

Legislation would be necessary to expand responsibility of the Virginia Port Authority, and appropriations were needed for the Authority to acquire the terminal facilities the individual municipalities already owned. I proposed these changes as a plank in my campaign platform.

I was unaware at the time that Senator Eddie Breeden, majority leader of the Democratic Party in the Virginia Senate who represented Norfolk, then headed a legislative commission to study ways to enhance development of the Port of Hampton Roads. This I learned the morning after a televised debate with my opponent, Bill Battle, on WAVY television, a station with broad cov-erage throughout the entire Tidewater area. During that debate I described my plan for coordinated development of the port and committed my support for the concept when I was governor. For reasons not clear to me, Bill Battle in that same debate opposed the concept. He summed up his opposition by saying it would make "the whole ball of wax come unglued." I felt pretty good after the debate, because my instincts were that a program to develop the full potential of that port would be very popular in Tidewater.

My good feelings turned to elation when I read the next morning's edition of the *Norfolk Virginian-Pilot.* A two-column headline on the right side of the first local page trumpeted, "HOLTON SUPPORTS COORDINATED DEVELOPMENT OF THE PORT THROUGH THE VIRGINIA PORT AUTHORITY." The story went on to report that Battle was opposed to it. Adding to my glee was a headline over a two-column story on the left side of the same page reporting the results of the Breeden Commission port study; it recommended assignment of respon-sibility for the development of the Port of Hampton Roads to an enhanced Virginia Port Authority. The majority leader, his commission, and I were all in accord—and my opponent was opposed! My campaign benefited materi-ally, particularly with the business communities in the Tidewater cities.

The really effective coordinated development of the Port of Hampton Roads came about over many years. Legislation to refine the necessary pow-ers of the Port Authority and to appropriate funds to support its development was required from successive sessions of the General Assembly. But the initial legislation—the first step toward coordinated development of the Port of Hampton Roads—was passed during my term. Chief sponsor of the legislation in the Virginia Senate was Eddie Breeden, fully supported by me as governor.

Some grumbling was heard here and there that funds were being appropriated for purposes that would "benefit only the Tidewater area." So it was great fun for me, during a speech I was making at the dedication of a new bank building in Appalachia in the far western corner of Virginia, to glance through the bank's front windows and see a big ocean shipping container prominently marked "Sea Land." It was being pushed down a siding on the Southern Railway not more than fifty yards from the front entrance of the bank. I was quick to point out how port activity in eastern Virginia was helping to make jobs for those Wise County trainmen who were at that very moment setting off that container for delivery to some distributor in downtown Appalachia.

I further contributed to the statewide importance of development of the Port of Hampton Roads by my appointments to the Authority's board of directors. Red English, CEO of English Construction Company in the town of Alta Vista—right in the middle of the state—was my choice to be chairman of the enhanced Virginia Port Authority. Red was a broad-gauged citizen who had just served a term as president of the Virginia State Chamber of Commerce. In discussing the chairmanship with him, I found Red quick to recognize the statewide importance of that development, and not just for the benefit of the Tidewater area. He accepted the responsibility with a will, and contributed importantly to acquisition of the municipal terminals and the early developments of a truly integrated port facility.

Others through the years, including especially Robert Spillman, CEO of Bassett Industries, headquartered in Henry County—again in the middle of the state, far from Tidewater—provided leadership for the continued enhancement of the port. The development has been phenomenal. Whereas something around 100,000 containers were being handled by the three municipalities when the coordinating legislation was first passed, the Port of Hampton Roads in 2004 handled over 2 million containers, and growth was continuing. More and more shipping companies are making Hampton Roads a port of call, and terminal facilities are being built privately as well as publicly. In September 2007, Maersk dedicated a new terminal near Portsmouth that will handle an additional million containers each year. The Port of Hampton Roads is now among the most important port facilities on the east coast of the United States—if not *the* most important. Financially, it is basically self-sustaining. Bobby Bray, who initially counseled with me about the concept of coordinated port development, was the CEO of the Virginia Port Authority for all of these years until his retirement in June 2007 and contributed mightily to its phenomenal success.

Noman Cole and the State Water Control Board

John W. Hanes, a personal friend and financial supporter of mine, brought to my attention Noman Cole and his activities relating to pollution of the Potomac River. Noman was a nuclear physicist who had worked successfully with Admiral Hyman Rickover in the U.S. Navy's nuclear submarine program. Rickover's standards for his associates were extremely high, and Noman Cole met or exceeded all of those standards. He was well-educated, knowledgeable, and an extremely thorough investigator whose self-confidence led him to believe he could solve any problem. He certainly solved a lot of problems for the Commonwealth of Virginia.

Noman lived on the banks of the Potomac River in Fairfax County and was acutely aware of the extent of that river's pollution. It was nearly a cesspool. In the years between 1968 and 1970, Noman had been instrumental in solving a serious pollution problem that had existed for years in Fairfax County. The County Board of Supervisors had imposed moratoria on new residential construction in order to avoid dumping any additional municipal sewage through its existing treatment facilities into the Potomac River. Litigation had been instituted by developers seeking to enjoin and end the moratoria. Noman in effect eliminated that confrontation by developing and demonstrating methods by which the existing Fairfax County treatment facilities could improve their operation and produce an effluent of sufficient quality to be acceptable for dumping in the river. He thus became a hero to the developers, and because of his deserved reputation as a supporter of a high-quality environment, even the most extreme environmentalists continued to have high regard for him and his ability.

Against that background, I appointed him chairman of the State Water Control Board, a policy-making body; as chairman, Noman became its hands-on chief executive officer, in effect overseeing and directing its day-to-day operations. Forthright and aggressive, Noman made one of his first acts the initiation of litigation against the District of Columbia and its Blue Plains sewage treatment facility that was intended to close the "Georgetown Gap." That gap existed because the collection system for sewage from suburban counties, including Fairfax, led to a collector pipe extending into the Potomac

River and terminating near Key Bridge, where 15 million gallons of raw sewage per day poured into the river. There was no trunk line to connect the collector pipe to the Blue Plains treatment facility, downriver from Washington. Noman's litigation forced the parties to install the necessary piping to close the Georgetown Gap and to improve operation of the Blue Plains plant. The improvement in the quality of the water in the Potomac River was almost immediately apparent.

The feathers of some state locality officials, whose cooperation was necessary to successfully implement our program to clean up Virginia's rivers, were ruffled by Noman's abrupt and aggressive tactics. I was concerned enough about reports of this that I called Noman into the office for a little Dutch uncle discussion that might help him take a more gentle approach. What I learned from that conference was that Noman had the facts, that his proposed solutions to pollution problems were meritorious, and that reasonable people would recognize that the implementation of his proposals was necessary to make all of our rivers swimmable again—a goal I had set for myself during my term as governor. I became convinced from our discussion that my job was to back him all the way. And I did.

A showdown of sorts developed some months after Noman became chairman of the Water Control Board. Roanoke, my adopted hometown, led by City Manager Julian Hirst, was extremely upset with Noman, the board, and me. Julian insisted that Roanoke's proposal for a sewage treatment facility designed by Chicago architect-engineers was adequate. Noman insisted that that facility proposed for Roanoke was already obsolete; in order to protect riparian owners downstream, a treatment plant that would serve the entire Roanoke Valley region and produce considerably higher-quality effluent was essential. Noman and the Water Control Board decided to withhold grant funds from Roanoke until his requirements had been met.

The Roanoke city manager was furious. He convinced his city council that their former hometown boy, now governor, had lost his marbles. They enlisted Ed Ould, then president of the First National Exchange Bank of Roanoke and a former client of mine, to go to Richmond, confront the governor, and convince him that his Water Control Board was requiring Roanoke to expend an astronomical amount of funds for an elaborate and unnecessary sewage treatment facility. Ed agreed to see the governor on behalf of the city, but only after he conferred with the chairman of the State Water Control Board. Noman had his facts; he showed Ed his color-coded bar graphs, demonstrated with facts and figures the inadequacy of the plant proposed by the Chicago firm, and convinced Ed that discharge from the Chicago-proposed plant would so pollute the Roanoke River it would destroy the viability of the downstream Smith Mountain Lake, whose potentially significant residential development was then just beginning.

Ed did not confer with the governor. He went back to the city council. His report: "The chairman is right; you'd better do what he says." The ultimate result was a regional plant. It collected sewage from all or most of the other localities upstream in the Roanoke Valley, and produced an effluent of Tahoe quality. (The treatment plant at Lake Tahoe, Nevada, was universally recognized as a most desirable model.) The effluent was of higher quality than the water of the Roanoke River itself. I received accolades from all the local officials (except the city manager) when the plant was dedicated some months after my term as governor ended. A picture of me drinking effluent from that plant appeared in the *Roanoke Times* the next day. I don't recommend the practice of drinking effluent from sewage treatment plants, but that act did demonstrate the efficacy of the new sewage treatment plant. Among other things, the millions of dollars of high-class residential development built on the shores of Smith Mountain Lake in the interim has been protected from pollution and enhanced by discharge of high-quality effluent from the Roanoke treatment plant.

A Governor's Cabinet

Another significant accomplishment of my administration was the creation of a governor's cabinet. Billy Zimmer's management study, supported enthusiastically both financially and with expertise by Virginia's business community, found that under the existing organizational structure, over a hundred agency heads were reporting (theoretically) directly to the governor. The management study recommended the creation of positions for five deputy governors, each of whom would have liaison responsibility between the governor and a group of agencies whose substantive responsibilities were related.

I approved the concept, though I thought that the title of secretary would be more politically feasible. Accordingly, I created an informal cabinet by executive direction, grouping agencies together and designating one of the senior agency incumbents as the liaison officer for that group. This informal arrangement served the purpose of the management study group's recommendation pending passage of legislation to confirm the arrangement that made it legislatively permanent.

Several members of the General Assembly quickly endorsed the idea, and when the legislation had been drafted, Roy Smith, the chairman of the powerful Appropriations Committee (and incidentally an employee of the A. H. Robins Company, where Billy Zimmer was his boss), became the chief patron of the bill. Speaker of the House John Warren Cooke, whose interest was always in the future of Virginia, was a co-patron. The reaction of these leaders gave us hope that we might obtain fifty-one co-patrons—a majority of the House of Delegates. But for once, my legislative counsel, Roger Hull, whose confidence in himself was always ample, was a little slow in getting the needed signatures on the bill. To our chagrin, James Thomson, a delegate from Alexandria and majority leader of the Democrats in the House of Delegates, announced his strong opposition to the bill and worked very hard to solicit votes against it. I tried reasoning with him but got nowhere. I concluded that as one of the most partisan Democrats in the House, he was simply determined that a Republican not get credit for such a major accomplishment.

With my staff, including Roger Hull, I therefore had to work very hard to get the constitutionally required fifty-one votes. Delegate Owen Pickett, whom I had lobbied earlier, was in my office for a final arm-twisting session as the debate in the House was concluding and the vote was imminent. When he finally committed to me that he would vote for the bill, I said, "You'd better get on down there. I'm afraid they're voting now." He slid into his seat on the floor of the House just in time to mash his voting button to send the electronic signal to give a green "yes" vote on the tabulating board. We had fifty-one votes—the minimum required!

The vote in the Senate was, if anything, tighter and scarier than in the House. Though we had significant support for the bill in the Senate, including that of Omer Hirst, a senior and highly respected senator from Fairfax County, we also had significant opposition. Senator Bill Hopkins vigorously opposed the bill. Billy Hopkins and I had met when I was a freshman at Washington and Lee in 1941 and he was a junior there. Billy and I had a pleasant, if not intimate, personal relationship during the twenty years that he and I had practiced law in Roanoke before my election as governor.

But there is not a stronger partisan Democrat in the world than Billy Hopkins, and he was the Democratic majority leader in the Senate. He was determined to kill that bill, motivated in part, I think, by his determination that a Republican would not get credit for a major restructuring. But in spite of his opposition, the House bill came over to the Senate, and after navigating the committee structure of the Senate, it was reported to the floor for debate and vote. Using the prerogatives of his position as majority leader, Senator Hopkins arranged for the vote on the bill to be scheduled late on Saturday, the last night of that session of the General Assembly.

The division among the senators was very close. Billy supported an amendment to the House bill, which, if passed, would require referral back to a conference committee to reconcile the difference between the bill passed by the House and the bill passed by the Senate. But there was no time for such a conference before the adjournment of the Assembly, so the adoption of that amendment would kill the bill. By a very close vote it was adopted.

Watching on the internal television circuit, I was heartbroken. But only momentarily. Freshman Senator Douglas Wilder, who had been elected to succeed J. Sargeant Reynolds in a special election just before the end of 1969— and who later became the nation's first African American governor—took the floor.

"Mr. President," Wilder said, "I voted on the prevailing side for the adoption of that amendment, and I now call for its reconsideration." What a thrill! Wilder was saving my bill.

On reconsideration, Wilder and possibly one or two others switched their vote and the amendment failed of adoption by a tie vote. The unamended House bill was then adopted by the Senate, sending the bill to the governor for signature. My pen was ready.

The White Burkett Miller Center of Public Affairs

In November 1969, I had just become governor-elect, and Jinks and I were on our way for some R&R in the Bahamas after the intensity of campaigning. Frank Rogers, Jinks's father—then rector of the University of Virginia Board of Visitors—suggested that we stop for dinner on the Miami-moored yacht of Mr. and Mrs. White Burkett Miller. He was a prominent Chattanooga, Tennessee, lawyer who had acquired substantial wealth in real estate transactions. Their college years at the university had overlapped, and as background and explanation for the invitation, Frank told me that Miller was a possible donor of a substantial gift to the university. Some discussion of this prospect had already taken place with various university officials, and he wanted me to know about the possibility.

Early in the conversation during the ensuing dinner, Miller dwelled on his concern about the decision-making process (or lack of process) in the office of the president of the United States. "We have backed into a war in Vietnam, and nobody at the White House ever made a decision actually to enter it," is an accurate paraphrase of his thinking. He speculated that a public affairs center in an academic setting where scholars, statesmen, politicians, and members of the public could be encouraged to express and exchange views on important policy issues could be an effective vehicle to improve the process for making decisions in the White House. He hinted strongly that he was inclined to make a financial contribution that would encourage such a center at the University of Virginia.

That dinner conversation was the first of many on this subject during the next four years. There were extensive group discussions with Mr. Miller that included Frank Rogers; former governor Colgate Darden (whose attendance at the university also overlapped that of Miller); Edgar Shannon, the incumbent president of the university and a close friend of mine; and several others who had been involved in preliminary talks about the idea. There was at least one trip in the state airplane when Governor Darden and I flew to Chattanooga for a visit that we had hoped—overoptimistically—would conclude the negotiations. I remember commenting to Darden on the return trip: "That man isn't going to make that gift; he just wants to *talk* about it!"

But in the end, he made the gift. An agreement creating the White Burkett Miller Center at the University of Virginia was signed in the Governor's Mansion on November 29, 1973. Darden, Rogers, Shannon, and Holton were named therein as life members of the Governing Council (I am the sole survivor), and for twenty-five years I served as chairman of that council. There were fits and starts in implementation of the November agreement, but President Frank Hereford, successor to Shannon, provided the final impetus to make it go.

Under the especially significant leadership of Professor Kenneth Thompson of the university's Department of Government, which began in 1978, the center became the leading entity for research and recommendations concerning the office of the president of the United States. Its effectiveness is easily illustrated with just one example: In press conferences under President Nixon, the press corps had resembled a bunch of monkeys hustling for bananas! "Mr. President! Mr. President!" the reporters shouted, vying to be called on. The strongest vocal chords usually won out. But under the leadership of Jim Brady, President Reagan's press secretary, the recommendations of the Miller Center Commission on the Presidential Press Conference, which had been chaired by Ray Shearer, of NBC News, and Linwood Holton, were followed. In his first news conference, Brady referred to the center's recommendations and said, "I'm going to follow them." And he did. Subsequent press conferences, contrasted with earlier ones, at least, became informative models of decorum.

Under the leadership of its current director, former Virginia governor Gerald L. Baliles, the center promises even greater influence.

National Center for State Courts

There was a big to-do concerning the judiciary in the spring of 1971. I think the initial impetus for a conference was the scheduled report of a commission headed by Justice Lawrence W. I'Anson of the Virginia Supreme Court to study the administration of criminal justice. Something about that coming report got everybody's attention, and "everybody" came to Williamsburg for what evolved into the 1971 National Conference on the Judiciary. President Richard Nixon was there, and he made a speech. Attorney General John Mitchell was there, and he made a speech. Chief Justice Warren E. Burger was there, and he made a speech. All dealt in some way with the administration of state courts as opposed to federal courts, especially relating to criminal jurisdictions.

Chief Justice Burger recommended the creation of an organization to act as a clearinghouse for ideas from any source that might be helpful to improve the administration of justice, particularly criminal justice, in the state court systems throughout the country. Out of this conference, and out of the chief justice's speech, the National Center for State Courts was created.

Paul Reardon, a former chief justice of the Supreme Judicial Court of Massachusetts who became a very good friend of mine, was selected to head the committee to select the place where the new center would be located. I recognized that the new National Center for State Courts would be both a valuable economic and intellectual asset, and I was determined to have it located in Williamsburg. I told Paul Reardon that I personally would raise $1 million from the private sector toward the construction of the new center building if it were to be located in Williamsburg. He told me later that my offer had been instrumental in having the committee decide to recommend Williamsburg, but I suspect my other "bribe" was equally effective, at least with the chairman of the Site Selection Committee. I knew of Chief Justice Reardon's affection for oysters on the half shell, and I heard he was making an overnight visit to a friend in our hunt country. What a pleasant surprise it would be for him, thought I, if upon arriving at the home of his friend in Virginia, he found a bushel of the best Chincoteague oysters delivered there for the enjoyment of

Justice Reardon and his friends, courtesy of the Virginia State Police Department and the governor of Virginia.

Getting a bushel of oysters from the Eastern Shore of Virginia to an estate in Fauquier County was an easy task for the Virginia State Police; raising the $1 million I had committed was a little more difficult, but several friends came through, even though by then it was 1973 and the lame-duck effect was limiting somewhat the power and influence of the governor. Nonetheless, Paul Mellon came through with $100,000. (I had supported his request for permission to move the Houdon statue of George Washington from the Virginia Capitol to the National Museum for the upcoming 1976 Independence Bicentennial Year.) And Hayes Watkins, CEO of what became the CSX Transportation Company, sent $100,000 even without the authority of his board. (I had helped CSX retain its status as a Virginia corporation by supporting legislation that overruled an arbitrary decree of the State Corporation Commission that would have prohibited CSX from becoming a holding company in Virginia. The commission decree would also have cast doubt on the legality of several Virginia bank holding companies whose charters had been authorized by the same statute relied upon by CSX.)

My friends the Colgate Dardens contributed $50,000; Justice I'Anson arranged for the Beasley Foundation, of which he was a member, to contribute; and enough others participated so we finally squeaked out the committed $1 million. The initial building was constructed by the Basic Construction Company of Newport News, and today the institution not only thrives, but it has had several expansions.

A collateral benefit came in the form of a modern physical plant for the Marshall-Wythe School of Law at the College of William and Mary in Virginia. William and Mary had agreed to contribute part of its land for the National Center for State Courts building, and there was adequate space adjoining the National Center site for the location of a new law school building.

Through the years, the Marshall-Wythe School of Law had not been adequately funded; hints were coming from the American Bar Association that the accreditation of the school could be terminated if definite plans were not adopted and implemented to provide adequate physical facilities, including library space.

In late 1972 or early in 1973, Tom Graves, president of the College of William and Mary, came to me with a representative of the law school to present a proposal they thought would satisfy the requirements for accreditation. It involved some rehabilitation of a chemistry building at William and Mary, one no longer in use for chemistry, and moving the law school into that cramped and unsuitable space.

After reviewing Tom Graves's proposal, I leaned back in my chair. "Tom," I said, "if I were president of the College of William and Mary in Virginia, and understood the heritage of that school and of its Marshall-Wythe School of Law, I'll be damned if I would present such a half-assed proposal to the governor. I would ask for a first-class facility, and I suggest you go back to Williamsburg and develop such a proposal." Tom had never received such a reception from a governor. Not many other presidents of colleges had either, but he followed my suggestion and came back shortly with a proposal to construct the very modern facility that houses the Marshall-Wythe School of Law today. True to my promise, I put the money for that law school building in the budget I submitted to the General Assembly in early January 1974. Legislative action took out the part of my recommendation for construction, but the planning money was left in the budget and appropriated, and construction funds were made available by subsequent actions of the General Assembly. The result: the Marshall-Wythe School of Law now occupies world-class facilities as part of the College of William and Mary in Virginia.

As a result of the contact with Chief Justice Burger in connection with the National Center for State Courts, and in connection with my response to his request for a portrait of Virginian Bushrod Washington (one of the early justices of the U.S. Supreme Court), Burger and I became good friends. A wonderful picture of the two of us was taken in the Virginia Room of the Williamsburg Lodge. The backlight in the picture was a recessed circular ceiling-light fixture, shining directly behind my head, providing me with a perfect halo. The chief justice did not have the same lighting effect, so I sent him a copy of the photograph with a handwritten question: "Where is your halo?" He was not to be one-upped. His response came just a few days later: "I never wear mine in public, and if I did, nobody would believe it!" It was signed "Warren E. Burger." (I regret that a copy of that photograph could not be found for inclusion here.)

The 1971 Williamsburg conference also provided another opportunity to spoof Chief Justice Burger—his tinge of pomposity made it great fun to tease him. When I found that no other provision had been made for his travel to the conference, I took the state airplane—a two-engine prop jet Beechcraft Kingair—to Washington and flew the chief justice and Erwin Griswold, my law school dean and the incumbent U.S. solicitor general, to Williamsburg. I could not join them after the conference, but I arranged for the same plane to return them to Washington. As the plane took off, two geese rising from a neighboring marsh near the little Williamsburg airport flew into one of the propellers. The result was a disaster for the geese; it was only somewhat dangerous for our two distinguished passengers, but the loud thump scared both of them nearly to death. On a trip to Washington not much later, I saw the chief justice eyeing me from across the room at a reception, moving deliberately in my direction.

"You know what happened as we flew out of Williamsburg the other day?" he inquired somewhat accusatively.

"Yes sir," I replied. "You killed two of my geese!"

Skinning the Cat Another Way

One very specific contribution made by my administration was to the environment of Virginia: we stopped the dumping of raw municipal sewage into Virginia's rivers. The so-called "Muskie legislation," passed by the U.S. Congress early in my term, provided an extra subsidy for the building of municipal sewage treatment facilities if the state provided grants for part of the cost of construction for those facilities. With subsidies from the state and federal governments, the cost to the municipality was reduced from sixty-five cents to twenty cents on the dollar.

In 1970 or 1971, I met with a small group of legislators, including delegate Vince Callahan of Fairfax County, in my conference room to discuss how we could finance a commitment by the state to pay grants to localities so they could obtain the maximum grants from the federal government under the Muskie legislation's formula.

The state actually had a lot of money. The proceeds of Mills Godwin's new sales tax were building up very nicely, in addition to funds from income tax and other normal sources of state revenue. But most of that was committed, and we didn't want to take money from other important commitments to pay the sewage facility subsidy. We considered everything, but a consensus developed very quickly when Vince suggested increasing the tax on whiskey and doubling the tax on cigarettes from two and a half cents per pack to five cents per pack. That would produce the needed revenue, and since Virginia's tax on cigarettes was the lowest in the nation, we assumed that the opposition to it, if any, would be very mild. It seemed so simple. And there was little expressed opposition to the increased tax on whiskey.

My wake-up call came just as soon as news of our cigarette tax–increase proposal hit the press. I was seated at the head table of a luncheon on the same day that news about the plan was published. When Tennant Bryan, publisher of the *Richmond Times-Dispatch,* came up to the table to give me a courtesy greeting, I asked him, in a voice that surely indicated how pleased I was with myself, "How do you like my new tax proposal?" "Don't like it at all," was the adamant reply. I had bitten the hand that feeds the entire community (Philip Morris Tobacco Company is headquartered in Richmond), and the *Richmond Times-Dispatch* was furious. They haven't forgiven me yet.

We soon realized it would be well-nigh impossible to clear a bill increasing the cigarette tax through the House Finance Committee, which was chaired by Delegate Willy Cleaton, a Southside tobacco farmer with a great deal of seniority in the House of Delegates. So we started on the Senate side, think-ing that if it passed the Senate, momentum might build sufficiently to over-come Chairman Cleaton's opposition in the House.

The process in the Senate turned out to be amazingly easy. I invited the members of the Senate Finance Committee to meet in my conference room to discuss the cigarette-tax proposal. The committee was chaired at the time by eighty-one-year-old Dr. Jim Hagood of Clover, Virginia, who had been in the Senate since 1942, and who was not in good health. Most of the other members of the Senate Finance Committee were equally mature. They re-tained instincts acquired during the old days when the Byrd Machine con-trolled politics, so after I suggested to the members of the Senate Finance Committee in my conference room that we needed revenue from an increase in the cigarette tax, Senator Melville Long, of Wise County, reacted with an Old Guard response: "Well, if the governor thinks that's what we ought to do, then I think we'd better go downstairs and do it!" And they did. It didn't make any difference if the governor was now a Republican—governors were gover-nors, and you did their bidding! The bill increasing the tax from two and a half cents to a nickel per pack of cigarettes passed the Senate by an approxi-mate two-to-one majority. I began to think that we might slip it by Delegate Cleaton in the House.

I also began to tease Willy a little bit when encountering him in the Capi-tol, and would toss him a jibe in passing, "Willy—gimme a chew of tobacco!" and he would smile wryly. We retained a very cordial relationship even if we were on opposite sides of the cigarette-tax issue. Surprisingly, we got commit-ments from almost a majority of his Finance Committee. If we did get the majority commitment, the committee members would report the bill out of his committee to increase the tax. On the other hand, they would not vote against their chairman unless they were sure to prevail. But Willy prevailed.

We fell short by one or two votes of the members of his committee, and the cigarette-tax bill was killed. The next day, upon returning from some downtown visit, I found on my desk a plug of Brown Mule chewing tobacco, compliments of Willy Cleaton. It was my turn to smile wryly.

Philip Morris executives apparently recognized that there was trouble afoot for them, all too aware of the narrow margin by which my proposal was defeated. In talks with me soon afterward about any future plans I might have that could affect them, they reaffirmed their opposition to a specific excise tax on their product, but recognized that additional revenue was necessary to improve the quality of Virginia rivers. They offered to support an increase in the income tax—a tax that would not single out their product as a source of those funds—if I would drop the plan to raise the excise tax on cigarettes. I agreed to their proposal; they arranged for the Virginia State Chamber of Commerce to endorse the idea, and a roughly 20 percent increase in Virginia's income tax (increasing the rate on the top income bracket from 5 percent to 6 percent) sailed through both bodies of the General Assembly almost unopposed. Roy Smith, chairman of the powerful Appropriations Committee (with help from Delegate Pete Giesen and others), tinkered with it just a little by amending the bill to levy 5¾ percent on the top bracket rather than an overall increase to 6 percent as the bill was originally introduced.

We got the money. And the General Assembly passed a very stringent law to require the localities to treat adequately the raw sewage they had previously been dumping in Virginia's rivers. Since the cost under our new matching grant formula was reduced for the localities to just 20 percent of the total cost of the treatment facilities, there was little squabble about either the cost or the more stringent cleanup requirements. The overall result was that at the end of my term I was able to proclaim, with approval from our Health Department, that "when the currently authorized cleanup projects have been completed, every river in Virginia will be swimmable again." That had to be said a little bit tongue-in-cheek because of the Elizabeth River, one of the most severely industrially polluted rivers in the country, which nobody would ever want to swim in, but the statement was substantially true.

The Governor's Schools
The Governor's Schools, which provide special opportunities for gifted young people, exist today throughout most, if not all, of Virginia. They are extremely popular and provide special opportunities in such areas as science, mathematics, the arts, and technology for thousands of especially talented kids. Cre-

ation of the Governor's Schools was a serendipitous development. Sometime in 1973, my appointments calendar noted that Bill Kelly, new president of Mary Baldwin College, was scheduled for a visit with me. Bill's older brother, John Jackson Kelly III, was my contemporary and good friend while we were growing up and going to school in Big Stone Gap. I was looking forward only to pleasant reminiscences with Bill about our hometown, so I was therefore a little surprised to find that Earl Shifflett, our newly appointed secretary of education following the new cabinet legislation, would also attend the meeting.

We did have the pleasant reminiscences I expected, but Bill had a mission: he had come to present the concept of Governor's Schools, which he had observed in action during his incumbency as president of an institution of higher learning in Kentucky. His glowing account appealed to me, and I suggested to Earl, "Why don't you look into it?" I don't remember what, if anything, I was called upon to do in the interim, but the next thing I do remember about the Governor's Schools was attending the "graduation" ceremonies (probably sometime after my term ended) of the two summer pilot programs Earl had quietly arranged, one at Mary Baldwin College and the other at Mary Washington College.

From little acorns mighty oaks do grow. The Governor's Schools have enjoyed tremendous legislative appeal—everybody wants one. And they exist all over the state, from the Thomas Jefferson High School in urban Fairfax County, which produces a record number of National Merit Scholarships annually, to the virtual Governor's School headquartered in Abingdon, offering a broad variety of programs from astronomy to world civilization for residents of twelve separate rural school districts in Southwest Virginia, using distance-learning technology. The Maggie Walker Governor's School, serving Richmond and its surrounding counties, has special significance for me. Our grandsons Nat Kaine and his brother, Woody, are both enthusiastic students there.

Virginia Is for Lovers
The now-famous slogan "Virginia Is for Lovers" began in an ad sponsored by the Virginia Department of Conservation and Economic Development in late 1969. The ad recalled that one of the first weddings in the British colony of Virginia was that of Englishman John Rolfe and the Indian princess Pocahontas. It noted that the couple honeymooned in the environs of Williamsburg, and it extolled the virtues of the Williamsburg area as a very desirable

twentieth-century honeymoon destination. The tag line "Virginia Is for Lovers" ran across the bottom of the ad.

Positive reaction to the ad was not instantaneous. Some of Virginia's traditionalists thought that maybe they should be offended by the ambiguous connotation of the slogan. Governor Godwin, for example, never mentioned it in the remaining weeks of his administration, and Mrs. Charles Beattie Moore (elderly daughter of Andrew Jackson Montague, Virginia's 1902–6 governor), openly expressed her contempt for it.

Bob Porterfield, founder of Abingdon's Barter Theater, Virginia's official theater, illustrated the double-entendre nature of the slogan in a little promotional talk in New York to an audience of actors, writers, and others associated with the theater. He referred to the slogan and assured his broad-minded audience that there was nothing offensive about it. "It means," he said, "Virginia is for history lovers; Virginia is for beach lovers; Virginia is for golf lovers; Virginia is for theater lovers. Why don't you come down and get a little?" At which point he probably flashed his famous signature grin.

My own initial reaction was to be a little wary of it; I wasn't at all sure how it would play with the public. But my inhibitions were destroyed completely soon after I took office, when I one day walked into the private quarters of the Executive Mansion, where my three older children were listening to a television jingle. Then eleven, twelve, and thirteen years old, they were enchanted by the ad and were singing along with the jingle "Virginia is for lovers." I recognized then that we had a promotional bonanza. I began to wear the lapel button every day. Its bold black background, with a large red Valentine heart and white-lettered "Virginia Is for Lovers," never failed to draw interest and comment. In Sun Valley, Idaho, in 1970 at a Republican Governors Association meeting, I was greeted by David Broder, a well-known political reporter for the *Washington Post.* He pointed to my lapel button and exclaimed, "I want one of those!" The one I "happened" to have in my pocket was immediately his.

Prior to New Year's Eve in 1970, our family attended a function of some kind at the Homestead Hotel, a popular resort in Bath County, Virginia. Tom Lennon, president of the company that owned that hotel, asked if I could supply him with enough of those buttons for all of his employees to wear during the coming New Year's Eve celebration, always attended by a capacity crowd— and I promptly had an adequate supply of buttons delivered to him. The buttons were meeting with approval from every level of Virginia's constituency.

In April 1971, the producer of a Roanoke TV talk show was on her way to trade programs with a TV station in Norwich, England. Jinks and I provided her with a bagful of the buttons, and a hundred or so made their way across the Atlantic in a British Airways duffel bag, to be pinned on the English TV station personnel. "Oh," said the managing director with great delight, "you've brought trinkets for the natives! We Brits did that for you *quite* a few years ago."

The fame of the slogan spread like wildfire, extolled in trade publications and publications of general circulation. Other states began to copy it. "New York Is for Lovers" was one of the first of the copycats, but Virginia is the only state that has kept that slogan going over the years. Even today, "Virginia Is for Lovers" bumper stickers are still available and are seen from time to time.

I continued to capitalize on the fame of that slogan any way possible. In the spring of 1973, it appeared that Secretariat, a Virginia-bred horse, was going to become very famous. After he won both the Kentucky Derby and the Preakness, I had a lapel button prepared with the same motif with the slogan "Breed More Secretariats." The wife of New York's well-known U.S. senator Jacob Javits was in our party at the Belmont Races in Governor Rockefeller's box. She seemed to be embarrassed about the button and favored me with disapproving glares as I spent some time pitching a pocketful of those buttons to the crowd below. If she was embarrassed, none of the rest of us was, especially when Secretariat won the final leg of the Triple Crown by thirty-two lengths.

Jinks took particular and very smug pleasure in showing off a button with the same black background, same white letters, and same red Valentine that somebody had given her that proclaimed, "I'M VIRGINIA!"

U.S. Route 23

Not too many months after I became governor in 1970, Jinks and I had sort of a homecoming when we attended the groundbreaking for the future Duffield Industrial Park, located in Scott County on U.S. Route 23, not far from my hometown of Big Stone Gap. This park project was a proposal to convert a floodplain into well-drained land suitable for use in economic development. Plans for the project were well along when I took office, and though my administration couldn't take credit for it, I was happy to see it coming to fruition. Route 23 had been widened to four lanes from Kingsport, Tennessee, to Duffield for egress and ingress to the proposed industrial park.

But the rest of U.S. Route 23 in that part of Virginia was a narrow, windy, dangerous road that Big Stone Gap folks knew as the "Wildcat" route, named for the section it passed through on the way from Big Stone Gap to Kingsport and Bristol. (Bristol was the "Big City," where those of us from Big Stone Gap went to do our serious shopping.) "Why not continue the four lanes and get rid of this tricky section?" I thought, and instructed Lynn Currey, Virginia's director of the Appalachian Regional Commission, to find funds to extend the four lanes of Route 23 on to Big Stone Gap. This was not entirely biased or provincial on my part. I envisioned the ultimate extension of the highway corridor through the depressed counties of Wise, Dickenson, and Buchanan on into Kentucky to help speed much-needed economic development in that region. In the shorter term, widening Route 23 to Big Stone Gap would facilitate access from the south to the proposed Mountain Empire Community College. The site for that college selected by the chancellor was on a delightful spot high on a hill just outside of my hometown. (I suspect the chancellor might have wanted to butter me up with this choice, and if so, I was happy to be buttered.)

"But Governor Godwin said that Duffield is far enough to widen Route 23," said Director Currey (apparently without thinking) in response to my instruction.

"Lynn," said I, "Governor Godwin is no longer governor. And Duffield is *not* far enough."

The four-lane road *did* get to Big Stone Gap during my term, and after more than twenty years and many difficulties, both fiscal and physical—a section of the highway north of Big Stone literally fell off the mountain in a landslide after it was built—Route 23 does now provide access to that depressed region throughout the entire north-south corridor from Tennessee into Kentucky and beyond to the entire Midwest. Duffield was indeed not far enough.

Housing Legislation

A significant piece of legislation articulating a Commonwealth policy against any racial discrimination in housing was passed without my active participation but with my silent blessing. William P. Robinson, an African American, represented a section of the city of Norfolk in the General Assembly. A highly respected educator on the faculty at Norfolk State College, he also quickly gained the respect and admiration of his colleagues in the House of Delegates after he was elected to that body in 1970. Somewhat to my surprise, the Fair Housing Bill introduced by Bill—which simply stated that the policy of the Commonwealth was to oppose racial discrimination in housing—did not bring forth any noticeable opposition. As a matter of fact, it seemed to be gaining support in the House. I assured Bill I would sign the legislation if it passed, but he and I agreed it might be better for me to "lay low" publicly. My integration policies had already approached the limits of acceptability, and I could well have become the lightning rod for opposition to Robinson's legislation. The tactic worked, and the House passed Bill's bill. Even more surprising, Delegate Robinson was able to quietly shepherd the Fair Housing Bill through the Senate, and in due course the legislation came to me for signature. No longer needing to "lay low," I expressed enthusiasm for the bill and labeled it "the most significant legislation passed by the General Assembly of Virginia since the Civil War." As policy, it ended generations of discrimination that had begun with slavery and had been maintained over the years through legislation, constitutional amendments, political activity, and tradition up to and including Massive Resistance.

My enthusiastic approbation of the legislation reported in the press disturbed my friend state senator John Dalton. He had his eyes on a statewide race in 1973, when he would be a candidate for lieutenant governor. He almost wept in my office when he came to protest my public support for the bill and said, "But Governor, I voted *against* the bill." There was little comfort that I could give him; he had just let an opportunity pass, and there was no way then for it to be recovered. Nevertheless, his political career was not in the least ruined. The son of "Mr. Republican," Ted Dalton, Johnny eventually became both lieutenant governor and then Virginia's governor in 1981.

Danville, 1973
Near-riots had occurred in the city of Danville in 1963 as the result of demonstrations and protest marches aimed at ending racial discrimination. The police had used fire hoses to quell disturbances, and several black ministers had been arrested and charged with criminal trespass, obstruction of justice, disturbing the peace, or what have you. There were no serious injuries, but it was a mess, and several of those ministers were convicted and given jail sentences. The convictions were appealed to the Supreme Court of Appeals (then the official name of Virginia's highest court), but for some reason there had been no disposition of those appeals by the court until 1973. I suspected that Chief Justice Nicky Snead, who had a great deal of common sense, had quietly seen to it that there was no disposition of the appeals. That suspicion was based on my guess that the chief justice, seeing that the situation in Danville had died down, simply decided to let sleeping dogs lie. But Attorney General Andrew P. Miller, in an apparent effort to clean up the state Supreme Court's old case docket, caused the court to send a decision back to the Danville court

ten years after the event and during my last year in office that affirmed the convictions of those Danville preachers.

The racial climate during that ten-year interim had improved significantly. There had been no racial incidents, and my chief of staff, Edward Temple, who had been city manager of Danville during a portion of that period, confirmed to me that there had been serious and successful biracial efforts to develop racial harmony in the Danville area. Conferring with Ed Temple; Bill Robertson, my special assistant for racial liaison; and John Ritchie, my executive assistant, I agreed with their consensus: if those preachers were put in jail in 1973 after ten peaceful years of progress, the situation would explode.

Exacerbating the potential problem, Ruth Charity, an African American attorney, represented the preachers. Ruth was a competent attorney, but something of a grandstander. She had attended a pretrial conference in chambers with the prosecuting attorneys and the judge, as a result of which she concluded that the sentences for those preachers would be suspended—meaning no jail time. She bragged to that effect at a meeting with some of her constituents, and the press picked it up. That violation of confidentiality of the pretrial conference upset the applecart, and risk was increased that the preachers would have to serve time. Bill Robertson's suggestion was that I be prepared, through a representative who was to attend the hearing at which sentences might be imposed, to pardon the preachers as nearly simultaneously as possible to the imposition of any jail sentence. Ed and John felt that was as good a solution as was feasible, and for the time being I acquiesced.

I'm not sure I had a martini at lunchtime following that conference with Bill, Ed, and John, but it would have been a good time for one. The idea of overruling the judiciary by exercising the peremptory powers of the executive to reverse the decision of the court just as it was handed down seemed to me to have explosive potential. It certainly would not have been a calming influence. Over a lunch break I came up with a different plan and called my friends back into a meeting on my return to the office.

I instructed Ed Temple to reach his friends in Danville, particularly those in the leadership of the chamber of commerce who he assured me would react favorably, and to line them up to testify at the hearing in favor of suspended sentences for the preachers. I telephoned Sam Tucker, a senior African American attorney who had a great deal of wisdom and a lifetime of experience with litigation to eliminate racial discrimination. Fortunately, I caught Sam just as he was about to depart for vacation. I urged him to postpone his vacation for a few days to go to Danville, first, to persuade Ruth Charity to step aside, and second, to take over the representation of those preachers himself. A third element developed serendipitously: the local judge recused himself from presiding over the hearing, and a considerably less volatile judge from far Southwest Virginia was called in to conduct the hearing.

Everybody did as hoped for. Somehow Ruth Charity was persuaded to step aside peaceably. The argument to the court at the hearing was made that the more sensible approach would be to suspend the sentences in order to continue the racial progress that had been made during the last ten years. Several leaders from the white community testified to that as well, and the judge complied with those arguments. A nasty picking at old sores was avoided, and progress toward racial harmony in the Danville area continued to develop.

There was still a long way to go toward racial harmony in Virginia. Old ways, old beliefs, old socially approved prejudices die hard, but every time goodwill and good sense prevailed in confrontations of any kind, I considered it a time for quiet jubilation—and then braced myself for the next challenge.

The Virginia Press
We had a wonderful group of political writers who covered the governor's office while I was in Richmond. Jim Latimer, of the *Richmond Times-Dispatch,* was dean of the group by reason of longevity and wisdom, although Melville "Buster" Carico of the *Roanoke Times* was not far behind him in either longevity or wisdom. Buster, as a matter of fact, had been closer to the development of the Republican Party by reason of his proximity to Ted Dalton's local jurisdiction centered in Radford, a town west of Roanoke and within the daily circulation area of his paper. Buster had a depth of knowledge and an informed respect for Ted Dalton's contribution to the early development of the Republican Party in Virginia.

Carl Shires covered Capitol Hill for the then-existent *Richmond News Leader;* Carl couldn't be relied on for the same degree of accuracy as most of the others, but in that respect he couldn't hold a candle to Joe Weeks, who covered news for WRVA radio. Weeks wasn't malevolent, but the absence of facts didn't bother him either. Once I was confabbing with one of his competitor reporters while leaning on the iron fence around George Washington's statue. As Joe passed by, he jibed facetiously, "Whatever you're talking about, don't bother to tell me; I'll just make it up!" He intended it as a joke, of course, but there was more than a grain of truth there. Weeks overtook me one Sunday morning as I walked back to the mansion after a brief visit to the office. We were both on our way to a Bloody Mary party I'd promised to hold for members of the press who had covered my campaign. He was ready with a jibe. "I'm sorry, sir, you can't get into this party—it's for journalists." "If you fiction writers can attend it, so can I," I replied.

George Kelly covered the Capitol for the *Norfolk Virginian-Pilot;* one time he acknowledged the confrontational dynamics between governor and press when he said to me at the conclusion of a press conference, "Well, Governor, we never laid a hand on you." I nearly always approached those conferences with some eagerness and never really felt that it had to be confrontational, but to some of them it was.

John Daffron represented the Associated Press, and at the beginning of my term Helen Dewar covered Richmond political activities for the *Washington Post.* She later went to Washington, however, and until recently was the lead political writer covering the U.S. Senate for the *Post.* Sad to report, she died in 2006 after a lingering battle with breast cancer. Ken Ringle, a feature writer for the *Post* today, and Carl Bernstein, of Woodward and Bernstein fame, took over after Helen Dewar left Richmond. Bernstein, who was there only a short time, was the only reporter of all I dealt with who left me feeling intentionally misled by some of the background statements for his questions. Helen Dewar had covered our campaign for the *Post* in some detail, as did Ann Compton, representing Roanoke's CBS affiliate, WDBJ-TV.

Ann continued to cover the governor's office for a good part of my term. Then a junior reporter headed for a very distinguished career in reporting political news, she was not above using feminine wiles to get answers to her questions. For example, she always sat during my press conferences on the floor of the center aisle, just in front of her cameraman. When she wanted to get my attention for a question, an appropriate or inappropriate amount of cheesecake would invariably appear and invariably get my attention.

Ann was equally creative when downtown Richmond was flooded and lost all electric power during Hurricane Agnes in 1972. In order to be able to cover the story, she ingenuously sought the company of Virginia's First Lady (my wife), and the two of them toured the flooded areas in an official limousine with full cooperation of the National Guard. Their tour included the lightless Executive Mansion, where Ann observed that the ceiling light over the landing on the ladies' stairway—the one with the wider stairs provided long years before to accommodate the ladies' hoop skirts—was burning steadily in spite of lost electric power everywhere else. One explanation for this phenomenon was put forth: that the well-known lady ghost said to inhabit the mansion supplied the power to light the ladies' landing. Could be!

I remember that late in my term Ann Compton jigged me a little bit about the State Police handling of a threatened uprising in the state penitentiary. Pictures on television and in the newspaper showed clearly that the State Police, garbed in heavy riot gear and carrying heavy weaponry, massively overwhelmed the potential rioters. Ann's questioning implied she thought we might have been too heavy-handed. "Why so much force?" she asked. But I had learned a lesson from Eisenhower's reply to my question about his sending the 101st Airborne Division to Little Rock, "Nobody got hurt." That was my response to Ann—"Nobody got hurt."

Ann continues her career as an ABC-TV reporter at the White House and was the only reporter on Air Force One with President Bush during the very hectic hours that followed the tragedies of 9/11, when three hijacked airplanes crashed into the Twin Towers in New York City and the Pentagon in Washington.

John Daffron's successor at the AP once bummed a ride from me on the state airplane from Roanoke to the Homestead Hotel at Hot Springs for some event I was to attend and he was to cover as a reporter. To my chagrin, we had some miscommunication, and I did not pick him up for the return ride. In a few days I received a present from him: a little model red biplane much like that in the Red Baron cartoons, labeled "Governor Holton's One-way Airline."

The press corps was always alert to call attention to any real or supposed deficiency. Early in my term, after I had been quite late for a scheduled press conference in my regular press conference room at the Capitol, I was alerted of the time for my next press conference by a nice little red alarm clock surreptitiously smuggled into my office, set to ring five minutes before the next press conference was to begin.

It was obvious that a competent press secretary would be needed to ride herd on this well-informed, intelligent group of observers whose curious eyes would be on all the activities of the new administration, as they say today, "twenty-four/seven." I was confident that we had the right person already on board from the campaign staff, but I did "clear" his appointment with my secret personnel committee. I also talked about him with Charlie McDowell, a highly respected political columnist based in Richmond and Washington. Charlie was a longtime friend, as were his father, a law professor and occasional interim dean of the Washington and Lee Law School, and his mother. As executive secretary to successive deans at the school, Mrs. McDowell really ran the place. I think Charlie was intrigued with my suggestion that perhaps he would like the job, but the stock option incentives he was accruing from long service with the *Richmond Times-Dispatch* precluded his giving that possibility any serious thought.

Charlie agreed with me without hesitation that Staige D. Blackford was the man. Staige was about forty, a University of Virginia graduate and a Rhodes scholar who had studied history at Oxford. He used to joke that he responded to one of the dons' inquiries about the time period of his intended academic concentration. He told the don that the period between 1870 and the beginning of the New Deal appealed to him. "Young man," said the don, "that's not history. That's journalism."

It was important to me that Staige had done a tour with the Southern Regional Council, where he was to report on and encourage the civil rights movement in the South. As editor of the *Cavalier Daily,* he was ahead of his time on racial issues while a student at the University of Virginia. He also knew the Virginia political scene and its participants from his work as political writer for the *Norfolk Virginian-Pilot.* And we had tested him: he had accepted my invitation to write press releases and speeches for the campaign. His performance there had been excellent—with one exception. On his first day at work he drove me to one of my campaign stops. I looked up suddenly from my notes to realize that he was driving the wrong way down a one-way street. He quickly corrected that but responded to my remonstrance with, "Well, I didn't sign on as a driver."

The press knew and respected Staige for his intellectual capacity, his wit, his candor, and above all, his integrity. He was a superb press secretary, and he was in a very large way responsible for the excellent relations my administration enjoyed with the working press. In the beginning—the very beginning— I worried a little about leaks, but I soon realized that regardless of efforts to maintain secrecy, whatever I even *thought* would soon be in the headlines. I therefore acquiesced without comment when I found that Staige, who knew everything about my affairs inside and out, was having coffee every morning with all the reporters, telling them everything they wanted to know. "Oh well," I thought, "it's the people's business."

Staige wrote most of my formal speeches. Some of them were intellectually superior to anything I could have come up with, but the inaugural speech, which he and J. Harvie Wilkinson III produced together, was just outstanding. They caught my speech patterns with precision, as well as my philosophy. The words "the era of defiance is behind us . . . let our goal in Virginia be an aristocracy of ability" set the exact tone I wanted to identify my leadership.

Following four years with me in Richmond and after serving as assistant to

Presidents Shannon and Frank Hereford of the University of Virginia, Staige became editor of the *Virginia Quarterly Review*, a fortuitous appointment for Virginia. He made his home permanently in Charlottesville, where he had grown up and his family had been leading citizens. He made the *Review* a highly respected, national literary publication, and he loved his work. Sadly, he met a premature death in 2003 in an automobile accident. It occurred while riding with his wife and his dog, just carrying out routine local chores.

Podiatry in the Jackson Ward
On one occasion while in office, I began to experience a pain in my right foot, probably caused by an ingrown toenail. This provided an opportunity to visit Dr. William E. Thornton, a podiatrist and president of the Richmond chapter of the Crusade for Voters, whose endorsement of me for governor contributed significantly to my winning majority. It was also an opportunity to further enhance my already strong approval in Jackson Ward, a center of professional, commercial, and social activity for the African American community in Richmond. Ordinarily on forays for little chores in Richmond I traveled in an unmarked police car. This time I asked my driver to take me in the "Number One" limousine. Dr. Thornton's office was, I believe, on Marshall Street. I told the Capitol policeman to double-park the limousine in front of Dr. Thornton's office while I went in for my appointment.

The receptionist received me with unawed professionalism. Yes, I had an appointment, but I would have to wait; Dr. Thornton would see me in just a few minutes. "Won't you please have a seat?" In due course, I was escorted into a treatment room where Dr. Thornton soon appeared, and after some minimal pleasantries, he gave my foot a very thorough examination and treatment. I returned directly to my office, and almost as soon as I was seated at my desk, Lois Firesheets, my secretary, announced a phone call from Lester Banks. Lester Banks was the longtime executive secretary of the Virginia Conference of the National Association for the Advancement of Colored People. He and I were friends, and he had been an important part of the effort to have the Crusade endorse me for governor. He had wisdom, a highly respected reputation in the black community, and a great sense of humor. "Well," he teased, "I see you found a good place to have your toenails cut." My little ploy had worked. I knew it would, but I had no idea that the word would circulate quite so quickly on the informal grapevine that was known to be an integral part of the Jackson Ward community.

Joe McConnell and the UVA Board of Visitors

While in Arizona attending a Republican governors conference, probably in 1973, I received a call from Joe McConnell. I was never very impressed with Joe McConnell. I could never understand how he got to be the CEO of ComSat; I could never understand how he got to be the CEO of Reynolds Metals Company; nor could I understand how he ever got to be rector of the Board of Visitors of the University of Virginia. But he did get to be all three at one time or another. When I took his call, Joe was the rector, and he reported that the Board of Visitors was having difficulty communicating with Edgar Shannon (one of my best friends), then president of the University of Virginia. The difficulty arose out of some disagreement about how to handle the contract of a football coach whose win-loss record was so far not impressive. But whatever the difficulty, Joe reported by phone to me that the Board of Visitors was going to appoint a committee comprised of some of its members to "communicate" with Edgar.

Joe didn't expect my response: "Good God, Joe! If you can't communicate with the president, why don't you fire him?"

"What?" He was obviously shocked.

I repeated, "Why don't you fire him?"

"Well, I don't think we can do that, but we think a communications committee would help."

"Joe—you can't appoint a watchdog committee over the president of the University of Virginia!"

"Oh, we're not going to call it a *watchdog* committee."

"But everyone else will."

That effectively ended the conversation, and I never heard any more about a communications committee. Edgar Shannon prevailed in the disagreement about the football coach and stayed in his job as president until he voluntarily retired some time after I left office.

Bonds and the Chesapeake Bay Bridge-Tunnel

That very expensive Chesapeake Bay Bridge-Tunnel connecting the Eastern Shore of Virginia with the mainland at Norfolk was paid for with revenue bonds issued in the mid-1950s. The old one-party political organization (headed by senior senator Harry Byrd) did pretty much whatever it wanted to do in those days. The Commonwealth of Virginia could *not* borrow money; that idea was a complete anathema to Senator Byrd. But revenue bonds issued by a local governmental authority created by legislation, to be paid off by tolls, were okay, even though such bonds were more expensive than bonds issued with the full faith and credit of the state.

In this instance, the bonds were particularly expensive. The financial community was wary of the high risk involved; that financially sophisticated group knew that the optimistic projections of traffic expected to use the bridge-tunnel—and the projected toll revenues—were overexuberant, and not certain to materialize. Therefore, in order to raise enough money to build the bridge-tunnel, three series of bonds were issued by the Chesapeake Bay Bridge-Tunnel Commission, each succeeding bond issue carrying a higher interest rate. The nominal rate for the series C, the riskiest, was 6 percent annually, a phenomenally high interest rate for these "municipals"—bonds that produced interest free of income taxation by either the state or federal governments. As many feared, the tolls on the completed project did not produce enough revenue to pay the required interest and principal payments as they came due, and the first default was anticipated to come during my watch on July 1, 1970.

In the spring of 1970, the very dignified senior executive of the very conservative, very traditional Virginia Trust Company came to my office to talk about the expected default of the Chesapeake Bay Bridge-Tunnel revenue bonds. That distinguished gentleman recommended that I arrange some way to use taxpayer general funds to subsidize the Bridge-Tunnel Commission and thereby avoid a default in its bonds. To me, this proposal had very socialistic overtones, something I had always thought was abhorrent to the ultraconservative financial community of Main Street Richmond. After pointing out that the holders of the C bonds had been paid a higher rate of interest to compensate them for the higher risk, I asked the gentleman to explain why the taxpayers should now bail them out. He condescendingly told me that default on the bay revenue bonds would adversely affect the credit of the Commonwealth and result in higher interest rates on full faith and credit bonds that might be issued in the future, now being authorized in the new amendments to the Virginia Constitution, which were pending in a statewide voter referendum.

"But," I said, "these investors are not little old ladies in tennis shoes; the holders of these bonds are sophisticated institutional investors like you. You mean to tell me that default on a revenue bond issue by some little local commission would adversely affect the interest rate on bonds to be issued with the full faith and credit of the Commonwealth of Virginia?"

"Yes," he asserted with authority.

"Bullshit!" was my reply. End of meeting.

A few days later I had a visit from Ben Alsop, whom I had appointed as director of the Division of Purchases and Supply at the request of Lawrence Lewis Jr., one of my chief financial supporters. Ben was part of that Main Street financial crowd. He seemed to me reserved, almost timid in his approach. He had been shocked, I'm sure, by the gossip he'd heard on "the street" about the Virginia Trust representative's disappointing conference with the governor and felt he had to straighten it out with me. I knew what he was trying to do, and I cut off his stammering by saying, "It's okay, Ben. Mr. So-and-So came up to my office the other day with a load of bullshit, and I simply described it for him." I'm not sure Ben ever recovered from the additional shock.

I held firm, and the state did not bail out the investors. They had to wait for payments until there was an upturn in toll collections. That upturn eventually came, though some time after the serial payments on their bonds were due. And there was never any detectable adverse effect on bonds issued subsequently with the backing of the credit of the Commonwealth of Virginia.

The U.S. Navy and the Chesapeake Bay Bridge-Tunnel

During my first two weeks in office, the navy had the misfortune of having one of its cargo ships, which was anchored off Ocean View without steam in its boilers, blown by a little gale through the Chesapeake Bay Bridge just south of the Thimble Shoals Channel. I learned of this incident from reporters who quizzed me about it as I was returning to my office from a breakfast speaking engagement in town. I had to confess to the reporters that I knew nothing about it, although it had happened several hours earlier.

When I got the facts, I found that the navy ship had completely severed the bridge, so the north–south traffic over that route was terminated, and it was unclear how long the termination would last. I felt sure the navy would accept responsibility for the mishap and would fix the damage. I therefore called my good friend John Warner, whom I had first met at Washington and Lee. When I was doing some graduate work there in the fall of 1946, he was a freshman who pledged my fraternity. On many occasions since, he has publicly referred to the fact that I gave him a pretty good whack with a paddle as part of the hazing that freshmen pledges underwent at the time. Now he was secretary of the navy, and I was governor of Virginia.

When he came on the phone to answer my call, I said, "John, you broke my bridge." His only response was, "I know." Warner pleaded a previous engagement that prevented him from joining me on a helicopter trip to inspect the bridge, but he did send a four-star admiral, Admiral Ephraim Holmes, then commander of the NATO sea forces based in Norfolk. I felt like I had "arrived" for sure when I boarded the luxurious helicopter that brought Admiral Holmes to Richmond to pick me up for the inspection trip over Hampton Roads. I had by that time spent about twenty-five years climbing the officer hierarchy in the U.S. Navy Reserve, but I was still only a senior commander, or a very junior captain. In either event, I was still very much in awe of a four-star admiral—more than I would have been of this current secretary of the navy. So when he stepped aside and indicated that I take the honor seat by the window in his premium helicopter, I felt like I'd reached the top of the heap!

I learned one good lesson in administration from that incident, and so did Colonel Harold Burgess, superintendent of the Virginia State Police Department. He and I had a nice talk, at the end of which the colonel understood that I was to be informed—day or night—of any such future incidents. There were to be no more surprises for me from members of the press about accidents or near crises during my term as governor.

B'rer Rabbit Outwits the Fox

Jinks and I were at home on the second floor of the Executive Mansion on a Sunday evening sometime after school opened in August 1970. I use that evening to establish the time of this event because I believe the motivation for what proved to be a hoax was an effort to embarrass me and possibly President Nixon by some of the right-wing nuts in the administration who were emotionally opposed to my support of the court decree that required busing to achieve integration in the public schools.

Our quiet Sunday evening together was interrupted by a telephone call from a caller who identified himself as Ron Ziegler, the president's press secretary. The speaker advised me that he was on Air Force One with the president, returning to Washington from a brief Florida vacation. I knew that the president had been in Florida, and it seemed logical for him to be flying over Richmond at about that time. I was therefore not at all suspicious when "Ron" said to me, in effect, "We are just flying over your capital, and the boss would like you come up and meet with him tomorrow morning at nine o'clock."

That was a little surprising, but consistent with some of Nixon's known impulsiveness, and I was not at all suspicious that the call might be fake. I assured "Ron" that I would be at the White House the next morning promptly at the designated time of 9 a.m. I flew to Washington in the state plane early the next morning, and a Northern Virginia state trooper picked me up and delivered me to the west gate of the White House just before my scheduled "appointment." The sergeant of the White House Capitol police recognized our unmarked state trooper's car and recognized me from previous visits.

"Well, good morning, Governor. Who are you going to see?" the friendly sergeant asked, and added, "I don't have you on my list." That statement still did not raise my suspicions. I thought the president's invitation to me had probably come as a spontaneous impulse while flying over Richmond the night before. So I replied with confidence, "the president."

The gates swung open, and I went freely into the West Wing entrance. Pat Buchanan's stately blonde wife was acting as receptionist to the West Wing office, and she too seemed surprised to see me, but when told I was there pursuant to an invitation relayed from the president by Ron Ziegler, she called Ron, and he came down promptly to greet me. He also seemed puzzled by my presence, and I repeated that I was there pursuant to his telephone call the night before. He looked startled, shook his head as if to clear his thoughts, and then said, "But Governor, I didn't call you!" I concluded immediately that somebody familiar with the president's schedule and who didn't approve of my integration activities had set up the whole ruse to embarrass me and possibly the president.

I told Ron what I thought and suggested that if the president were available, we could turn the tables on the hoaxer by having me meet briefly with the president. Further, Ron should let the press corps report (with pictures) that the president and the Virginia governor had met that morning about an undisclosed matter. Ron agreed both with my analysis and with my recommendation about a short meeting for me with President Nixon. The president approved, and it turned out even better than I could have dared hope. The president had had a meeting scheduled with some real estate folks in the Cabinet Room, and, for no explained reason, I was seen in the photographic record of that conference, sitting at the cabinet table on the president's right.

He and I both wore a little smirk of satisfaction at the ultimate outcome. The hoaxer had been outfoxed.

The Story That Never Was

There were three hoaxes, or attempted hoaxes, that occurred during my term between 1970 and 1974. We outfoxed the false appointment-with-the-president story. We ignored a false bomb-scare-in-the-mansion story (described in chapter 12). The hoax behind the story-that-never-was has never been completely revealed.

I was scheduled to attend a function in Lexington on October 12, 1973, the same day that President Nixon selected to announce his choice for a nominee to succeed Vice President Agnew, two days after the veep had resigned. I had flown from Richmond in the state's Kingair and planned to continue on to Washington after the Lexington appearance because I'd been invited to attend the White House announcement scheduled for later the same day. Speculation was rampant because there had been no really reliable indications about whom the president might nominate. I was as eager to hear his choice as the press was.

Charlie McDowell, longtime friend, syndicated columnist, and Washington bureau chief for the *Richmond Times-Dispatch*, showed up at the Lexington function, which did not have any obvious national or Washington significance, so I was surprised to see him there. The reason for Charlie's unscheduled trip to join me in Lexington became clear when he confided that he had had a "reliable tip" that I, Linwood Holton, would that day be nominated by President Nixon to fill the vice-presidential vacancy created by Agnew's resignation. Charlie clearly intended to be in at the beginning of a story that would be big nationally as well as in Virginia.

"Absurd!" was my response to Charlie, but he persisted. "It's a strong, reliable tip, and I believe it's true," was the substance of his counter to my disclaimer, and he asked to ride with me to Washington on the state plane. I was happy to have him come along, but I explained the reason I knew the rumor was untrue: "Charlie, when Nixon pulls one of his surprises—this one would have been typical—he always has the 'brides' present, and I know that Jinks is in Richmond, not Washington." That dampened but did not erase Charlie's certainty.

Substance was added to the rumor when we landed at Washington National Airport. A *Time* magazine reporter (I think his last name was White) met us as we deplaned. He had heard the same rumor. Despite my insistence that it was not true, he also hitched a ride with us to the White House in the trooper's car. When the three of us and the trooper showed up at the southwest gate, the secret service officer stopped us. "Governor, you'll have to wait a few minutes; I don't have my list yet." I turned to my journalism friends, flapped my arms bird-wing style, and said with some glee, "Well, boys—there goes your rumor, flying away." We all realized the unlikelihood of an imminent new vice president having to wait while the bureaucracy delivered a list. We were in due course admitted to the White House, and watched in the East Room as Nixon announced his selection of U.S. House minority leader Gerald R. Ford.

Charlie and Mr. White were not the only journalists fooled by the false tip. The folks in the news department of the *Washington Post* were also duped, and almost carried the story-that-never-was. It would have been phenomenally embarrassing to the *Post* if they had, but the rumor got only as far as the galley proof of a story written by Carroll Kilpatrick, a veteran *Post* political writer, in which the paper would have reported that Nixon would nominate Governor Holton. When he retired as a White House correspondent in September, 1975, Carroll presented a photocopy of the false story to President Ford on Air Force One. He also thoughtfully gave a copy to me.

The source of the tip is still the subject of speculation. Carroll told me that he thought it came from well up in the White House hierarchy and was leaked to top management at the *Post*. In 2004, *Post* publisher Katharine Graham and I were both attending a Miller Center political forum in Charlottesville. I asked her then about the rumor, but she had no memory of the incident. My belief is that someone on Nixon's top staff floated it. There was a good bit of displeasure around there with Holton: he was too liberal, he supported busing, and he did not approve the Southern Strategy. Also, the White House staff dislike of the *Post* was well known. Why not embarrass both Holton and the *Post* with one false story tip? It almost worked.

Memories:
Up Close and Personal

Trooper Compton

One of the warmest memories of my four years as governor comes from the association with "my" trooper. There was no twelve-person security detail from the State Police Department as there is now. On the day I took office, Colonel Harold Burgess, State Police superintendent, advised me that—subject to my approval—he was assigning Charles R. Compton as my trooper.

Compton was a six-foot-five-inch, good-looking, twenty-seven-year-old state trooper who had grown up in Hampton, Virginia, and had served in the department long enough to have impressed the management. (Once, on a later occasion, when I commented to Colonel Burgess that another young trooper had impressed me as being "outstanding," the colonel gave me a comeuppance: "They are *all* outstanding, Governor." I found out during my term that he was about right.)

As for Trooper Compton, I wanted to avoid any possibility that this young man's assignment to the governor would have any adverse effect on his career; I wanted to be sure there was no feeling on his part or any perception of others that the post was a "teacher's pet" assignment that would avoid less desirable but perhaps more important posts for him. So I suggested to Compton that we both look upon his assignment as a six-month trial period. If, at the end of six months, either of us preferred a different arrangement, there would be no questions asked and other assignments would be made. We both enthusiastically renewed our pact at the end of each of two six-month trial periods. After that, both of us considered it a permanent assignment until the end of my term. Compton's performance was nothing less than outstanding. He not only knew where we were going and how to get there, he also arranged for parking without any interruption of my schedule. He anticipated and supplied my every need.

He seemed to take pride in being able to handle any emergency, but I thought I had him one day at Pawleys Island, South Carolina. I was stung by a bee, something to which I had become very allergic. When Compton offered to wield the hypodermic needle for an antiallergy shot, I protested that he didn't have to go that far—I could certainly do it myself. "But, Governor, I'm a medic in the National Guard, and I've given these shots many times." I gave up. He *could* do it all.

On one occasion, I asked Compton to drive the "Number One" limousine out to Wise County ahead of me, where I would be making a ceremonial appearance of some sort. The plan was for me to fly out later in the day and meet him there. It was a time of some slackness in the coal fields, and the coal truckers were very upset with me for having vetoed a bill the Assembly had passed that would have increased the weight permitted on their coal trucks. (I had vetoed it because the Highway Department engineers predicted that the heavier weight would cause fatigue in bridge structures, possibly resulting in a tragedy such as dumping a school bus in a creek.)

When I arrived by plane at the Lonesome Pine airport, we could see maybe sixty coal trucks lined up as a reception committee for the vetoing governor. I told the pilots, "If you don't see Compton out there, wind this thing up and let's go back to Richmond!" But Compton *was* there and had the situation well in hand. He had "explained" to the truckers that "Yes, Governor Holton would be glad to participate in their welcome parade, but of course the governor's car always leads the parade." After shaking hands all around with the disgruntled drivers, who didn't quite know how to respond to Compton's announcement, we "paraded" to Big Stone Gap, leaving the trucks and truckers a good way behind, their protest confounded by Compton's diplomacy.

Compton became a real part of our family, and he quietly extended the range of his responsibilities. One time we were having target practice with clay pigeons at Camp Pendleton, the National Guard complex at Virginia Beach where one of the officers' cottages was dedicated to the use of the governor and his family. I think the shotgun involved was a 12-gauge Remington given to each of the governors attending a Little Rock meeting of the Republican Governors Association by our host, Arkansas governor Winthrop Rockefeller. I had fired a few shots, and the older children—the girls and Woody—had fired a few. Five-year-old Dwight was not one to be dissuaded by any argument that shooting this weapon was beyond his capacity. Dwight was not, and *is* not, of a mind to be deflected by any suggestion of his limitations.

So we let him try it, with Compton standing behind him, helping him hold the weapon with appropriate firmness to the young would-be Nimrod's shoulder. It didn't work. In spite of Compton's support, when Dwight pulled the trigger, the recoil kicked him down on his very surprised butt. He was one embarrassed lad, but Compton gently led him away from the group and did his best to comfort him. He later reported that Dwight's comment, in an attempt to recover from his loss of face, was, "Well, I didn't want to shoot the damn thing anyhow."

Though I came to believe that Compton was perfect, thankfully there were a few minor glitches. One seemingly occurred on a Sunday afternoon early in my term, when Compton was driving part of the family and me at a fairly leisurely pace on Interstate 95/64. The highway was as smooth as a table, the weather perfect, and we were traveling at a moderate speed. Even so, an axle on the brand-new Cadillac limousine broke, and we were stranded on the side of a road in the middle of Richmond. It was a very simple matter to radio the first division about our predicament and have a patrolling trooper rescue us almost immediately. But wouldn't you know—the nearest patrolling trooper turned out to be "Shakey" Shields, the trooper assigned to Governor Godwin during the four years preceding my term. Shields was a great tease, and this situation was irresistible to him. "What's the matter, Compton?" Shields asked, grinning broadly as he came up beside our limousine. "Did you run out of gas?"—implying that Compton's neglect was the cause of our plight rather than the unexpected and unavoidable broken axle.

On another occasion, Compton actually did make a mistake. One day in White Stone, he had gone at least a half mile before he realized that his last turn should have been to the left and he had turned to the right. My subsequent teasing was not unmerciful, but close to it.

There was one other opportunity to goad him a little. We had arranged that the two of us would join a group for duck hunting at Ed Allen's, a commercial recreation area on the Chickahominy River less than an hour's drive away from Richmond. I had arranged with Compton to pick me up at the Executive Mansion at 5:30 on the morning of the hunt. I put on my hunting clothes, got my gun, and went out the front door of the mansion, just at the appointed hour. No Compton. When I telephoned the dispatcher, he checked and advised that "201" (Compton's car radio number) was not responding. Realizing that Compton had overslept, I asked the dispatcher to call him at home and advise him that I would be going on down Interstate 64 toward the Chickahominy River with a Capitol Police driver and that Compton could overtake us in just a few minutes.

As we drove down I-64, I wondered why Compton hadn't checked in by radio, and then realized, "Well, of course! Compton isn't going to broadcast to the entire first division that he was late picking up the governor." Sure enough, his little blue and gray trooper's car very shortly drew up behind us, and we stopped so I could transfer to his patrol car. I couldn't let this rare moment go by. I jumped out of the car, and as Compton approached, I said, "Godammit Compton! You haven't been working for me but three years and you're late once already." He was relieved, I'm sure, that I responded with some levity, and I have many times enjoyed telling that tale.

He was deservedly promoted several times and, because he was later moved into management, continued his service in the department much longer than twenty years, the average term of service for most troopers. His last post was as the commanding officer of the sixth division of State Police headquartered in Salem, Virginia. In the early part of the Allen administration, I recommended him for appointment as superintendent. But Governor Allen had his own idea about the person he wanted for that job, and I think his consideration of Compton was minimal at best.

Jinks and I braved a snowstorm to attend the retirement party the department put on for him near Bedford in 2004. There was—in spite of bad weather—a standing-room-only crowd, and enthusiastic praise of him and his career came from many associates and law enforcement colleagues who had dealt with him through the years. He and his wife, Jane, are now enjoying his retirement in their home near Blue Ridge, Virginia, where his hobby of raising goats has turned into an almost full-time bustling goat meat and milk business.

Holton Management Style

While governor, I tried not to micromanage the actual operating functions of government. There were great numbers of people available—staff members, appointees, and career professionals—with expertise much superior to mine in their specific fields of responsibility, so I tried as far as possible to be the policy decision maker, not the implementer.

My approach did not work so well when the question concerned where the very large and elaborate new headquarters for the Division of Motor Vehicles should be located. I think Vern Hill, the commissioner of the Division of Motor Vehicles, had visions of a nice suburban location with all of the amenities that a slightly rural setting could provide. The rumor mill had suggestions of various other locations. This was to be a major project, so I thought it should be placed where it would become a hub around which there could be additional desirable development. I therefore instructed the Division of Planning in the governor's office to explore the possibilities and make a professional recommendation for the most suitable site. Several weeks later, a report from the Division of Planning came for my review. I was disappointed. This document was merely a descriptive catalog of six or eight possible sites, but there was no recommendation, professional or otherwise.

I was in a fairly good mood at that time, so I decided not only to try to teach a lesson to the two planners who authored this document, but to have a little fun as well. I sent instructions to have the governor's "Number One" limousine parked at the west entrance to the Capitol and to invite the two planners to come from their office, be seated in the limousine, and wait for me. I gave them a little time to ponder just what this summons was all about and what might be happening next. Then I joined them. The Capitol policeman, who had been given our destination beforehand, drove us to the area of Broad Street in Richmond just east of the old Broad Street Station of the RF&P (Richmond, Fredericksburg, and Potomac) Railroad. I led the way after we left the car and walked up to the pedestrian bridge that then crossed in a northerly direction over the railroad tracks.

When we reached a high point on the bridge, I stopped and surveyed with my planners the area east of the Broad Street station, north of Broad Street itself, off the railroad tracks and extending easterly toward the Pleasants Hardware operation.

"Why," I asked, "isn't this the best place to locate the new Division of Motor Vehicles building? It seems to me that it would attract new development and prevent the deterioration of an area that will definitely take place otherwise."

"Yes sir," came the ready reply. "It certainly *is* the very best place in the whole Richmond area."

"Then why in hell didn't you all recommend it?" I asked with an edge in my voice.

"Oh—well, we didn't know what you wanted!" they responded cheerfully.

This gave me an opportunity to deliver a short but earnest lecture on how people in my position needed a professional staff who could be counted on to provide candid and objective evaluations based on their own professional expertise.

I was rude on another occasion when Ed Temple, my excellent chief of staff, and John Garber, the state director of personnel, came to my office for something they considered to be in urgent need of a gubernatorial decision. They described the problem and found to their dismay that I was not in a very good mood that morning.

"I believe you two can make that decision," I said coldly.

"I beg your pardon?" queried the always very gentle Ed, apparently taken aback.

"Each of you has over thirty years in public administration," I said. "I believe you're competent to make that decision."

A very meek "Yes sir" came from Ed, and the chagrined pair departed. I was immediately sorry I had not been gentler myself, but my tone had reflected my impatience with the failure of competent professionals to get on with their work without stumbling over trivia.

Sometimes I didn't realize quite how much weight my management style carried over into lesser matters. One hilarious experience I had concerned the fountain in front of the Executive Mansion. On a bright but cold March morning, I walked out the door and down the front steps. It was brisk, my favorite kind of weather. I commented on the beauty of the day to the Capitol policeman on watch nearby: "What a beautiful day! Spring is on the way! It won't be long before they'll be filling up the fountain." (The fountain in front of the mansion was always drained to prevent freezing during the winter.)

When I returned from the office at suppertime, the fountain was full of water. I had a good laugh to myself, and in a day or two sought out my friend Turpin, our inmate-gardener and a regular attendant on the grounds of the mansion. When I asked him what sort of message he had received about the water in the fountain, he replied, "They told me the governor said, 'Fill up the damn fountain!'"

Woody in Israel

Leonard Strelitz was a member of a prominent Norfolk family that headed an extensive retail furniture empire. Leonard was an avid and persuasive salesman, whether for furniture, for a favorite political candidate, or for any other cause he considered worthy. In 1973, it was the United Jewish Appeal (UJA) that brought him to me.

On behalf of the UJA, Leonard invited me to be the celebrity host for a group of Virginia Jewish citizens for a weeklong tour of Israel. The Virginia governor was to be the bait to encourage Virginians to join what was obviously (to me) a fund-raising expedition. Since it was to benefit the state of

Israel, I was happy to join in. Not incidentally, I looked forward to a very interesting experience, not inconsistent with the national interest of the United States.

"Jinks and I would be happy to go along," was the substance of my response. I knew that Jinks had long wanted to visit Israel. But a red light, or at least a yellow light, flashed through my mind when Leonard countered with, "No, Governor. This will be a strictly stag trip." My instinctive reaction was that the Virginia governor had better have a chaperon. So I told Leonard that I would have to be accompanied by a couple of aides; one would be Sandy Gilliam because of his foreign service experience, and the other would be Woody, my twelve-year-old son, whom I privately considered my chaperon.

A very congenial group of thirty or forty Jewish male Virginians (with one wife who somehow invaded the group) left Kennedy Airport on an Israeli El Al 747, with only Woody, Sandy, and me going first-class. Woody's face and eyes reflected major excitement as we entered Israel airspace and our crowd began to sing loudly "Shalom! Shalom!" I expect I felt a pretty special emotion myself, realizing that this group was about to visit the traditional Jewish homeland, and some of them—maybe most—for the first time.

The three of us gentile outlanders attended some of the group's fundraising sessions, but we were essentially just invited guests, and so were sent with a security officer/guide on a fairly extensive tour. We saw Nazareth, Haifa, the Dead Sea, the Masada, irrigation projects near Bathsheba, and a great deal of Jerusalem including the Via Dolorosa (the street of sorrow), and Yad Vashem, Israel's Holocaust Museum.

With Leonard Strelitz, Norman Sisisky (a wealthy beer distributor from Petersburg who later represented the Fourth District of Virginia in Congress), and one or two others, we had an audience with Prime Minister Golda Meir in her office in Jerusalem—which the Israelis would like to be their capital instead of Tel Aviv. I had a pleasant conversation with the prime minister of Israel, and at first we covered mostly noncontroversial subjects. When the talk turned to more serious areas such as the future of Israeli-Arab boundaries, I suggested that Woody describe his plan. (He had told me of his thinking in our hotel room the night before.) "Is it all right?" Woody asked me cautiously in everybody's presence before taking my cue. When I gave him a go-ahead, he proposed to the prime minister that Jerusalem become an international neutral territory to which all rival groups would have unfettered access. Tel Aviv would be the capital—not neutral Jerusalem. He got a muffled laugh when he said earnestly to Mrs. Meir, "Of course, you'd have to move your desk." The former Wisconsin schoolteacher listened attentively, but then explained calmly to the fifth-grader that a similar plan had been tried before, but hadn't worked. The current arrangement with Israel's forces in control, but with protected access for all, was just fine. "So I won't have to move my desk," she concluded with a warm schoolteacher smile.

That Woody had really charmed the Virginia travelers became evident toward the end of the trip. That he had been very observant also surfaced. He had noticed the arm-twisting going on to persuade potential donors in the group to give considerably more than they'd planned. One story—probably apocryphal, but given a good bit of circulation through the crowd—was that Strelitz and Sisisky assured one reluctant prospect that they hadn't realized he'd had such a bad year in his business. Therefore they would contribute $50,000 on his behalf, and he could pay them back when his business improved. At the final banquet, Woody was presented with a special award. Jerry Gumenick, a member of the visiting group and a major contributor, was particularly effusive in his presentation on behalf of the group. Woody listened in some disbelief to the extravagant praise and brought down the house when he began his response by saying, "But Mr. Gumenick—I don't have any money!"

There is a postscript to the Jerusalem trip through Woody's eyes. After his return, an older friend at Sunday school asked him if he had visited Bethlehem, where Jesus was born. "No," said Woody, "but we did visit Nazareth, where he grew up." His friend continued, "Well, did you see Joseph's carpenter shop where Jesus worked when he was a boy?" Woody's eyes rolled up, and you could almost hear his brain going click, click, click. We had visited the carpenter shop authenticated by the Jesuits; we had visited the carpenter shop authenticated by the Greek Orthodox; and the one authenticated by the Methodists, among others.

"Well," said Woody, "you see—Joseph had a *chain* of carpenter shops."

How Sleep the Brave (or Foolhardy)
One of the riskier decisions that flowed from my superabundant ego followed our return to the mansion from a trade mission to Japan and Australia. Jinks and I were exhausted from the very long flights from Canberra, but we had a short welcome-home visit with the children before falling into bed. The bedside telephone jangled loudly at about 2:00 a.m. "Governor, this is Officer Harris. We've had a bomb threat, and the major says we must evacuate the mansion while we conduct a search." That really woke me up—enough to say,

"Harris, you tell the major that there will be no evacuation. He can conduct any search he wants, but if he wants me, I'll be up here asleep." I reported that conversation to a half-awake Jinks when she asked, "What was that all about?" We both went back to sleep without further discussion.

Next morning when I went to the dining room for breakfast, twelve-year-old Woody was already there. He greeted me with these words: "Dad, Mom told me what happened last night. If that happens again, how about waking me up and letting me make my own decision?"

J. Sargeant Reynolds

My warm association with my Democratic lieutenant governor, J. Sargeant Reynolds, ranks high in my inventory of memories of my days as governor.

I hardly knew Sarge before the campaign, though I was familiar in a general way with his political career, first as a member of the House of Delegates representing Richmond, and then as a Virginia state senator. I knew he had been a very successful legislator, that he was extremely charismatic, that he was from a wealthy, influential family, and that he was very popular with a broad spectrum of voters who expected him to go far in the political arena—even to the presidency. But I don't remember that I ever met him before our respective elections, except for briefly crossing paths a time or two during the 1969 campaign.

He changed all that. A day or two after the inauguration, he came to my office to pay a courtesy call on the new governor. We had a pleasant visit, and then he made the following statement, which in the ensuing fifteen months he more than made good on: "Governor, you are a Republican, and I am a Democrat. When election time comes again, I will support the Democrats and you will support the Republicans. That's as it should be. But in the meantime, if you can think of anything I can do to help you help Virginia, please give me a call." To the extent he was able—as lieutenant governor he had no vote except in a case of a tie vote in the Senate—he supported substantially everything I proposed. I can recall no opposition to any part of my platform.

I wasn't sure how Sarge would regard the powers of the lieutenant governor in the event of the governor's absence from the state. This was 1970, and there were occasional press reports of a lieutenant governor's seeking to exercise gubernatorial powers in the absence of the governor from the state or the country. This was particularly so in connection with racial and antiwar protests and demonstrations that were occurring frequently—and occasionally getting out of hand. The deaths on the Kent State campus in Ohio resulting from the discharge of live ammunition by troops of the Ohio National Guard certainly provide the most flagrant example.

The Kent State shootings caused great consternation. While there were threats of disturbances in Virginia, I was determined that nothing would interfere with the orderly processes of the government of Virginia, even in my absence. In a way, my confidence in our administration was something of an anomaly among other governors: when Jinks and I went to Santa Fe, New Mexico, to attend a Republican governors conference, we found that Pennsylvania's governor and chairman of the conference, Ray Shafer, and I were the only governors to show up; all of the others for various reasons had hesitated to leave their states during that disruptive period.

On another occasion, when the time of departure was imminent for a group of governors (including me) to return an exchange visit with French prefects, I asked Sarge to stop by my office for a little visit. I told him that I had not made a study of whether any powers of the governor would transfer to the lieutenant governor in my absence from the state or nation, and that I would be inclined to respect his opinion on that subject. I told him Jinks and I were scheduled for a trip to France and that I had some advice for him in case he felt he had to take charge because of out-of-bounds protests or rioting in my absence. "Our National Guard is simply not trained for riot work," I said. "On the other hand, the Virginia State Police Department is a highly professional, well-trained, and disciplined organization, completely competent to handle almost any kind of foreseeable disorder."

"Thank you, Governor," was all Sarge said. He called me the next day and asked for another meeting in my office. It was short. He reported, "Governor, I have done some research and studied the matter very carefully. *You* are governor wherever you are." We therefore did not, in Virginia, have any dispute between the governor and the lieutenant governor about authority.

It was a sad, sad day when thirty-two-year-old Sarge called me to tell me he had been diagnosed with a cancerous brain tumor. He had even diagnosed it himself. Following severe headaches, he had visited the library on his own to make an extensive study of his symptoms and concluded that he had a brain tumor. His diagnosis was confirmed but only after three medical opinions were sought. The first was yes; the second was no. But the third confirmed the existence of an inoperable, terminal brain tumor. "I've been dealt a bad hand," he reported to me on the telephone in a very matter-of-fact voice.

In the spring of 1971, most everyone knew his time was limited. Even so, Sarge accepted an invitation to speak at the notorious "Shad Planking" in Sussex County. Up until that time, the Shad Planking—where baked or broiled fish are served on a wooden board—was an all-male, all-white gathering, widely regarded by nonparticipants as the annual convergence of the white supremacists from the days of the Byrd Machine. I had declined to attend the year before when the sponsors refused to honor their own tradition of inviting the entire Virginia Senate because Doug Wilder, an African American, was now a member of the Senate. The Senate therefore had been excised from their guest list.

Bill Thornton, president of the Richmond Crusade for Voters, and Lester Banks, executive secretary of the Conference of the National Association for the Advancement of Colored People (NAACP), were shocked to read of Sarge's acceptance of the invitation to be the featured speaker for that racist gathering. Each telephoned to urge me to dissuade Sarge from attending. They said he should "change his mind and stay away from that crowd." I agreed only to report their concerns to Sarge, and I did. His response was typical: "Thank you, Governor."

Apparently Sarge had his own good reasons for speaking at that event. We nonparticipants were much relieved and much inspired to read the newspaper account of his speech at the Shad Planking. Columnist Guy Friddell of the *Norfolk Virginian-Pilot* described the gathering as "a roll call of the former leaders of Massive Resistance." Nevertheless, Sarge poured it on:

> I tell you one thing is not going to happen, and it is an open defiance of that order [of the Supreme Court announced the day before favoring busing to integrate schools] the way we attempted tragically years ago. School means too much to the children of tomorrow, and it won't happen again. Nor will we fight another Civil War; nor will we be intimidated by those who cry for impeachment of the Court. Virginia will not be propelled into Massive Resistance again, forward, backward or bilateral movement. Its efforts were futile and very expensive for the present generation of Virginians.

You could hardly ask for stronger support of the positions I had taken on integration and cross-town busing. "Atta boy, Sarge," I said to myself as I read press accounts of his speech and learned more later in a personal phone conversation with him.

The only mitigation of my sadness over the catastrophe of Sarge's illness came through watching the courage and grace he and his wife demonstrated during the following months. They both attended a gathering in Capitol

Square near the bell tower on a beautiful day shortly before his death, attended by hundreds of adoring friends who knew, as Sarge and Mary Ballou knew, that it was time to say good-bye.

On June 14, 1971, Mary Ballou gave one final demonstration of her courage, at the private terminal of the Reynolds Metal Company. Their jet arrived there from New York, where Sarge had died, returning his body and his widow home to Virginia. With all the eyes of those who were there to welcome him home focused on the door of that airplane, Mary Ballou emerged. She stood on the top step, looked out over the crowd, and gave us the sweetest, most beautiful smile anyone ever saw.

The Supremes

It was fortunate for me that Chief Justice Warren Burger was serving on the U.S. Supreme Court during my term as governor. We became acquainted because he was extremely interested in the history of the Court and sought in various ways to permanently memorialize that history. Our first contact came when my secretary, Lois Firesheets, announced over my desk intercom, "The chief justice is on the phone." Lawrence l'Anson, nicknamed "Red," was then chief justice of the Supreme Court of Appeals of Virginia. He and I were fishing buddies, and I assumed the call was from him, maybe trying to set up a fishing date. So I picked up the phone and said casually, "Hi, Red—how're you doin'?"

"This is Warren Burger" came the response. I gulped a couple of times and passed off my seeming impertinence with a weak comment to the effect that, "Well, we do have a chief justice down here, too." Mr. Chief Justice Burger was very gracious, seeming to enjoy my informality, and went on to explain his call. He was tracking down portraits of all the associate justices of the U.S. Supreme Court from the beginning of the Republic, intending to exhibit them in the U.S. Supreme Court building. He wanted me to help find a portrait of Bushrod Washington, George Washington's nephew, and of Philip P. Barbour, both Virginians, and early justices of the Supreme Court. Portraits were soon located in our archives, and copies of each are now part of the U.S. Supreme Court collection. I believe the persistent chief justice was ultimately able to acquire portraits of every single past associate justice.

Some time later, following my help in implementing his idea of forming a National Center for State Courts, he asked me to be president of the U.S. Supreme Court Historical Society, an organization created at Burger's initiation to collect and maintain documents, artifacts, and memorabilia of the

Court. I was happy to accept and served as the first president of that organization, continuing in that capacity for several years. During my tenure, the society began a project to fill in the gaps in the Court's records, a gap caused by the burning of some of its files during the War of 1812. Also during my presidency we raised the money to buy a building on First Street, across from the rear of the Court building, which housed the headquarters of the Supreme Court Historical Society for a number of years. One of the largest contributions came from Ambassador Walter Annenberg, and I had the enjoyable task of negotiating the details of his gift directly with him.

The chief justice was appreciative of my efforts, and there followed a number of years during which Jinks and I visited several times in the Burger home and attended social functions hosted by the Burgers at the Court. Their hospitality was returned at a number of social functions in our home in McLean. After the National Center for State Courts moved into its new building in Williamsburg, the chief justice was the moving force to have the principal meeting room named "Holton Hall" in appreciation of the efforts I had made to find financing for its headquarters.

Through that association, Jinks and I had unique opportunities to meet and enjoy very pleasant relationships with several members of the Supreme Court. Among them were Justice Sandra Day O'Connor, Lewis Powell's successor as the balance wheel on a divided Court, and Justice William Brennan, a perfectly marvelous man. Justice Byron White (who did not like to be called by his nickname, "Whizzer") and his wife, Marion, traveled in some of the same circles in McLean as we did. Jinks and Marion White occasionally got in some good games of tennis.

Justice Tom Clark became a dear friend, and on several occasions he introduced me, or referred to me, as the governor of Virginia who woke his teenage children each morning with the loud announcement: "It's Opportunity Time!" I did indeed do that, and Tom Clark was enthusiastic in telling about it. I once had the opportunity to ask Justice Clark whether, in his opinion, the school desegregation cases of *Brown vs. Board of Education* were the most significant in which he participated during his tenure on the Court. Somewhat to my surprise at the time (but upon reflection, not so surprising), his answer was, "No. The most significant decision while I was there was the one that required one man—one vote." He was referring to the *Baker vs. Carr* case, decided in 1962; he voted in that case with the majority and wrote a separate, concurring opinion.

Justice Thurgood Marshall had a great sense of humor. During a fairly large reception in the Supreme Court building, I was asked by one of the guests to help her locate Justice Marshall. "I am a cousin of his," she explained, "and I would like to speak to him." By pure happenstance I spoke to Justice Marshall shortly after that and told him his cousin was looking for him. "Governor," he said, "you can't believe how many 'cousins' I've acquired since I got this job!"

Justice William O. Douglas and I happened to occupy adjoining seats on a flight back from the West to Washington, D.C. We talked about the society and, among other things, his project to restore and preserve the C&O Canal. His heroic personal effort saved that historic canal and towpath from development and destruction, and he was quite effusive in expressing appreciation for my help on that project. I don't remember that I ever gave it much more than a little nudge, but it was most agreeable to hear his gratitude. He continued to show enthusiasm for our historical society for the rest of his life.

Our friendship with Justice Lewis Powell and his wife, Josephine, came about independently of the historical society, though he strongly supported it. Jinks and I met the Powells at meetings of the Virginia State Bar Association, held in alternate years at the Greenbrier and Homestead hotels, soon after we were married. The Powells were close friends of Jinks's parents, Frank and Anne Rogers, and the six of us were together many times through the years thereafter.

By the time of Nixon's election in 1968, Lewis Powell was one of the outstanding lawyers in the United States. He was the leading partner in the firm of Hunton and Williams, headquartered in Richmond and one of the outstanding firms in the entire nation. He was a beautiful thinker, fiscally conservative, a responsible and influential citizen, and a highly competent lawyer—a professional in the very finest sense of that word. He had favored the election of Richard Nixon as president, and he was an obvious choice for the Supreme Court, particularly since Nixon was eager to appoint a southerner. Ambassador Walter Robertson, assistant secretary of state for Far Eastern affairs in the Eisenhower administration and others, wanted me to press the administration to nominate Powell in 1970 to succeed Justice Fortas, who had resigned from the Court in 1969. But Lewis would have none of that. (He later told me, after he had finally agreed to accept an appointment to succeed Justice Black in 1972, he had thought it would be "ridiculous" to start a new career at the age of sixty-five.)

Because Powell declined an appointment to the vacancy created by the Fortas resignation, in 1970 Nixon tapped Judge Clement Haynesworth of South Carolina for the Supreme Court. A member of the U.S. Court of Appeals for the Fourth Circuit, he failed Senate confirmation because of alleged conflicts of interest related to his investments. Nixon next nominated Judge G. Harrold Carswell of Florida, who was pretty obviously not qualified for the Court vacancy. The American Bar Association rated him "mediocre," and though U.S. senator Roman Hruska argued on the Senate floor that "mediocre Americans also deserve representation on the Court," again the Senate promptly rejected the nomination.

These two failures of confirmation put the heat on the Nixon administration to come up with a candidate who was unqualifiedly acceptable, and Nixon, abandoning for the moment his desire to appoint a southerner, nominated Harry Blackman of Minnesota, who was unquestionably acceptable. The story of how Lewis wilted two years later under the heat and reluctantly agreed to accept the appointment to succeed Justice Black has been well told by John Jeffries Jr. of the University of Virginia Law School faculty in his book *Justice Lewis F. Powell, Jr.*

John Mitchell, attorney general in the Nixon administration, was unable to pull it off by himself; it took a call to Lewis Powell from Richard Nixon himself, and with that call Lewis capitulated. He agreed to accept the appointment because of his conviction that if you were asked personally by the president of the United States to accept a civic responsibility, you just couldn't say no.

In one of the few telephone calls I had from President Nixon after I was elected governor, he called to tell me he was putting Lewis Powell on the Court and that Lewis had agreed to accept the appointment. I, of course, was delighted. Early the next morning, I violated the Hunton and Williams firm protocol and betook myself to Lewis's office to congratulate him and express appreciation for his acceptance of the position. (In that law office, it was unheard of for a governor to come to you; if there was to be a meeting with the governor, you went to visit him.) To my amusement, Lewis had not arrived at the office when I got there a little after 9 a.m. I had caught the prominent lawyer coming in late, so I made his secretary promise to let me know when he arrived, and I would return. She did so; I returned—and was rewarded with some of his great reminiscences. He also emphasized again his reluctance to go on the Court, but he was resigned to embarking on a new career. I had great confidence in Lewis's thoughtfulness and fairness in spite of his reputation as a conservative—which in his case did not include any element of racism. I said to Lewis during that conversation, "Your conservative friends will be surprised at some of the opinions you'll write." He grinned, knowing exactly what I meant, and said, "Yeah—they'll say I sold out to Bill Douglas, won't they?"

Some of Lewis's opinions, such as the *Bakke* decision in which Lewis wrote the Court's opinion permitting some affirmative action in school admissions, confirmed that prediction. He was not as liberal as Bill Douglas, but he was always fair.

Lewis Powell became a distinguished justice. He was the balance wheel between opposing factions on the Court and earned universal admiration for service that extended into his eighties. I was present in the Supreme Court room when Lewis Powell and Bill Rehnquist, whom I had met while we were both campaigning for Nixon in 1968, took the oath of office and became associate justices of the U.S. Supreme Court in 1972. That was icing on my cake.

Colgate Darden

Colgate Darden: "The noblest Roman of them all." Thus did Benjamin Muse, the token Republican candidate for governor in 1941, describe his Democratic opponent Colgate Darden, in a reflective article written several years after being handily defeated by Darden. Darden was indeed the Elder Statesman of Virginia throughout the period of my active involvement in Virginia politics.

Born on a farm near Franklin in Southampton County, he maintained a distinctive Southside accent his entire life. He volunteered for the French Ambulance Corps during World War I, later flew airplanes in the same war for the U.S. Navy and the Marine Corps, and sustained a back injury in a plane accident that remained painful all his life. He earned a bachelor's degree from the University of Virginia, a law degree from Columbia University, and, on a Carnegie Fellowship, studied at Oxford University in England. He was married to Constance du Pont, one of the heiresses of the well-known DuPont chemical fortune.

Darden had a genuine and not unseemly confidence in himself that enabled him to "call 'em as I see 'em" throughout his career and to maintain a political independence that was unusual, if not unique, during the period of Virginia's history so completely dominated by Harry Flood Byrd. Although he supported Byrd for governor in 1925, as a member of the House of Delegates in the Depression year of 1932 he bucked the Byrd organization's "pay as you go" policy with an effort to divert some of the highway trust fund for the support of public schools. He was elected to represent the Norfolk area in the U.S. House of Representatives in 1932 and 1934. In 1936, he was defeated by a more ardent New Dealer, but he was reelected again in 1938 and 1940. He resigned in 1941 to run for governor. He supported Franklin Roosevelt's third-term candidacy, although Byrd opposed it, and he supported the candidacy of

Congressman John Flanigan, whose performance was more anti- than pro-Byrd in the Ninth District of Virginia. Darden's independence and universally recognized impeccable integrity built broad support for his candidacy for governor in the 1941 election.

As governor, he gave priority to the needs of the war effort, deferring non-defense spending as much as possible, and concentrated on needs of civil defense. He supported efforts at penal reform, improvement of teachers' salaries, and enhancement of retirement plans for state employees. Importantly, he convinced a special session of the General Assembly in 1942 to invest surplus funds of state revenue in war bonds to create a sinking fund for paying off the long-standing debt that the State of Virginia incurred in connection with Reconstruction activities after the Civil War.

He skillfully steered the Democratic state convention in 1944 through a potentially divisive contest between the liberals, who were pushing to endorse Roosevelt for a fourth term, and Byrd forces, which were not eager for that. Part of the compromise he engineered prohibited the Virginia delegation to the national convention from endorsing the renomination of Henry A. Wallace, who was too liberal for Virginia, and sent the Virginia delegation to the national convention without being committed to any presidential candidate. Everyone, including Byrd, was satisfied.

Colgate Darden's streak of independence was never more evident than when he turned down the opportunity, offered by the overwhelming majority of the Democratic Party, to succeed Carter Glass in the U.S. Senate. He chose other arenas of public service, with major emphasis on higher education. He became chancellor of the College of William and Mary at the end of his governor's term, and in 1947 he began a twelve-year term as president of the University of Virginia. While there, he raised academic standards, enhanced the physical plant of the university, created the now-famous Darden School of Business Administration, and played a major role in the creation of what is now the four-year University of Virginia College at Wise, an important educational and economic development engine in what is still a somewhat disadvantaged southwest section of Virginia.

Everybody was after him. Truman wanted him for the United Nations, Eisenhower for advising the National Security Council, and in 1960, Governor Lindsay Almond convinced him to serve on the State Board of Education. Governor Albertis Harrison invited him to a meeting early in that governor's term and prevailed upon him to undertake probably the toughest assignment of all: to reopen the public schools in Prince Edward County, which had been closed for four years to avoid court-ordered integration. With characteristic humor, Darden's acceptance of that task concluded with the words, "And what would you like me to do this afternoon when I finish in Prince Edward County?" (His oil-on-troubled-waters approach enabled him to convince local county leaders to open public schools on an integrated basis in 1963.)

Following the lead of so many others who valued his wisdom and influence, and recognizing that everybody has to have a governor, I relied upon Darden as "*my* governor." He had welcomed me when I stopped by his Norfolk office during my initial campaign for governor in 1965, and during repeated visits in the interim between then and my election in 1969, we became fast friends. He encouraged my more progressive leadership, and he also encouraged the political efforts of Henry Howell, the very liberal state senator from the Norfolk area. I wonder if his failure, as a member of the Southern Regional Council, as president of the University of Virginia, and as a supporter of the Gray Commission, to more strongly oppose Massive Resistance or support integration served as partial motivation for his tacit support of some of us who did take those positions.

Darden never openly supported me, and I don't know how he voted, but he was always a comfortable confidant. I can almost recite his telephone number from memory even today, forty years later. I could count on a libation of Virginia Gentleman and soda in his living room on short or no notice, and I was pleased one day when he was available to join me on Virginia's state yacht, the *Chesapeake,* at a Norfolk dock where we indulged in Scotch for him, bourbon for me, and soft-shell crabs for a late luncheon. With ironic humor, he "allowed" that he should "complain as a taxpayer" about the affluent luxury we were enjoying, just before he took another sip of Scotch and another bite of soft-shell crab. My family always enjoyed hearing how Darden inevitably concluded his telephone remarks to me in pure Southside accent, "Be of good chee-ah; ahm glad you're they'ah and ahm he-ah."

To appreciate one of Darden's most endearing satiric *bon mots* requires a little background: The *Richmond News Leader* endorsed my candidacy for governor and later changed its editorial mind. The original endorsement was unusual because the *News Leader,* with its history of support for very conservative causes including Massive Resistance to public school integration, had a much more conservative outlook than mine. I think Ross MacKenzie, editor of that paper's editorial page, did give some credence to my argument in favor of two-party democracy and was impressed with my advocacy of a designated state agency both to hear and then try to respond to legitimate consumer complaints—a sort of governmental "Mr. Fix-it." But Ross was really won over during a northeast blow when he had accompanied our campaign tour to Virginia Beach in early October 1969. I suggested to him that we "take a little dip" in the boiling surf we watched from the window of the oceanfront hotel where we were staying. MacKenzie's mentality is such that he could not resist the macho appeal of that suggestion. We took the dip; the water was still warm, but the surf was indeed a challenge, and I'm sure it convinced MacKenzie that I was tough enough to be governor!

But the *News Leader*'s endorsing sentiment was short-lived. My support of the increase in the cigarette tax to five cents per pack sent both Richmond newspapers into an opposition orbit, and when I failed to oppose the consolidation of the Richmond public schools with the public schools of the surrounding counties, as ordered by U.S. district judge Robert Mehrige to maintain some sort of racial balance, the *News Leader* just couldn't stand it. One of its critical editorials was entitled "Waffling in a Cottage by the Sea," a reference to the fact that my family and I were relaxing at the National Guard camp at Virginia Beach while the segregationists' lawyers were in court opposing Judge Mehrige's city-county consolidation orders.

Aware of all this editorial backlash, and after a very pleasant telephone visit during which we discussed several matters, Darden began to wind up the conversation by saying, "Well, what else is on your mind?"

"Oh," I said, "Everything else seems to be okay—though if there were a little something I could do to be even a tiny bit pleasing to the Richmond newspapers, I would be glad to give it a try."

"Well," said Darden, "I can help you with that. Just advocate a return to slavery, but explain it to them in very simple terms." Priceless! As was my friendship with him.

13 Past as Prologue

Sometimes a crystal ball is not required to predict the future. In this chapter, I recount four separate stories stemming from my political life, starting in 1965 and ending with my observations and thoughts in 2007. All have something to do with the black vote, the Republican adoption of the Southern Strategy, the decision not to give Senator Byrd a free ride in 1970, and the ultimate impact these factors have had and, I believe, will continue to have on the Republican Party in Virginia.

Godwin, Thurmond, and the Black Vote

Mills Godwin beat me in the governor's race in 1965 because he got the endorsement of the Richmond Crusade for Voters. The Crusade—created to make the vote of the African American community matter—had become a potent organization. It endorsed Godwin in 1965 in spite of his avid support of Massive Resistance to school integration in the 1950s, essentially because its leaders believed Godwin would win anyway, so "let's be on the winning side."

I doubt if Mills ever admitted this, even to himself, because he did not like to feel obligated to that group. It is a fact, however, that if the vote totals in the African American communities were reversed—that is, if I had gotten the vote from them that he got, and he got the vote from them that I got—I would have won.

In retrospect, I can see it was fortunate both for Virginia and for me that Mills won that year. Virginia needed a substantial addition to our state revenues to support (among other things) an expanding education establishment, including an entirely new system of community colleges. When he was elected, Mills was able to convince the General Assembly to levy a general sales tax, which produced essential revenues. I had campaigned *against* a sales tax because of a $100-million surplus anticipated in that biennium—a tremendous amount of money in those days. I was a young, inexperienced, and—before the election—unknown Republican. It would have required some kind of a political miracle for me to have reversed my position and convinced the Democratic General Assembly to increase revenues with a sales tax when we were already creating huge surpluses.

Though the surplus did amount to $113 million, it was insufficient to meet educational needs, especially increased state assistance for teachers' salaries, even before adding the cost of the new statewide community college system then being established.

The election result was different four years later. The endorsement of the Richmond Crusade for Voters came to me, partly as a result of my developing friendship with its leadership and partly because of their disappointment with Mills Godwin's performance between 1965 and 1969 on issues of importance to them. Other factors contributed to my victory, but educated guesses are that I got a minimum of 30 percent of the vote from the African American communities in 1969, and those votes constituted a good portion of my margin of victory.

At the end of my term, when Godwin ran again in 1973 (this time as a Republican), he won, but not by much. His opponent, Henry Howell, Godwin's major nemesis and the darling of the African American communities, had both the endorsement of the Crusade and almost *all* of the African American vote. Godwin's victory was not clear until substantially all the precincts throughout the state reported, coming in at a very late hour. I was not able to reach Mills to congratulate him until late in the morning following election day.

I got the impression from my conversation with Godwin that he couldn't believe he had had such a close call. I asked him if he could explain the difference between the vote results for governor in the Fifth District in Virginia and the Fourth District. Both were Southside districts, and Godwin had done substantially better in the Fifth District than he had in the Fourth, where Byrd-type candidates like Godwin had historically run the strongest. "It was all that black vote," he said with what sounded like resignation.

I also asked him if he could explain why Russell Carneal, a senior member of the House of Delegates who had represented the Williamsburg area for many years, had been defeated. Again: "It was all that black vote." I just didn't have the heart, because Mills was so sensitive and so easily offended, to say what I wanted to say. But I thought it: "You fellows realize they count that vote now?" It is a fact that many like Godwin, who had spent a lifetime as part of the racist Byrd organization, simply could not grasp the reality that votes from the black community could now have a significant effect on the outcome of a statewide election.

Further evidence of what I casually refer to as the "plantation attitude" came when I recommended to Godwin, based on my positive experience with Bill Robertson as my liaison to the black community, that Mills put a black professional on his immediate gubernatorial staff during his second term. After he had been elected to succeed me, I made that suggestion to one of Godwin's speechwriters. The speechwriter declined to take the message to his boss, but agreed that I was correct and urged me personally to give Godwin the benefit of my advice. I did, but his response was an impatient, "I'm going to do something for 'em, Lin."

He just didn't get it: "They"—the members of the African American community—don't want "something done for 'em." They want to be heard. They want to be considered. They want an opportunity to use all the talents they possess and be compensated for the use of those talents on the same basis and at the same level as anyone else. But they're not looking for a handout.

When I had a similar discussion in 1976 with Senator Strom Thurmond of South Carolina, the reaction from him was different from Godwin's. Strom, of course, had established himself as the world's leading segregationist when he ran for president as a white supremacist on the Dixiecrat ticket in 1948. His principles were fairly flexible, though, and throughout his entire career he was carefully attuned to election returns. When Jinks and I moved to McLean in 1974, Senator Thurmond was about seventy-five years old. He lived approximately one hundred yards west of us on Claiborne Drive in McLean, and the route of his daily jogging path included the street in front of our house. When I went out to pick up the *Washington Post* on the day after Jimmy Carter had been elected president of the United States in 1976, I encountered Strom in the middle of his jog.

"What do you make of the election?" he asked.

I replied, "Well, the press says Carter got about two-thirds of the black vote."

"Got more than that in my state," the senator rejoined.

Then I said to the senator what I hadn't had the nerve to say to Governor Godwin: "You fellows realize they count that vote now?"

His gaze focused on the horizon, and he uttered a very convincing, "Yeah, they do, don't they?"

"Strom," I said, "why don't Republicans realize they should go after some of the black vote? I got more than 30 percent in my race."

"How you git 'em?" was his abrupt response.

"Well, you talk to them. They like to be considered."

"Do you 'point 'em?"

"Yes . . . 'pointing 'em does help."

"I 'pointed one to the Court of Military Appeals," he said.

"But Strom," I argued, " 'pointments up in Washington, Dee Cee, won't do; they want to be 'pointed to something in South Carolina."

The senator "got it." Within the next few weeks, his children were transferred from private schools in the Washington area to integrated public schools in Aiken, South Carolina. He actively sought blacks' views on issues, blacks shortly became members of his staff, and soon election returns showed him receiving substantial votes in the black community.

Bill Cahill

Bill Cahill had been elected governor of New Jersey in November 1969, the same day I was elected governor of Virginia. We first met the day after the election at a luncheon in the private quarters of the White House hosted by President and Pat Nixon, attended by Vice President Ted Agnew and his wife, Judy; Bill Cahill and his wife, Betty; and Jinks and me. The luncheon was an exhilarating experience, with Nixon really elated over the beginning success of his program to generate a majority Republican Party in the United States.

During that luncheon, our youngest child, Dwight, then just barely four years old, earned the nickname "Motormouth." He was so dubbed by George Wayne Anderson, the pilot who had flown us to Washington for the luncheon, and who had also been drafted to babysit our four children while we were celebrating at the White House. Characteristically chatty, Dwight had apparently more than talked the ear off our waiting pilot and was forever thereafter, in George Wayne Anderson's mind, "Motormouth."

Governor Cahill and I developed a warm friendship through the next four years, though our contacts were largely at meetings of the Republican or National Governors Associations. I didn't know a great deal about his gubernatorial performance, and I doubt that he knew much about mine. We did know enough of each other to realize we were both pretty close to being clas-

sic "moderate" Republicans. Being "moderate" caused him some real problems with the right-wing Republicans in New Jersey, and I'm sure I had some
of the same disaffection on the ideological right of our Virginia party. It was
not so bothersome to me because I was constitutionally barred from running
for reelection, but it was really troublesome for Bill; he *could* run for reelection, subject to being nominated in the Republican primary in New Jersey.

As the end of our four-year terms approached, it became apparent that the
right wing of the New Jersey Republican Party was going to support a very
conservative New Jersey congressman, Charlie Sandman, in the Republican
primary, to oppose the nomination of Cahill for a second term as governor.
However, it was pretty clear from polls and press reports that Bill Cahill would
be easily reelected in a general election if he got the Republican nomination
in the primary. It was equally clear from the same sources that if Charlie Sandman were nominated, he would likely lose to the Democrat in the general
election.

In the summer of 1973, Bill asked me—as chairman of the Republican Governors Association—to urge the president to support him for the nomination
for reelection. He believed (correctly) that some members of the White House
staff, perhaps including John Ehrlichman, Bob Haldeman, and Harry Dent,
were urging the president to support the more conservative candidate, based
solely on ideology. Of course I was happy to comply with Cahill's request, although I wasn't certain I could get in to see the president, even as a Republican governor and chairman of the Republican Governors Association.

But the Watergate noises were getting louder, and my close ties to Congressman Caldwell Butler were generally known. Caldwell, my former law partner
and a former member of the Virginia House of Delegates, was a member of
the House Judiciary Committee, which would decide whether an impeachment proceeding against President Nixon would be referred to the floor of
the U.S. House of Representatives. Thus, "magically," I got in to see President
Nixon about Bill Cahill and his race for the renomination.

My message to him was very simple: "Bill Cahill, if nominated, can be reelected and continue as the Republican governor of New Jersey for another
four years. If Charlie Sandman is nominated, he will be defeated by a Democratic candidate in the general election. Please, Mr. President, support Cahill."
The president well knew what I said was correct, and he all but committed to
me in that conversation that the White House would support Cahill.

Alas, mine must not have been the last voice to reach the president's ear on
this subject, because evidently the safely anonymous White House staff urged

the president to support Sandman, which he surreptitiously did. Sandman was indeed nominated for governor—and defeated, as I predicted. The real loser was the moderate wing of the Republican Party—and the nation. It does not surprise me that New Jersey, once again, has a Democrat in the governor's mansion.

Why Not Reagan?

Ronald Reagan made two appearances to support me in Virginia in 1969. He and his political advisors were probably acting on the assumption that the South, including Virginia, would be very important if one were to seek the Republican nomination and win the election for president at the expiration of Nixon's term, or terms. In any event, his first appearance was as the celebrity attraction at the state convention in Roanoke on March 1, 1969. This convention would nominate me, Buzz Dawbarn, and Richard Obenshain for the three statewide races that year.

I don't remember how he came to be the star invitee, but I do not think that I, or any members of my immediate staff, initiated the invitation. I do remember that he received a warm and enthusiastic welcome from the state delegates. He got a good laugh after describing the many troubles he was facing as governor of California, including mud slides along his state's Pacific coast, and then said, "In desperation I called Dial-a-Prayer, but the only response I got was a busy signal."

Reagan campaigned specifically for me in October at a breakfast in Norfolk. Caldwell Butler was the moderator for that event, and he got a good laugh while introducing the VIPs with the comment, "And on my far right, John Birch—but he couldn't come." Several of my advisors had questioned whether we should have Reagan appear in Norfolk, where the most significant union labor vote was concentrated. Of all the outsiders who campaigned for me in Virginia, Reagan was the most antiunion, at least by reputation.

Jinks and I met him at the airport on the day before his speech and were amused to watch his security detail conduct a sweep of the motel, including a look under the bed in which he was to spend the night. His speech for me had the usual Reagan rhetoric, he drew a good and enthusiastic crowd, and there appeared to be little if any negative fallout for my campaign from union supporters.

While governor of California, Ron attended the meetings of the National Governors Association and the Republican Governors Association pretty regularly. His effervescent personality was always on display, but he did not seem to have any really close friends among the governors. He generally seemed preoccupied with his own agenda, which included frequent interviews with members of the press who covered those meetings.

When it was Virginia's turn to host the Republican Governors Association in 1972, I announced the invitation in an open meeting of the association. I addressed the chair, referred to the next scheduled meeting of the association, and invited them to "meet in Williamsburg—which is in old Virginia, which is for lovers!" With that great smile and a twinkle in his eye—Ronald Reagan trademarks—he said, "Mr. Chairman, I move we accept that invitation!" That motion carried, of course, and we had a very pleasant social occasion, attended by most of the Republican governors, but without conducting any particularly significant business. A highlight of the meeting was the closing banquet, where the magnificent choir of the Fifth Baptist Church of Richmond sang. That choir, which our family discovered when we attended that church soon after we moved to Richmond, was comprised of several professionally trained singers as well as church members. They happily accepted our invitation to sing in Williamsburg, and their performance simply wowed the governors and the whole audience. The ovation was overwhelming.

My negative bias against Reagan's desire to be president was not based on anything personal. I was as charmed by his personality as anyone else. But he represented the more conservative faction of the Republican Party, tinged with racism. His reference to states' rights when he opened his 1980 presidential campaign in Philadelphia, Mississippi, was an obvious appeal for the votes of southern segregationists. He was also less enthusiastic than I to provide and pay for governmental services such as education, treatment of the mentally ill, environmental enhancements, and deserving welfare recipients.

We never had any public disagreement, but on one occasion I expressed dissent regarding a major Reagan proposal. This was a much ballyhooed program that he had originally described to a secret meeting attended by governors only—no staff—in 1973. The essence of his proposal was to limit the amount of revenue the states could raise from the taxpayers. The theory was that this would limit government. When he concluded his presentation to the governors, he was met with silence for some several seconds. I then spoke up and asserted that Senator Byrd had effectively conducted such a program in Virginia for a whole generation. I pointed out that there was no legal restriction on the amount of revenue Virginia could raise, but the attitude of the Byrd leadership had kept Virginia public revenue well below the amount required for essential governmental services. "The result," I said, "was that the municipalities, lacking appropriate state contribution to the costs, had therefore been required to raise all of the money to meet the needs demanded by the constituents. This was done largely through bonds issued by local governments, which resulted in overall higher cost to the taxpayers." Ron looked at me as though he thought I was crazy, but made no comment.

I missed an opportunity to keep my mouth shut about the same subject when Jinks and I visited an educational conference in San Diego in 1973. Some California reporter there asked me about Reagan's revenue limitation proposal, and I publicly stated my opposition to it and gave the above rationale. Michael Deaver, one of Reagan's top staff people, responded to my impertinence by saying that "the last time Governor Reagan was in Virginia he was campaigning for the election of Linwood Holton as governor." I was appropriately put down.

In 1976, I tried—and succeeded—in helping to break the momentum building for Reagan in his contest for the Republican nomination against President Gerald Ford. Even Governor Godwin was publicly leaning to Reagan. He explained in a luncheon speech in Richmond that his prior endorsement of President Ford had come "BC—before Carolina," when Reagan had amassed a winning vote in the North Carolina Republican presidential primary. Jim Baker was managing Ford's campaign for the nomination, and at his request I contacted Willard Forbes of Portsmouth, Virginia, one of our delegates to the 1976 National Convention, to urge his support for the nomination of Gerald Ford. Willard, after some reflection, did publicly come out for Ford and several other national convention delegates from Virginia followed Forbes's lead. That helped break the snowballing Reagan drive in Virginia.

It was really repulsive to me that when Reagan opened his 1980 campaign for president in Philadelphia, Mississippi, he declared his vigorous support for "states' rights." To me that phrase, especially when used on that occasion in that locality, was simply code for white supremacy, and his campaign and subsequent actions as president helped to enhance the so-called Southern Strategy. That appeal to racism in the South, which Nixon had used in 1968, helped produce the divisive leadership with which the Republican Party is saddled today.

Southern Strategy: A Trojan Horse

Senator Harry F. Byrd Jr., who was then still nominally a Democrat, announced in March 1970 that he would run for reelection as an independent. He had been appointed by Governor Albertis Harrison to serve out the unexpired term of his father when the latter died late in 1965. Some of the members of the Nixon staff in the White House, and Nixon himself, believed that Byrd's move to independent status could become the first step of a move by Byrd either to actual membership in the Republican Party, or at least to vote with the Republican senators to organize the Senate.

Though I was not sure how an independent Senator Byrd might vote on organization of the Senate, I was extremely confident that he would never become a Republican. Nor did I have any enthusiasm for him to become a Republican. I had been elected from a much broader base than Byrd, including votes from black voters and labor unions. His constituency was the very narrow, conservative base of the Byrd organization. That base included traditional white supremacists who had been enthusiastic about the Massive Resistance policies that Senator Byrd's father had advocated to prevent implementation of the U.S. Supreme Court decision in *Brown vs. Board of Education.* I devoutly hoped to build a permanent broad-based Republican Party without that element. I knew that to bring Senator Byrd into our party would inevitably also bring his hard-core Southern Strategist fans right along with him, their racism still raging to dominate Virginia's politics.

But Richard Nixon was obsessed with a desire to create a majority Republican Party in his time. He accepted the Trojan horse—Southern Strategy—urged on him by Senator Thurmond, now strongly advocated by Harry Dent, a former Thurmond staffer who in 1970 held a prominent policy position in the Nixon White House. Dent attended, and may have instigated, a meeting with President Nixon in the Oval Office on April 23, 1970. I was there, as were Harry Flemming and Bryce Harlow. Flemming had been cochair of Nixon's Virginia campaign, and currently held a personnel position in the West Wing. Harlow was a presidential confidant whose legendary reputation was secured as a valued advisor to former president Eisenhower. I knew before the meeting that its purpose was to lock in my commitment to invite Senator Byrd to accept the nomination of the Virginia Republican Party in 1970 and to assure the senator of my support for that nomination if he agreed in advance to accept it.

Though I had no enthusiasm for this approach, I knew that if Harry Byrd agreed to run for the Senate as a Republican, the Republican Party of Virginia would nominate him. Neither I nor anyone else could stop that. I had so advised the president before his April 23 meeting, and I had assured him that I would support the Byrd nomination if Byrd spoke the magic words: *as a Republican.*

The president understood that, and he told me: "Of course, if he won't run as a Republican you have to run a candidate, because you are building the party. But if he runs as an independent, I will have to remain neutral, and that will be construed as support for Byrd." The president was forthright; I was forthright. There was no duplicity on my part when I supported the nomination of Ray Garland as the Republican candidate after Senator Byrd declined the offer of the Republican nomination. Harry Dent's opinion, as described in Frank B. Atkinson's *The Dynamic Dominion,* that the president was "infuriated" because he believed Holton had "misled him" is categorically contradicted by the president's express statement of his awareness that we, as party builders, would have to run a Republican candidate if Senator Byrd declined a Republican nomination (p. 216).

I was disappointed in the president's position because I too knew that Nixon's neutrality would be construed as support for Byrd, but I also knew that the president was determined to take that course, and I did not voice any opposition. I should have tried to get Nixon to commit to support the Republican Party nominee, even if Byrd refused to run as a Republican, but I was realistic enough to know that he wouldn't have done so in response to any entreaty that I might make.

At the April 23 meeting, the president outlined his plan for an invitation to Byrd, from him and from me, to join the Republican Party and to run with our support as the Republican candidate for the U.S. Senate from Virginia in 1970. He would thus be assured of the support of the president and the Virginia governor for his nomination by the Republican Party of Virginia, and everyone knew that election in November would follow almost automatically. I readily assented, and no conversation took place in that meeting about what would happen if Senator Byrd did not agree to run as a Republican.

After receiving assurance of my agreement, the president turned to Bryce Harlow, who was to be the emissary to carry the invitation to Senator Byrd, and said, "Bryce, put it to him cold turkey." I was a little surprised at the "cold turkey." "Cold turkey" implied that Byrd would have the president's support only if he ran as a Republican, but he had forewarned me of his plan for neutrality even if Byrd declined. There would be no leverage on Byrd if he could have the president's tacit support (neutrality) without changing parties.

As it turned out, the invitation from the president and me was not sufficient to move Senator Byrd to the Republican Party, and he persisted in his decision to run as an independent. Although the Republican state convention in 1970 clearly would have nominated Senator Byrd if he had given even minimal assurance of future cooperation with the Republican members of the U.S. Senate, it just as clearly, in the absence of such assurance, would not adopt a resolution that the Republican Party not nominate a Senate candidate, thus leaving Senator Byrd without opposition from us in the general election. Congressman Broyhill vigorously supported the motion that we not nominate any candidate. Harry Dent buttonholed everyone he could find on the state convention floor to insist that President Nixon did not want the Republican Party to nominate a candidate, and he urged delegates to vote for no nomination.

I made my "fire engine" speech against the "no nomination" position. In that speech I said, "We're the biggest, strongest, and the best party in Virginia. I can't believe we'll do nothing. Doing nothing would be like having the biggest, shiniest, newest fire engine and not taking it to the fire." The "no nomination" motion was rejected by a vote of over 60 percent of the delegates.

In 1970, Ray Garland was a member of the Virginia House of Delegates representing Roanoke. He was well educated, extremely articulate, and enjoyed independent means. He recognized that the Republican Party of Virginia had a responsibility to nominate a candidate for the U.S. Senate in order to continue progress toward a true two-party system. He would have supported a candidate better known than he was, such as Jim Turk or William Whitehurst. (Turk was a long-term, well-known state senator from Radford, and Whitehurst was a very popular congressman from the Second District of Virginia in Norfolk.) However, they did not want to run, so Garland agreed to accept the nomination. The state convention nominated him in a two-way race between him and Ken Haggerty of Arlington, a moderate Republican who had served one or more terms as a very popular member of the Arlington County Board of Supervisors.

To say that any race against Harry Byrd was a long shot is an exercise in understatement. But Garland campaigned mightily, and the Republican leadership—including me as governor; Joel Broyhill, a popular Tenth District congressman; and Dick Obenshain, popular leader of the conservative faction and former candidate for attorney general of Virginia—all gave his candidacy loyal Republican support. But financial resources were extremely limited because the business community was for Harry Byrd, and, in view of Nixon's "neutrality," the national Republican Party was of no help. As I feared—and as the president had predicted—it was in fact construed by most Republicans as support for Senator Byrd.

How well I remember my conversation with Garland after he was nominated when he asked me about the possibility of help from Nixon for his campaign. I had to give him the bleak negative news. (I am still embarrassed that I let him be nominated before I told him this bad news.) "We are in deep trouble," he replied. We were. That race was a short-term disaster for me and for the Republican Party of Virginia. Byrd got 54 percent of the vote; George Rawlings, the very liberal Democratic nominee, got 30 percent, including most of the vote in the black communities; and Garland was on the short end of the stick with only 15 percent of the vote.

By nominating a candidate for the Senate in 1970, the Republican Party of Virginia, however, maintained its integrity as a viable political party. It had won its first statewide race with my election less than a year earlier, and the fact that it nominated a candidate against superman Harry Flood Byrd Jr. put great pressure on Mills Godwin to run *as a Republican* in 1973 rather than as an independent, which he strongly preferred to do. Dortch Warriner and Dick Obenshain, longtime leaders of the conservative faction of the Republican Party of Virginia, and Smith Ferrebee, a very conservative and effective fundraiser for conservative candidates, were the liaisons between me and Governor Godwin as he contemplated running again for governor. (I was never able to talk candidly with Mills Godwin; he did *all* the talking!) They told him in no uncertain terms that he would have to run as a Republican if he expected to receive the support of the Republican Party of Virginia. They assured him that the Republican Party would most definitely nominate a candidate for governor even if he ran as an independent. Godwin responded that the resulting three-way race would result in the election of Henry Howell as the candidate of the Democratic Party and predicted that the candidate of the Republican Party would surely lose. Dortch's response was classic: "Governor, we are Republicans. We are used to losing. We would rather lose than sacrifice the principle."

With great reluctance, Godwin—well aware of the 1970 precedent when Republicans nominated a Senate candidate when Senator Byrd insisted on running as an independent—finally agreed to run *as a Republican*. Those three words were added to the original mimeographed text of his press release announcing his candidacy for governor in 1973 to succeed me. Forcing Godwin to run as a Republican in 1973 proved to be a positive step in the maturity and maintenance of two-party politics in Virginia. One can only speculate about what turn politics in Virginia might have taken if he had run as an independent (multiparties?), but it is a fact that his participation, even as a reluctant Republican, confirmed the Republican Party as a significant force in Virginia politics and helped ensure its permanence.

The downside, as far as I am concerned, is that the elements Godwin brought to the party have made it far more conservative than I have always believed is right for Virginia. That conservatism has strengthened through the years, and the extremism that dominates the leadership of the Republican Party of Virginia today is the same type of thinking that killed the Byrd Machine.

There are better ways to win. A broad-based, inclusive coalition elected Virginia's first Republican governor (me!) in 1970. South Carolina's Democratic governor John West was elected in 1970 over Southern Strategist Strom Thurmond's handpicked racist candidate, Albert Watson, by a coalition of blacks, conservatives, and moderates almost identical to the coalition that elected me; Reubin Askew beat Florida Republican governor Claude Kirk, who ran a racist campaign for reelection in 1972; and Dale Bumpers beat racist icon Orval Faubus in the Arkansas gubernatorial primary in 1972. Southern Strategists may have taken comfort from the Virginia gubernatorial victories of Governors George Allen in 1994 and Jim Gilmore in 1997, but Mark Warner and Tim Kaine won gubernatorial races in Virginia over extreme right-wing Republican candidates in 2001 and 2005 with coalitions comprised of the same groups of voters who defeated Southern Strategists in an earlier day.

The amazing defeat of the once-popular Republican George Allen in his run for reelection to the U.S. Senate in 2006 was the most recent illustration of the ever-increasing distaste of Virginia citizens for racism. Senator Allen entered that race with a lead that pundits, politicians, and press agreed was all but insurmountable. But while addressing an otherwise all-white audience during the campaign, Allen called attention to the presence of a dark-skinned young man known to be a supporter of Allen's opposition. With a piece of pointed ridicule that proved costly to his campaign, he referred to the young man with a word of double meaning: macaca ("a monkey from the Eastern Hemisphere" or "a town in South Africa"). Widely reported, his wisecracking was perceived—and I believe rightly perceived—as racist. It evoked public and press recollections of other symbols thought to be racist in Allen's life, such as a Confederate flag in his living room and a hangman's noose on the wall of his law office. Bloggers had a field day. All the reports of the incident brought more than enough outraged independents, moderate Republicans, and most especially African Americans to defeat Senator Allen at the polls and quashed what were thought to have been his presidential aspirations.

The public's response to Allen's self-revealing name-calling is but one more confirmation that time is not on the side of the Southern Strategy or the well-being of the Republican Party in Virginia.

·

Rockefeller and a Tour
at the State Department

Before the end of my term, I had developed a very friendly relationship with Nelson Rockefeller, then governor of New York, and I respected him enormously as a dedicated public servant. He genuinely believed that public office was the best opportunity for him to serve people, and he went at it with a will. His reputation and sometimes his performance as a "liberal" made him anathema to the more conservative members of the Republican Party, and even I was not in agreement with him on some issues. For example, in view of the highly unionized state of New York, he could not support a right-to-work law, and it would have been equally damaging for me in Virginia to oppose those laws. Nevertheless, I admired him, and we became very close friends.

He was always available to me by telephone or for a visit in his office when I was in New York. He had a highly capable and most attractive staff, including Ann Whitman, whom I had met in Gettysburg when she was President Eisenhower's chief secretary, and who was now serving in the same role for Governor Rockefeller. I had great fun teasing both of them (Nelson had a great sense of humor) about a well-worn rug with a fairly large hole caused by long use. It served as a pad for Ann's desk chair in his New York office. "The poor Rockefellers!" I grinned during one visit. On my next trip to New York, I took a 3 x 4-foot bright red carpet, manufactured in Buena Vista, and presented it to Ann as Virginia's contribution to the Nelson Rockefeller office. Everyone had a good laugh, but the rug's term in that office was short. Apparently the red clashed with everything in the office and offended Ann's sense of color.

Until the ramifications of Watergate became so serious, 1976 had afforded an opportunity for the moderate forces of the Republican Party to confront the conservative wing with a strong candidate for the presidency. Richard Nixon would be completing his second term and would then be constitutionally barred from seeking a third term. Ronald Reagan would lead the conservative forces, and I urged the more moderate Nelson Rockefeller to compete vigorously for the nomination.

I knew it would be tough to beat the conservatives, but if Nixon had served out his second term, the 1976 election would have been a fork in the road for the Republican Party. It could either have followed what I considered to be the problem-solving moderate wing with its appeal to a broad spectrum of voters, or turn to the fervent conservative wing, with concentration on Southern Strategy and its racist overtones.

I had been opposed to the development of the Southern Strategy that began to be articulated in the middle of the Nixon campaign in 1968. It came out of South Carolina, with Senator Thurmond the symbolic head of it, and Harry Dent, one of Thurmond's principal young staffers, probably the most prominent exponent at that time. Later, Lee Atwater of South Carolina became chairman of the Republican National Committee. Both of them articulated the Southern Strategy. Dick Obenshain also sought to amalgamate conservative Virginia Democrats into the Republican Party (though Dick himself never exhibited any tendencies toward racism), while I was coming up as leader of the moderates. As the 1976 nomination contest approached, Dick was the chairman of the Republican Party in Virginia. Once when he happened to be in the same area of National Airport at the same time as Nelson and I were, I tried to get him to come over and speak to Governor Rockefeller. Dick and I always got along, although we were ideologically at opposite poles, so he grinned at me when I said, "Come on over and speak to Governor Rockefeller." He replied, "Governor, you're trying to get me in trouble." And he didn't come over.

The Southern Strategy was designed to combine the more conservative Republicans with the conservative Democrats, who had been headed by people like Senator Harry Byrd Sr. of Virginia. Proponents believed that a majority party could be developed on a conservative basis combining those two groups. Nixon was obsessed with the desire for a Republican majority in the Senate, so he followed the strategy through, which he believed could result in a Republican majority becoming a reality during his presidency. Senator Strom Thurmond of South Carolina had already switched from Democrat to Dixiecrat to Republican, but there were others such as John Stennis and James Eastland of Mississippi and Senator Russell of Georgia, all open and avid segregationists, who might be persuaded to convert. Nixon may never have admitted it in so many words, but that was what he hoped when he followed the advice of Dent and Thurmond. What I objected to was that the basic tenet of the strategy was an appeal to white supremacy, exactly counter to my goals.

As part of my encouragement to Nelson to build his support with those who controlled the machinery of the Republican Party, I suggested that he host a meeting of the Republican Governors Association in Manhattan. Also as a part of my campaign to have him seek the presidential nomination, I visited him a couple of times in New York. One time his security officer met me at the airport in Newark. Since we had arrived early he took me on a little sight-seeing tour of one of the two World Trade Towers. Though it was still unfinished, we took an elevator to the 110th floor anyway. When I stepped out of the elevator, my acrophobia kicked in with a vengeance. There was nothing in front of me but a bare concrete slab extending to the outer edge, where there were as yet no windows or walls. Later I was able to laugh and joke that I had pressed so tightly against the wall of the elevator shaft that the impression of my silhouette was clearly visible. I truly think it made a permanent mark on the building!

On that particular visit, Nelson took me for an overnight visit to the family's Kykuit estate, located in Pocantico Hills north of New York City. We traveled from a heliport on the East River in Manhattan, accompanied on that trip by Nelson's brother David, and Pete Peterson, a prominent economist who had served as secretary of commerce in the Nixon administration. Nelson and I had a very pleasant visit, while David and Pete met on another part of the estate. I don't remember the dinner menu, but I do recall that the next morning there were delicious blueberries covered with cream so rich it was like having blueberry ice cream for breakfast.

Nelson did indeed invite the governors to meet in Manhattan, and in typical Rockefeller fashion, he went all out. Memorable favors appeared for each governor at various meals. At one meal, it was an expensive electronic watch recently developed and just then coming on the market. Another favor was an elaborate Corning glass sculpture of a trout jumping for a golden fly. A huge outdoor barbecue was staged for the governors and their families at Kykuit, and the final banquet was held in the Rainbow Room on the top floor of Rockefeller Center in Manhattan. Clare Boothe Luce was one of the many celebrities who joined the governors on that occasion.

In a private moment toward the end of my term, I told Nelson: "I have made no commitments for the period between January 1974 and the presidential campaign in 1976. I'm available for whatever you might like me to do to help your campaign for the nomination and, hopefully, the election." He reflected on that offer for a short period, then suggested that I take the position of assistant secretary of state for congressional relations on Henry Kissinger's staff, which would be vacant early in 1974. (I assumed he would find a way for me to be considered for the nomination to that position.)

Nelson pointed out that my taking the post would provide me an opportunity to get to know more members of Congress and to learn something about foreign policy. Jinks and I discussed that possibility and decided it might well be a sound idea. A phone call came from Henry Kissinger exactly at the end of my term as governor, who said he wanted me for that position. I was a little wary, concerned about whether Henry—who had a reputation for secrecy—would confide in me. In response to my verbalized concern, he assured me: "Of course you'll be kept informed. I wouldn't want you running around like an unguided missile!" I figured that was just one of Henry Kissinger's blandishments, but I agreed to be nominated.

But after that Kissinger phone call, no one at the State Department seemed disposed to explain why my nomination didn't seem to be moving through the Senate for confirmation. The weeks of January and early February passed, and nothing happened. Finally I was able to wangle out of Kenneth Rush, deputy secretary of state, the fact that Wayne Hays, a congressman from Ohio and chairman of the U.S. House Operations Committee, was responsible for the delay. Hays had grumbled to the State Department that he didn't want that position used to "promote the possible candidacy of some former elected Republican official." Since he had considerable influence on State Department appropriations, his displeasure was alarming to State Department functionaries.

When Ken came clean with me, I suggested that I might be able to resolve the problem by talking to Congressman Hays myself. After consultation with an anonymous somebody, Ken called and gave me the go-ahead to talk to Hays. After my very congenial visit with Mr. Hays—whose reputation as something of an ogre was probably accurate—the problem was solved. I had assured him I understood the needs of the members of Congress, that I had no future political ambitions—which was true at that time—and that I understood the wishes and needs of the members of Congress were to be respected. To my relief, Congressman Hays authorized Charlie McDowell, then at the Washington bureau for the *Richmond Times-Dispatch,* to announce his approval of my appointment. Charlie had received a tip from Roger Mudd, TV anchor for CBS, who ran into me as I was leaving Congressman Hays's office, that there might be a Virginia story in the fact that I had had a visit with Congressman Hays. And indeed there was. Charlie's story reporting Hays's approval of my nomination was in the *Times-Dispatch* the next day.

Things moved smoothly thereafter. Senator Fulbright, chairman of the Senate Foreign Relations Committee, which would consider my appointment for confirmation, commented publicly that "this is the sort of person they should have in that job." Fulbright himself did not conduct the hearings because he was in the midst of a tough primary fight for renomination with a contemporary of mine, Dale Bumpers, former governor of Arkansas. Senator John Sparkman, who chaired the committee in Fulbright's absence, expedited the relatively uncontentious committee hearing on my appointment, and I was confirmed without opposition.

So I went to Washington and joined Kissinger's office on March 1, 1974. Working with Kissinger proved a little frustrating, but I had a lot of fun anyhow because Larry Eagleburger, Kissinger's closest staff person, became my friend immediately. Larry had known about and approved of my term as governor, though I hadn't known anything about him except that he was from Wisconsin. I later learned he was something of a protégé of former congressman Mel Laird, secretary of defense in the Nixon administration.

Ken Rush continued to be very friendly to me during my tenure at State, as did Joe Sisco, foreign service careerist, then undersecretary for political affairs. But the people to whom I became closest during my year at the State Department were Larry Eagleburger and Carl Maw. Larry was very welcoming to me, and we soon reached complete confidence in each other. Because of that relationship, I quickly became a participant in some of the inner workings of the U.S. State Department at a very intriguing time. As I had predicted, Kissinger was difficult to approach, but I could always get to him through Eagleburger if I needed to. In many ways, Larry ran the State Department. Larry understood Kissinger's eccentricities, he was not in awe of that gentleman, and on every issue he called 'em as he saw 'em. From the very beginning we understood each other perfectly, and through him I always knew pretty much of what was going on at the State Department.

Carl Maw, a partner in the prominent New York law firm of Cravath, Swaine and Moore, was serving as legal advisor to the State Department as a public service. Befriending me immediately, he provided both a warm friendship and extremely valuable advice, always forthright and complete because he enjoyed the full confidence of the secretary. Carl shared State Department information with me I would never have known otherwise.

There were four significant developments during the short twelve months I served at State. First was a series of negotiations conducted personally by Kissinger (aided by a large staff) to help reach some kind of interim settlement among the rival parties in the Middle East. There was a lot of publicity during the thirty-three-day shuttling between Tel Aviv and other capitals, which ended with a degree of success. I was in the party to welcome home the tired returning delegation, and it was clear they had experienced enormous stress. Carl Maw, then about eighty-five years old, looked absolutely exhausted.

The success of that Middle East mission made Henry K. something of a national hero. Most of his prior appearances at the Capitol had been off-the-record meetings with the Senate Foreign Relations Committee, unannounced and largely unnoticed by the ubiquitous Capitol tourists. After his success in the Middle East, Kissinger was invited to testify before an open, publicly announced session of the Senate Finance Committee. As his assistant, I escorted him to that meeting. Along the way, the adulation from the hordes of tourists at the Capitol, who had been alerted to his visit by the press reports of his expected appearance, was equivalent to that for a rock star. He received similar approbation from the members of the Senate Finance Committee, and his ego, never needing much nudging, was securely parked on a highly elevated cloud nine.

As we left the Capitol en route back to the State Department that day, he turned to me in the back seat of his official car and asked huskily, "Do you t'ink Nelson can get da nomination?" (Obviously, Governor Rockefeller had confided some of his presidential aspirations to Kissinger prior to my appointment at the State Department.) I responded by observing that it would be tough to nominate the liberal Nelson Rockefeller, but I thought the possibility existed, and I thought it was worth a try. Nonetheless, we discussed others who might more easily be nominated. By the time we reached the State Department building at the end of Constitution Avenue, it was clear to me that in Henry's mind there was only one really potent presidential possibility: Henry Kissinger. Knowing he was German-born and therefore constitutionally ineligible for the job, I held the door for him as we reached the secretary's elevator and said, "Okay, Mr. Secretary, you go on upstairs and practice your accent." (His accent had become an almost mystical—and positive—trademark.) "I'll go back to the Capitol and start working on the constitutional amendment."

Another Kissinger-needling I couldn't resist occurred the morning after a formal dinner had been held in the State Department diplomatic reception rooms in honor of one of the uncles of the royal family of Saudi Arabia. We had assembled for a staff meeting. Henry sat at the end of the table, and on his right sat Joe Sisco, undersecretary for political affairs. I was not at the table itself, but close by in one of the row of chairs against the wall at Kissinger's right. There was a brief period of silence before the official meeting got started, so everyone heard Henry's audible rasping mumble to Sisco about the visiting Saudi royal guest: "It's very hard to talk to that man. He doesn't know anything except women and horses." At that point, I asked in a voice audible to all, "And what do *you* know about horses?" There was spontaneous albeit suppressed laughter around the table, and the look on Henry's face directed at me clearly said, "Holton, if you hadn't already announced your resignation, you would now be fired!"

Secondly significant during my service at State was the beginning of the end of the Vietnam War. We had reached the stage in Richard Nixon's Vietnamization strategy for U.S. troops to be withdrawn. Arms and supplies were to be sent to enable the Vietnamese to defend themselves against the invading Communists. But in spite of maximum effort on the part of all concerned to have Congress continue to fund the war in that way, and in spite of the efforts of both President Nixon before his resignation and President Ford after he assumed office, the Congress of the United States, responding to serious antiwar pressures, terminated all sources of funds for armaments destined for the South Vietnamese army. Since the whole Nixon program of Vietnamization was dependent on U.S. bullets and other armaments, when the bullets were finally cut off, that ended the South Vietnam effort. The photo of U.S. ambassador Graham A. Martin's very dramatic escape by helicopter from the roof of the embassy in Saigon, leaving panic-stricken Vietnamese begging to be taken along, became an icon of the end of our involvement there.

A third significant event during my tour occurred when the Turks invaded Cyprus. I was amused to hear Secretary Kissinger's descriptions of his telephone calls with his former Harvard student Bülent Ecevit (who had subsequently become prime minister of Turkey) in Henry's attempts to get the Turks to back off and help maintain some neutrality with Greece about Cyprus. My own involvement with that problem was limited. I did try to ward off the belligerent and pro-Greek resolutions of Congress that were thwarting Kissinger's efforts to maintain neutrality between Turkey and Greece. We got almost nowhere in that effort, and the reason we got nowhere was pretty well summarized by a statement from Joel Broyhill, congressman from the Tenth District of Virginia. When I tried to persuade him to vote against the anti-Turk resolution, he responded honestly and tersely, a political rarity, "Lin, I don't have a single Turkish restaurant in my district."

The last and by far the most significant of the major developments during my stint at State was President Nixon's resignation. My confidant Carl Maw and I both strongly preferred a course of action that would permit Nixon to serve out his term. However, in a conversation right after the Supreme Court made the "smoking gun" tapes public, we had to concede that it was just a question of twenty-four hours. Nixon left his office at noon the next day.

The transition was nothing short of phenomenal. My personal observance of the process was limited to hearing Kissinger telephone diplomatic representatives of significant allies to assure them that the transition would be peaceful, effective, and without disruption. It was. That fact, in circumstances having traumatic potential, is irrefutable evidence of the unassailable and enduring strength of our republic and its institutions.

As soon as it was announced that the president's resignation would be forthcoming the next day, I left Washington for the Grayson Highlands State Park near Galax, Virginia, where I would be meeting my family for a previously planned short vacation. I heard the resignation speech on the radio in my car. There was mixed reaction to Nixon's resignation throughout the land, but universal sadness that our country had been brought to this crisis. For me, there was both personal and political grief; I had been a Nixon supporter, and he had been a supporter of mine. On the long drive to that beautiful park in the Blue Ridge in Southwest Virginia, the wistful lines of Whittier filled my mind: "For all sad words of tongue and pen, the saddest are these, 'It might have been.'"

At a politically pragmatic level, Nixon's resignation ended the possibility of a 1976 contest between Reagan and Rockefeller. Nelson accepted Ford's appointment of him as vice president to help preserve national unity. I'm sure he did this with some reluctance, because his philosophy, often expressed to me, was, "I am not stand-by equipment." I believe strongly that Ford made a mistake when he replaced Nelson Rockefeller with Bob Dole as the candidate for vice president when Ford sought the renomination in 1976. Bob Dole is a friend with whom I have worked a great deal, but Ford's replacement of Rockefeller with Dole was an unnecessary concession to the conservative wing of the Republican Party. That group would have supported Ford's reelection against Jimmy Carter without regard to his vice-presidential running mate, and Nelson's active campaigning in that year would have added votes from the middle of the political spectrum that, in my judgment, would have resulted in

Ford's election. Though Reagan contested Ford's nomination as president, our presidential plans for Nelson in 1976, which had counted on a race without an incumbent president, ended with Nixon's resignation. For Rockefeller to have joined the contest, vying for the nomination along with Ford and Reagan in 1976, would simply have split the more moderate vote and resulted in Reagan's being nominated in place of Ford.

Even though the effort to nominate Rockefeller in 1976 was quashed by Nixon's resignation, I was glad to have had one year at the State Department. I expect I would have stayed longer were it not that tuition expenses were beginning to assume gigantic proportions in my eyes. Tayloe had entered Dartmouth in the fall of 1974, and Anne was to enter Princeton in 1976. These two college expenses exceeded $15,000 annually; my salary at the State Department was $35,000, pretax, and there wasn't going to be much left to live on. As I put it at the time, I had to "quit and go to work." I left State on the last day of February 1975, exactly one year after I had gone there on March 1, 1974, to join the Washington law firm of Hogan and Hartson at a very comfortable salary.

John Warner and Our Occasionally Parallel Paths

John Warner supported me in 1965 at a time when his three-thousand-dollar contribution to my first gubernatorial campaign was a tremendous amount of money. As mentioned earlier, John and I met each other when he was a freshman and I a special graduate student at Washington and Lee in 1946; we were friends from then on. By 1965, both of us had married, he to Catherine Mellon of Middleburg, Virginia, daughter of the philanthropist Paul Mellon, and I to Jinks Rogers.

It was apparent from the beginning of our friendship that John was as interested in a political career as I was. I was pleased and flattered when, after my statewide campaign in 1965, he asked me to introduce him to some of my political contacts in the Seventh Congressional District. I realized that my "pupil" had a lot to learn when he showed up at our scheduled rendezvous in the Shenandoah Valley (where John was thinking of running for Congress), in a two-engine private airplane, dressed in a dark blue pinstriped suit with a buttoned-up vest—hardly a suitable costume to create a favorable first impression on some of my Republican farmer friends in what was then primarily a rural district. However, he was a quick study, and by 1968 John had gained the confidence of the leadership of the Nixon campaign and was asked to lead an independent organization called something like "Volunteers for Nixon." He spent a lot of time with that organization and did a good job. When the election was over and Nixon had won, John confirmed to me his interest in being appointed secretary of the navy, first showing me the courtesy of making sure I wasn't interested in that appointment myself. (I wasn't.)

Because of the role I had played in both the nomination and election campaigns of Nixon in Virginia and in some of the border states around Virginia, John was confident that I could influence the decision of who would be secretary of the navy—much more confident than I was. Though I protested to

John that I probably wouldn't be very much help to him, he insisted that I go to New York in the period between election and inauguration and importune Nixon to appoint him. He even bought and delivered personally a round-trip airline ticket from Roanoke to New York for me. At that point I didn't know if I would even be able to see the president-elect at his transition headquarters in the Pierre Hotel; nevertheless, I undertook the assignment.

I had to smile ruefully as I walked down the hotel hall toward the room where John Ehrlichman (future counselor to the president), John Mitchell (future U.S. attorney general), and Richard Nixon were holding forth. I had passed a room where a group of television cameras were focused on John Chafee, former governor of Rhode Island and a Nixon supporter. It was clear to me right then that John Chafee had already been selected to be secretary of the navy in the Nixon first term. Having pointed out that very possibility in my earlier conversations with John Warner, I mentally dropped back to plan B: I would ask for the undersecretary's job for John.

I was welcomed into the group surrounding Nixon, and after the amenities, I nevertheless made the case for John Warner to be named secretary of the navy. Nixon confirmed then that John Chafee was going to be appointed to that post, but that he was likely to be a short-termer in the job. Nixon thought—and I did too—that Chafee would seek and win a seat in the U.S. Senate in 1970. He suggested that if Warner were to serve now as undersecretary, he would then be in position to move up to the top job in the navy when Chafee went to the Senate. That made sense to me, and I was beginning to think my mission would be at least partially successful. The only hitch was that Mel Laird, who would shortly be appointed secretary of defense, also had to approve the appointment.

Ehrlichman was about to depart for Washington to discuss appointments with Laird, and within my hearing, the president seemed to make it very clear to Ehrlichman that he should let Laird know that Warner was Nixon's personal choice for the undersecretary's job. Laird apparently had no objection to Warner, nor did he have a candidate of his own, so the Warner appointment was announced shortly thereafter. It was a most appropriate appointment. John had enlisted in the navy and served as a sonar technician at the end of World War II, and he had also served in the Marine Corps in the Korean War. I was delighted that he was delighted with the undersecretary appointment and the prospect of future promotion.

John Warner was not my only friend and political ally involved in this particular cabinet appointment. My friendship with John Chafee went back a long time too. During a two-week period of training at the Naval War College in Providence, Rhode Island, in 1965, I had invited myself to meet with the then Republican governor of Rhode Island—John Chafee. He was very interested and very helpful in my effort to help create a two-party system in Virginia. In view of our friendship, which began then and lasted until his death in October 1999, I welcomed his appointment as secretary of the navy, even though my friend John Warner had to delay his turn in the post. As anticipated, Chafee became a U.S. senator from Rhode Island in 1970. He probably concentrated on environmental issues more than anything else while in the Senate, and he was always a leading member of the fairly small group of moderate Republican senators.

He was succeeded in the U.S. Senate by his son, Lincoln, who is also a problem solver and is classified with the moderate Republican senators whose political ideology is close to mine. His defeat in strongly Democratic Rhode Island in 2006 was apparently due to aversion to anyone even nominally supportive of President Bush.

As predicted, John Warner was moved up to the secretary's job when Chafee went to the Senate, and nobody could have been happier with a job. It was great training and background for John's later career in the U.S. Senate, especially because he worked directly for about three years under the leadership and influence of Secretary of Defense Mel Laird, arguably the most outstanding member of the Nixon cabinet.

I had at least one very pleasant visit with Secretary John Warner while he was in office and while I was governor. John and I were just socializing, so one of his staff members felt free to interrupt our conversation to announce a brief visit from Admiral Louis Strauss. Strauss was a Virginian who had supported my candidacy, and I was flattered when—in spite of the obvious confidentiality of his suggestion—in my presence he recommended to Secretary Warner that the nuclear carrier then under construction at Newport News be named for President Eisenhower. John readily assented, and I think that deal was pretty much done on the spot.

By chance on another occasion, I ran into Secretary Warner on the Pentagon steps just as I arrived for a luncheon with the then chief of naval operations (CNO), Admiral Elmo "Bud" Zumwalt. In view of the traditional rivalry between the CNO (military head of the navy) and the secretary (civilian head of the navy), I would just as soon have completed that social visit without the secretary's knowledge. But, having no worthy excuse when Secretary Warner asked, "What are you doing here?" I said, with something of a smirk, "I'm going up to have lunch with your boss," and beat a hasty retreat down the hallway.

The Holton-Warner friendship continues to this day. It continues in spite of the fact that John had every right to resent my failure to support him for the Republican nomination to the U.S. Senate upon the expiration of Bill Scott's term in 1978. I should have supported him; he really wanted a place in the Senate more passionately than I did, and I knew in my heart he would make a good senator. But in the context of the time, I convinced myself that John would not be able to get the nomination of the Republican Party in a contest with Richard Obenshain, then state Republican Party chairman and leader of the more conservative faction of our party in Virginia.

It's quite possible, however, that with my help John could have been nominated. Again, in the context of my beliefs at the time, I convinced myself that though Obenshain, in a two-way contest with Warner, would probably be the Republican nominee, I didn't believe he would be able to defeat Andrew Miller in the general election. Miller had been elected attorney general of Virginia twice and was the Democratic nominee.

Maybe my rationalization about Warner and Obenshain was because I was restless. My plans for a Rockefeller-Reagan contest for the presidential nomination in 1976 had been derailed by Nixon's resignation. My very pleasant one-year tour at the U.S. State Department was cut short by my aversion to borrowing the money necessary for our daughters' college tuitions, so I'd joined Hogan and Hartson, a prominent Washington, D.C., law firm, in order to earn enough money to pay-as-they-went. But without the flow of political adrenalin flowing, I was bored.

On top of the boredom, my gubernatorial vanity had convinced me I could easily gain the Republican nomination for the U.S. Senate, even with the opposition of Dick Obenshain and John Warner. After all, I was the only person who had ever won a statewide race in Virginia as a Republican. "Win Again with Lin" seemed to me to be a slogan everyone would remember and support. Wrong!

Jinks knew it was a mistake, but she went along with my decision to enter the race for the Senate nomination. I conferred with Dick Obenshain in his Virginia office, optimistically and rather naively thinking he would stand aside if he knew I was going to enter the race. Wrong again. Dick made it clear he was going to make an all-out effort to win the nomination himself. I think I also assumed that John Warner would not be much of a factor in a three-way race among Holton, Obenshain, and Warner. John had only Washington experience, and he hadn't paid a great deal of attention to the people in Virginia who would select the nominee. Wrong a third time. John was also going all-out for the nomination.

I didn't think the presence of Elizabeth Taylor in that campaign as the wife of John Warner would be particularly significant. After all, this was her seventh marriage, and I just could not believe that the members of the Republican Party with their intense vocal support for "family values," would pay much attention to the appearance of this particular celebrity. Once more, how wrong I was—1978 was surely my year for being wrong. The glamour of John's new wife was no small asset. She joined him enthusiastically in campaigning for the nomination throughout the whole state, a sensation wherever she appeared. Even rumors of her excessive drinking—and I personally never saw any evidence that they were more than rumors—failed to dampen enthusiasm for her. Even one of my longtime committed supporters, Ryland Heflin of Stafford County, told Jinks at a political rally that he would break his commitment to me and vote for John Warner for the nomination. He rationalized to Jinks that "Elizabeth Taylor would help me establish a race track on my property," one of his fervent ambitions. In telling Jinks of his change of support, he conceded, "I know Lin will be disappointed." I was.

The nominee was to be chosen by a state convention in Richmond. John and Elizabeth brought in support and attracted unbelievably large crowds. Dick's state organization, which he had prepared so very carefully over a five-year period, made a prodigious effort on Dick's behalf. The amount of funds raised in that race was incredible to me, and most of it wasn't raised by or for me. I've always been uncomfortable raising money by direct appeal, and all of the money-raising in my gubernatorial races had been done by finance committees. But this time I got on the phone, and by personal efforts and the efforts of a finance committee, we did raise an amount adequate to support my campaign.

The result of the convention, which drew ten thousand delegates to the Richmond Coliseum—by far the most people who had ever attended a Republican function in Virginia—placed Obenshain first, Warner second, and Holton third on the first ballot. I knew it was over for me, but I went through the motions of visiting several delegations in the stands, seeking support based on what I proclaimed was my best asset: the ability to win the general election in November. But the only positive reaction I got was from one little group who promised I would gain one hundred votes on the next ballot if I would announce support for their antiabortion position. I took some inner satisfaction from declining their offer, unwilling to go further in the race if I had to abandon my principles.

Failing to gain significant, if any, votes on the next ballot, I gathered the family, all of whom were with me there, and we went to the rostrum. "Jinks, Tayloe, Anne, Woody, and Dwight and I are happy to join you in welcoming me to the status of senior statesman." Thus we withdrew. That chapter was over for us, and shortly afterward it was over also for John Warner. Obenshain was nominated by those dedicated loyalists whom he had recruited for the statewide organization during his tenure as state chairman of the Republican Party.

It was tough to lose, but it had been a positive campaign—no mudslinging—and all of us remained friends. Jinks and I didn't hesitate to join the "unity" breakfast the Obenshain folks scheduled for the John Marshall Hotel on Sunday morning following his nomination that Saturday night. We suspected that John Warner and Elizabeth Taylor would not appear at the breakfast, but somewhat to our surprise, they were getting out of a car in front of us when we pulled up to the hotel. We all wore our "unity" smiles as we greeted each other and prepared to join the breakfast. As we moved from the street to the hotel, Elizabeth leaned over to Jinks and whispered, with her unity smile in full glow, "Shit, Jinks—just *shit!*" And so the disappointed candidates went in, all smiles and charm, to the unity breakfast.

A day or two after the convention, the *Washington Post* ran a story about the convention under a headline that ascribed my loss to my stand on busing and civil rights. When our daughter Tayloe, who was particularly disappointed by my not having been nominated, saw that headline, she commented to the effect: "If that's the reason we lost, then I don't feel so bad about losing." She and I had the satisfaction of knowing I had done the right thing about busing and civil rights. It far offset for all of us the disappointment over losing the Senate nomination.

In August of that year (1978), I found a new opportunity as vice president and general counsel of the American Council of Life Insurance (ACLI). My good friend Blake Newton, a distant cousin of Jinks's, was president of that organization. I had not been interested in a lobbying job, particularly with the federal government, but Blake convinced me that the ACLI was not a typical trade association (i.e., lobbyist). He summarized his approach to federal government relations with the slogan "We do well by doing good," and pointed out one very convincing example: the life insurance industry had recently made $100 million available for low-cost mortgages to support the construction of low- and middle-income housing. At that time, the ACLI did not have a political action committee (PAC), and Blake was committed to the position of the organization's *not* seeking to obtain favorable federal action by making huge contributions to political campaigns of candidates for Congress. Though that policy was changed after Blake retired, it remained in effect through most of my tenure. Illustrative of the fact that the policy worked was the appearance of Senator Robert Dole, Republican chairman of the Senate Finance Committee, on the Senate floor in 1982, commending the life insurance industry for the positive contributions that we had made to the development of major changes in the U.S. tax laws adopted by the Senate that year.

The story of the 1978 Senate race did not conclude with the unity breakfast. Tragedy followed. Jinks and I were awakened by our telephone at about 3:00 a.m. on August 2, 1978. Kathleen Lawrence, a major member of my former Senate campaign staff, gave us the sad news that Dick Obenshain and two others including the pilot had been killed when their plane was attempting to land at the Chesterfield County airport while returning from a campaign trip to Winchester. We were horrified. Dick was a competitor, an opponent, but he was also a friend, and this was a tragedy for us as well as for his family and other friends.

In spite of the entreaties of various members of the press, neither John Warner nor I speculated about any successor candidate to Obenshain until after his funeral. The selection would be made by the State Central Committee of the Republican Party of Virginia, and I knew there would be very little chance of that very conservative body nominating me even if I sought the nomination. At any rate, by that time I'd joined the American Council of Life Insurance and was not inclined to change course again, so I advised Judy Peachee, one of the leaders in the State Central Committee, that I was not interested in being considered by the committee for the nomination. Though there was some concern among some of the members of the State Central Committee about whether John Warner was conservative enough for them, they did nominate him. He won a close general election victory over Democratic candidate Andrew Miller.

John Warner has been a very successful and increasingly popular U.S. senator. Throughout most of his elected career, he has been supported and aided in a very material way by his chief of staff, Susan Magill—one of the really outstanding political analysts of our time. Her political acuity can be called nothing less than perspicacious.

From barely squeaking by with about five thousand votes in 1978, John was reelected in 1984 with 72 percent of the vote; in 1990, he received 84 percent of the general election vote. Though he has been a team player on the Republican side of the aisle, he has cooperated with Democratic administrations, and there has been no trace of the objectionable racism of the Southern Strategy in his career. On important occasions, he has voted against the positions of the extreme right wing of the Republican Party: he voted against the nomination of Robert Bork to the U.S. Supreme Court; he has supported some gun control and voted pro-choice on some of the abortion issues; and he opposed the election of Michael Ferris, the extremist Republican candidate for lieutenant governor in 1993.

John Warner's most serious crime, from the perspective of the right-wingers of our party, was to oppose the candidacy of marine colonel Oliver North when he ran against Senator Chuck Robb in the general election in 1994. North was the Republican nominee, and he was the adulated hero of all of the zealots on the right wing of our party. John had some rather harsh things to say about Colonel North, but to avoid outright support for a Democrat, he sponsored J. Marshall Coleman, a former Republican nominee for governor of Virginia and a longtime Republican member of the General Assembly, as an independent candidate in the general election. The effect was to take the votes of more moderate Republicans away from Oliver North, making it possible for the incumbent Democrat, Senator Chuck Robb, to win the election, though with a plurality of only 46 percent. Coleman got 11 percent of the general election vote, leaving only 43 percent for Colonel North. John Warner effectively performed another good turn for Virginia.

If that right-wing element of the Republican Party of Virginia could have forced Senator Warner to seek renomination in a state convention in 1996, they would have punished him by declining to renominate him in spite of his eighteen years of seniority and service to Virginia in the Senate.

But a statute that had been passed to protect incumbents in the General Assembly of Virginia many years ago gave the incumbents—including, in this case, Senator Warner—the option of seeking renomination in a primary or in a convention. The right-wingers did not give up when John chose the primary; they entered a candidate, Jim Miller, who had been budget director in the Reagan administration, to oppose Warner in the primary. Their vindictiveness was of no avail because Warner was renominated going away, with thousands of independents and Democrats entering the Republican primary to see that he was renominated.

Warner is an outstanding senator; regardless of potential consequences, he does what *he* thinks is right. As recently as the summer of 2004, he asserted his independence of partisanship by supporting the joint effort of Republican moderates in the Virginia General Assembly and the Democratic governor to raise state revenue to pay for essential needs, particularly in education. And in 2005 he was active in the group of moderate Republicans who forced a compromise to avoid a rules change that would have entirely eliminated filibusters to oppose extreme U.S. court appointments.

Until January 2007, when the Democrats took over as the majority party, he served with distinction in the position of his fondest dreams: chairman of the Armed Services Committee of the U.S. Senate.

The Metropolitan
Washington
16 Airports Authority

There's no denying that a letdown followed my four years as governor of Virginia. I left office when I was just over fifty; what hill was there now to climb? The year at the State Department was somewhat exciting, but that was Henry Kissinger's ballpark; I was just a supporting functionary. The time in the big Washington law firm was dull—deadly dull. Lobbying for the life insurance industry under Blake Newton, my friend and president of the trade association, was more fun, and I think we made contributions to the public with the work we did to help develop reforms of tax policy with amendments to the U.S. Tax Code in 1982. But amendments to tax codes represent mundane accomplishment at best; I really wanted another challenge. I always wanted to *do* something. I *did* the governor's job. Then, happily, in 1984 it was Opportunity Time again, out of the blue.

In the spring of 1984, Dr. and Mrs. Edgar Weaver of Roanoke (Tuffy and Evelyn) and Jinks and I were enjoying a Chesapeake Bay cruise on our small, old, but comfortable jointly owned yacht, the *Wind Song*. We sailed south from our home port in Deltaville, made some stops in the Hampton Roads area, traveled up the James River past the old "ghost fleet"—a group of obsolete cargo ships moored there because nobody knew what else to do with them—and stopped at the Kingsmill on the James marina near Williamsburg. To my surprise, the marina operator there delivered a phone message asking me to call Elizabeth Dole, the incumbent secretary of transportation in the Reagan administration.

I was a little dumbfounded because even my office had no information about our specific itinerary. Someone had done great detective work. I promptly returned the call, only to find that Mrs. Dole was traveling. Instead, her chief of staff spoke to me, saying Mrs. Dole would appreciate it if I would meet with her in her office as soon as possible regarding a matter she would like to discuss personally with me. He didn't reveal the subject. I recall thinking later that may have been because she feared that forewarned, I might be inclined to respond negatively to the request she was about to make.

When I met her a few days later, she was all smiles, evidently prepared to lavish her renowned charm on me. Our following discussion involved the Washington National Airport and Washington-Dulles International Airport, the only two carrier airports still owned and operated by the federal government. Mrs. Dole detailed the overcrowded and outmoded conditions at National Airport, which of course I already well knew. She told of the several past attempts to transfer ownership and operation of the airports from the federal government, acknowledging the difficulty that would confront her proposal to make that happen. Nonetheless, she was determined to accomplish such a transfer during her term as secretary of the transportation department.

She had already appointed a broad-based commission and charged it with the responsibility to determine, not whether, but *how* to accomplish the desired transfer. She had selected as commission members the mayor of the District of Columbia, the governors of both Maryland and Virginia, U.S. senator Sarbanes of Maryland, and U.S. senator Warner of Virginia, along with several representatives in the House, including Frank Wolf of Virginia's Tenth District and Stenny Hoyer of the District of Maryland, which included the area near Washington, D.C. Several representatives of local governments in the area were also members of the commission she had already selected.

After describing that background and her proposal, she looked me straight in the eye, turned on all of her impressive charm, and said, "I need a strong chairman for that commission, and I want you," pretty obviously prepared to twist my arm to accept this challenge. Responding with what I'm sure was great surprise, my unhesitating and immediate response was, "Madam Secretary, I am your man."

I was intimately aware of the deficiencies at National Airport. The old main terminal was hopelessly obsolete and overcrowded, and the expansion to the north was in a series of shacks, a disgraceful entrance to the capital of the free world. I recognized that first, federal appropriations would never be sufficient to correct these deficiencies, and second, an authority that could issue bonds and pay interest that could not be taxed by the states or the federal government could probably raise sufficient money to make the improvements so badly needed at National Airport. Both of us knew that the Dulles International Airport was badly underutilized, but that factor was not stressed in the initial con-

versation. Mrs. Dole continued to emphasize that the commission's assignment was to determine how, not whether, to transfer the airports out of the
federal government's aegis; she made no suggestions about the how, except
one glancing reference to the possibility of a "leveraged buyout." That phrase
was just then becoming faddishly popular to describe an old-fashioned purchase money mortgage: a buyer purchases a piece of property and agrees to
pay the purchase price out of revenues to be received from the future operation of the property.

Mrs. Dole assured me she would actively support the work of the commission, and arranged for both Greg Wolfe, a young lawyer in a career position in
the law department of the Department of Transportation, and Shirley Ybarra,
one of her special assistants, to give their full time to me to assist in the endeavor. Greg was somewhat reluctant to join what I'm sure he felt was a futile
enterprise, given past efforts to transfer the airports. From his several-year
tenure in the department, he knew of eleven failed past efforts to transfer these
airports. Shirley was enthusiastic from the beginning, and Greg became so
after I convinced him that I, at least, was convinced that the time for transfer
was now ripe.

Most importantly, Mrs. Dole promised she would exert every effort to use
all the resources available to her, both personal and official, to implement the
recommendation of the commission to transfer the airports, if it came up with
a reasonable plan. She didn't mention it, but I was well aware that her husband was then chairman of the powerful U.S. Senate Finance Committee.
(Before the commission finished its work in December of that year, Bob Dole
was elected Republican majority leader of the U.S. Senate for the Ninety-ninth
Congress.) I sincerely believed we had a good chance to get the job done.

Not everyone shared my optimism. A day after the formation of the commission and my chairmanship were announced in the press, I was quizzed by
my next-door neighbor, recently retired four-star U.S. Air Force general
Richard Ellis. He had heard my name on the radio but couldn't remember the
reason. When I reminded him, he smiled, looked at me quizzically, and asked
bluntly, "Are you *crazy*?"

As the work of the commission got under way, a few friends as well as some
old and new acquaintances encouraged me to think my optimism was well-
placed. Jim Wheat, CEO of Wheat First Securities and an old friend, expressed
optimism and offered professional assistance to determine the financial feasi-
bility of the proposed transfer. Bob Crandall, then chairman of the American
Air Lines holding company, agreed during my telephoned request to him to

encourage the major airlines to withhold their decisions about possible change of ownership of the airports (which might be negative) until they saw the results of the commission's studies. Colonel Frank Borman, former astronaut and then CEO of Eastern Air Lines, was even more encouraging; he openly expressed his opinion that a change from federal control was a good idea. Paul Ignatius, then president of the Air Transport Association, the important lobbying organization of the major commercial air carriers, agreed to try to maintain neutrality among his members. This wasn't really easy for him because his members instinctively believed any kind of change would be bad.

Sweetness and light pervaded the first meeting of the commission. The principals were there: Mayor Barry, Senator Sarbanes, Senator Warner, Congressman Hoyer, Congressman Wolf, Governor Hughes of Maryland, Governor Robb of Virginia, and several representatives of the local governments. Mrs. Dole personally described her goal of transferring control of the airports out of the federal government and explained her rationale.

My impression was that there was a willingness to explore the possibilities, though perhaps not enthusiasm. Subsequent meetings were basically routine, with emphasis on determining whether revenues from the operation of the airports were sufficient to support bond issues large enough to pay for needed improvements. Walter Craigie, a representative of Wheat First Securities, was very helpful on this issue and was also very optimistic that those revenues would suffice. I pushed strongly for the airports to be transferred to an authority created by a compact between Virginia and/or Maryland and the District of Columbia; such an authority could issue bonds on which the interest would be tax-free. A consensus developed pretty quickly: if the airports were to be transferred, this was the way to do it.

I don't remember how much discussion the commission had on the issue of how much, if anything, the proposed authority would pay the federal government for the transfer of the airports. I do remember that at some point Jim Wheat suggested that the authority could buy the airports from the federal government and pay the purchase price with the proceeds of its bonds—a natural bias for Wheat, who was in the bond-underwriting business. His idea of buying the airports was consistent with the "leveraged buyout" concept Mrs. Dole had referenced in our initial conversation. At some point, I proposed that *nothing* be paid to the federal government for the airports; I argued that if the operation of the airports became self-sustaining under the authority, then the government would come out ahead. We would be doing the federal government a favor; federal funds would no longer have to be appropriated for annual operations, and there would be no need for federal appropriations to pay for capital improvements. This issue was ultimately resolved by a plan under which the authority would pay rent sufficient to reimburse the government for all the past capital funds it had invested through the years in the creation of the airports—a sum relatively nominal when compared to any theoretical present market value of the properties.

The biggest contention was over allocation of representation on the board of directors of the proposed authority among the political entities involved: Maryland, the District of Columbia, and Virginia. The Maryland representatives, whose interests were mainly to protect its investment in the Baltimore-Washington International Airport from competition by Dulles, didn't seem particularly concerned about its representation on the board of directors. However, Governor Robb of Virginia insisted that since National Airport and Dulles Airport were both located in Virginia, he could not accept a board of directors with less than a majority of its members from Virginia. Mayor Barry was equally insistent that since National Airport was really Washington's airport, he could not accept a board of directors on which the District of Columbia had fewer members than Virginia. When this impasse began to develop in one of the meetings of the commission attended only by surrogates, I suggested it was time to consult with the principals directly. I peremptorily adjourned the meeting before people dug in to irreconcilable positions.

Governor Robb, in a spirit of compromise, seemed willing to back off somewhat from his requirement for a majority, but Mayor Barry continued in his insistence on having just as many representatives as anybody else. Two collateral developments helped to resolve the impasse. First, Presidential Airways, a small start-up airline, began flying to East Coast destinations with its headquarters at Dulles Airport, the initiation of hub-and-spoke operations that became a model for the industry. It had apparent early successes, and there were rumors that United Air Lines was considering a similar operation, also to be initiated at Dulles Airport. The second development came in a telephone conversation I had with my friend John T. "Til" Hazel, a very successful and wealthy real estate developer in Northern Virginia. Til was aware of the commission discussions and suggested in this private conversation that the commission consider a recommendation to sell Dulles Airport to a syndicate of businessmen he thought he could put together in northern Virginia. I didn't consider that practical, but the suggestion became very valuable to me. I used it effectively when fortuitously I discovered on a business trip to New York that Mayor Barry was also in New York on that very day, and that he was basically free, awaiting departure late in the day for a trip to Europe. So I filled his waiting time with several phone calls.

That phone dialogue turned out to be crucial to the success of the commission's deliberations. I recommended to Mayor Barry that he accept a plan in which Virginia would have five representatives on the board of directors of the proposed authority, the District of Columbia would have three, and Maryland would have two. That would create a balance of five each for the respective sides of the Potomac River. I talked about the activities of Presidential Airways and the rumors of possible participation by United Air Lines, as indications that development at Dulles Airport on a possibly explosive basis was imminent.

I also told him that if the commission failed to come up with a recommendation that would keep the two airports under single ownership in a way satisfactory to all of the parties, there was a possibility that Dulles Airport would be sold to a group of private investors. I stressed to him that if that happened, the District of Columbia would have no influence on the operation or ownership of what might become the major airport in the Washington region. This rationale impressed him. Referring to my recommendation, he said, "Governor, you've got a winner!"

That recommendation, with a slight adjustment suggested by Senator Warner later, settled that. Warner proposed that a "tiebreaker" be appointed by the president of the United States, to protect the continuing interest of the federal government in the two airports, and to act as something of a mediator among the five representatives from each side of the Potomac River. Further, my suggestion that the transfer legislation provide that board members would serve as a civic responsibility, without compensation, was passed unanimously.

With the board representation issue resolved, it was easy for the commission to recommend the transfer of the airports by a long-term lease or sale, for a nominal consideration, to an authority to be created by a compact agreed to between the District of Columbia and Virginia. (Maryland was not interested in joining the compact, fearing that the whole concept was going to be competitively damaging in the future to the Baltimore-Washington International Airport.) The authority to be created by the compact between the District and Virginia could issue bonds on which the interest would be free of taxation by the United States, the District of Columbia, Maryland, and Virginia. Revenue projections were more than adequate for operations and financing improvements. This recommendation went to the secretary of transportation in December 1984, within the six-month deadline Dole had originally hoped we could meet. The recommendations were essentially adopted unanimously by the commission, though the Maryland representatives, again with their eye on the future of BWI, filed a mild dissent. I would describe the Maryland vote as acquiescence rather than positive concurrence or serious dissent.

The Airports Transfer Legislation

Secretary Dole initiated her promised major effort to implement the recommendations of the Holton Commission in January 1985, less than one month after she received the report of our commission. She instructed the senior members of her staff, including Jim Burnley, her deputy secretary, and assistant secretaries Mari Masseng Will and Rebecca Range Coxe, her congressional relations specialists, to give top priority to the preparation and passage of the legislation necessary to transfer the airports. Shirley Ybarra, one of her special assistants, and Greg Wolfe, the lawyer at the Department of Transportation who had assisted the commission with its work, were both assigned to the legislative effort on a full-time basis.

Mrs. Dole asked me to take a lead role in the effort to "educate" Congress on the necessity of passing the transfer legislation and to lead the effort to create the desired authority. (There was some kind of crazy rule that prohibited the Department of Transportation from "lobbying" for legislation, so we sought to "educate" Congress.) She suggested that she appoint me as an assistant secretary of transportation to perform that task, but I declined and convinced her that I could be more effective as an outside attorney for the department than if I were to approach Congress as just another member of the federal bureaucracy. She therefore instructed Jim Burnley to find the funds to pay reasonable compensation for my services as an independent contractor, and he did so.

With the goodwill I had maintained with the members of the Virginia General Assembly over the years, and especially with the cooperation of Senator L. Douglas Wilder, then chairman of the Virginia Senate Rules Committee, I was able to obtain prompt passage of legislation in Virginia to create the Metropolitan Washington Airports Authority (MWAA). A little later, Mayor Marion Barry was able to get similar legislation passed by the District of Columbia City Council; these actions adopted the two-pronged compact that established an entity that could receive the airports from the federal government and operate them. Most importantly, that entity, the Metropolitan Washington Airports Authority, was authorized to issue bonds to pay for improvements to the airports, and the interest on those bonds would be free of taxation by the federal and the two state governments.

The two Virginia U.S. senators, John W. Warner and Paul Trible, were the principal sponsors of legislation to transfer the airports, introduced early in 1985. The final legislation was passed by Congress near the end of 1986, just before it adjourned sine die, largely because there was near-consensus that there would never be sufficient federal appropriations available to pay for desperately needed improvements, particularly at Washington National Airport. It was also apparent to almost everybody that operation of the airports by the Metropolitan Washington Airports Authority would generate funds sufficient to pay operating expenses as well as the costs of needed capital.

Nonetheless, there were collateral issues that constituted obstacles to passage of the legislation that required two full years of major effort on the part of many people. For instance, in the mind of practically every member of Congress, admitted or not, was the question: "Will I lose the free parking privilege which I have had for years at both airports?"

I simply took this bull by the horns and volunteered to every member I talked to that the free parking privileges would be continued under the authority's management. With tongue in cheek, I several times promised, "We will even maintain a free parking space with your name on it." That always produced a look of consternation, so I would quickly add, "your name in code." I felt that the sacrifice of a few parking spaces was a small price to pay for the advantages to be gained by the authority's ownership and operation of the airports.

Governor Hughes and some of the Maryland Transportation Department officials were concerned that the contemplated transfer of Dulles Airport would create an unbearable competition for Baltimore-Washington International Airport (formerly "Friendship Airport"), which had recently been acquired by the State of Maryland from the City of Baltimore. Senator Sarbanes therefore participated in what ultimately became sixty-four hours of filibuster in opposition to the transfer legislation. The senator, governor, and other Maryland officials were placated when unexpected discretionary federal funds were made available by Secretary Dole for some needed runway improvements at BWI.

The so-called "perimeter rule" became the subject of wrangling and constituted another obstacle to the transfer legislation. Congressman Snyder of Kentucky wanted to retain the existing limit that required airliners departing from National Airport to serve destinations within one thousand miles of

Washington National; that limit protected Congressman Snyder's Louisville destination, flights to which might be switched to other more distant destinations if the perimeter rule were extended. On the other hand, Congressman Jim Wright (who just happened to be Speaker of the U.S. House of Representatives and who represented a district in Texas) wanted any airports legislation that passed the House to extend the perimeter rule so that airliners from National Airport could directly serve the airport at Dallas–Fort Worth—in his district. Texas senator Benson was also interested in a little extension of the perimeter rule so that airliners from National Airport could serve Houston. Though Senator Trible, who was really the manager of the legislation in the Senate, had committed that the transfer bill would not extend the perimeter rule, Senator Warner intervened with Senator Benson, and together they worked out a compromise that did in fact extend the perimeter rule to 1,250 miles. I don't think the compromise upset any real applecarts, but the tensions at times were intense.

There was an underlying reluctance on the part of many members of Congress, particularly of the House and their staffs, to support the transfer for fear that any legislative change might reduce their influence, or even control, over the operation of what they considered to be *their* airport—Washington National. A proposal developed by the staff of the House Public Works Committee, which would have transferred the airports to a federally created corporation similar to that which operates the Saint Lawrence Seaway, gained enough headway to be somewhat alarming to those of us who preferred a transfer to the MWAA. That effort lost steam when the financial experts who were testifying in support of a federal corporation had to admit that it would be politically impossible to get the U.S. Treasury and the Office of Management and Budget to agree to a federal corporation that could issue tax-free bonds, a disadvantage that killed that proposal.

Another proposal under which Congress could keep a controlling hand in the operation of the airports was that of Arkansas congressman John Hammerschmidt, ranking Republican member of the relevant House committee. His proposal would create a so-called "review board" made up of members of Congress who would have a veto power for certain important decisions made by the MWAA, including selection of a chief executive officer and adoption of a budget. I was certain that provision for such a review board was unconstitutional under the separation of powers provisions of the U.S. Constitution. It was apparent, however, that Congress would not pass transfer legislation without such a provision. Someone in the Department of Justice was prevailed upon to write an opinion that this particular review board would pass constitutional muster. In recognition of the inevitable, I agreed to go along with the provision for the review board, though I made plain to all concerned my opinion that such a provision was unconstitutional. However, I committed the MWAA to retain the best available constitutional counsel to defend the constitutionality of the review board in the litigation that was certain to follow passage of the act.

The MWAA did in fact later retain the services of a prominent constitutional lawyer, William Coleman, former secretary of the U.S. Department of Transportation, who vigorously defended the legislation before the U.S. Supreme Court, which nonetheless ultimately declared the review board invalid. Subsequent review board legislation in the second attempt by Congress to retain control met a similar fate in the U.S. Court of Appeals, whose opinion the U.S. Supreme Court declined to review.

After Congress lost its battle for the review board, it consoled itself by a requirement that two additional federally appointed members be added to the board of directors of the MWAA. The composition of the board of directors of the Airports Authority therefore became five from Virginia, three from the District of Columbia, two from Maryland, and three members appointed by the president and confirmed by Congress.

Congress again demonstrated its muscle over the airports in the late 1990s by a congressionally mandated name change from Washington National Airport to Washington Ronald Reagan National Airport. The fact that the change required extensive modifications to signs, airline guides, and substantial advertising seemed of no moment to the right-wingers in Congress who insisted on the name change. Nor did the fact that the federally mandated name change flew in the face of Ronald Reagan's personal philosophy, which clearly would have left the name of the airport to a decision of the local government entity—the Metropolitan Washington Airports Authority.

The most effective obstacle to the passage of the legislation was one man: Senator Fritz Hollings of South Carolina. Fritz was still chairman of the Senate Commerce Committee, which would consider the transfer legislation when the Holton Commission reported in December 1984. Though the Republicans would select new committee chairmen when they acquired a Senate majority early in 1985, John Warner and I recognized that Hollings would be a key player anyhow. We therefore had called on him late in 1984 to seek his support for the transfer bill. He made no commitment in that meeting, but I sensed from his manner and body language that he was going to cause trouble. Little did I realize just how much trouble.

Throughout the parliamentary path of the bill through the U.S. Senate, Hollings—with assistance from Senator Sarbanes of Maryland—filibustered against the passage of the bill for a total of sixty-four hours. Were it not that Senator Robert Dole became Senate majority leader in 1985, the legislative effort to pass that bill would have failed. Because of his belief in the merits of the bill—and incidentally because of his devotion to his wife, the secretary of transportation—he was able to keep the bill moving toward eventual passage.

It was a close call, though. Late in the nighttime on a legislative day very near the end of the 1986 congressional session, Senator Warner made an effort in the Senate to attach the Senate version of the bill to a must-pass piece of legislation coming over from the House. Senator Hollings, on the floor of the Senate, blocked that move by a direct filibuster threat: "I have a thick file in the office which I'm prepared to read to you." Congress being so close to final adjournment, there was little time for any further legislative maneuvering. It appeared that our two-year legislative effort had ended in failure.

But the next day, we found that Senator Hollings had a price. Secretary Elizabeth Dole received a surprising and unsolicited early-morning call from Senator Strom Thurmond, Republican and senior senator from Senator Hollings's state of South Carolina. I, of course, did not hear that telephone conversation, but the substance of the call was quickly reported by Secretary Dole to me and the members of her staff. Having been a next-door-but-two neighbor of Senator Thurmond for over ten years, I feel confident that the following reconstruction of that conversation, complete with South Carolina accent, is accurate: " 'Liz-beth—if the pri-oties on those South Ca'lina highway pro-jecks could be re-arranged, I b'lieve Sen'ta Hollins could be bro't along." Secretary Dole was able to rearrange those priorities, Senator Hollins was thereby "bro't along," and the bill passed.

Events moved very rapidly after the legislation was signed by the president late in October 1986. The board of directors was selected and convened at its first meeting by Jim Burnley, deputy secretary of the Department of Transportation, in January 1987. I served on that board for a six-year term as an appointee of Virginia's Governor Baliles, and was elected chairman by the board for each of those six years. My first meeting as chairman began on the stroke of the appointed hour with a loud bang of my gavel, and it was apparent from the beginning that a very strong board of directors was in charge of policy making for the Metropolitan Washington Airports Authority. The board selected as staff essentially the same cadre of employees who had operated the airports under federal control, and general manager Jim Wilding was retained in that capacity. The essential difference was that now net operating revenues, which previously went to the U.S. Treasury, were available to pay expenses and generate profit adequate to support bond issues to pay for capital improvements.

It was a gratifying experience for me. I was able to lead an effort that made possible almost unbelievable improvements at National Airport, and equally incredible and essential expansion in the capacity of Dulles International Airport. This included the Caesar Pelli terminal at National, now the envy of the world, and doubling the Sarinan terminal size at Dulles. A subway system is now under construction that will provide access to the expanded concourses. On the aviation side, there are new taxiways and a new (fourth) runway. From almost 3 million passengers using Dulles in 1984, over 20 million passengers were served there in 2005.

I hope I may be forgiven for closing this chapter with a flattering quote from a 1987 memorandum from the Department of Transportation files:

> A second critical decision was to call former Virginia Governor Linwood Holton, who was floating somewhere on the Chesapeake at the time, to chair the Advisory Commission.—He often speaks of that phone call—Holton's standing and political skills made the Commission work, while so many other Federal advisory committees failed to agree. More important, Holton had long specialized in accomplishing what all others assumed could not be done.*

*Transportation Department fax, "MWAA, Washington DC," August 30, 2004.

The Ongoing
Amtrak Saga

Legislation passed by Congress in 1997 placed the management of the National Railroad Passenger Corporation (Amtrak) under a newly created seven-member board of directors. When I read this in the newspaper, I became very eager for an appointment to that board. I was, and am, convinced that a national rail passenger system is essential to help solve the nation's transportation congestion. If I were to be appointed, I hoped—during a five-year term on the board—to help convince Congress and the administration that such a system was needed, and that it should be subsidized as a public utility.

My son Dwight was able to arrange the appointment for me. Dwight had worked very closely with John Podesta, who was chief of staff to President Clinton when Dwight did a two-year tour in the Clinton White House as a special assistant to help design a plan for health care. At Dwight's behest, his friend John Podesta arranged for President Clinton to nominate me for the Amtrak board.

The 1997 legislation had authorized a substantial one-time capital subsidy for Amtrak, theoretically sufficient to pay some of Amtrak's deferred charges and provide some working capital. But there was also a requirement that Amtrak become self-sufficient for its direct expenses within a period of five years. I was sure that the requirement for self-sufficiency was impossible to fulfill, so I ducked that issue during my confirmation hearing. I hinted in my testimony that reaching that goal would be difficult. But I did, in substance, promise Senator John McCain, chairman of the Senate committee conducting the confirmation hearing, that if confirmed I would support every effort to reach that goal. However, my remarks to the Senate committee made it plain that if the money wasn't there, it couldn't be done. I referred to my experience with the Chesapeake Bay Bridge Tunnel Authority's inability to pay coupons on its series C bonds when they came due during my term as governor. If you don't have the money, you can't pay the bill. Nevertheless, I was confirmed.

George Warrington, who had had considerable experience in management positions in passenger mass transit systems in the Northeast, was the interim president of Amtrak when I went on the board in September 1998. George was elected permanent president and CEO shortly afterward. He was the obvious choice of the chairman, Governor Tommy Thompson of Wisconsin, and the incumbent members of the board appeared to agree with Governor Thompson. The only other candidate under consideration who seemed to be competitive with George Warrington was a female officer of the Norfolk Southern Railway—Nancy Fleischman, then general attorney and later vice president corporate in that organization. I would have liked to examine her credentials more thoroughly, but she withdrew her candidacy before we interviewed her so I therefore joined the consensus and voted with the others to elect George unanimously.

I think all of us on the board were aware that no successful passenger rail service anywhere in the world operates without subsidies from its government. But we were of a single mind to leave no stone unturned in an effort to comply with the statutory requirement that Amtrak produce revenue sufficient to pay all of its direct expenses.

George Warrington was an eternal optimist, and under his leadership we tried everything. A principal source of our board's optimism was the potential revenue we hoped would be generated by a fancy new train, the Acela, which had long been on order and was supposed to provide 125 mph service between Boston and Washington. Delivery dates kept being delayed, and delayed, and delayed. When it *did* arrive, it didn't perform as hoped; it never met schedules based on 125 mph speeds, and it continued to experience serious maintenance problems with consequent repair expense. Needless to say, optimistic revenue projections for it were never met.

We approved contracts for mail and small express packages. We approved contracts to transport perishables from the West Coast to the East Coast. We heard optimistic reports of opportunities to participate jointly with Norfolk Southern to produce new revenues. We jumped at a chance to provide high-speed rail service to Las Vegas from Los Angeles, with capital expenditures to be furnished by the State of Nevada and some gambling interests. But none of these various hoped-for opportunities to earn operating revenues panned out, and we lost money on most, if not all.

We even succeeded in fooling ourselves that we were making progress toward self-sufficiency by selling capital assets. We all knew that such sales would produce only nonrecurring revenues and thus not help the long-term income situation, but we were doing everything we could to operate that railroad without asking Congress for more money. In the end, we went back in desperation to the Department of Transportation, which reluctantly loaned us $200 million to avoid otherwise certain bankruptcy.

The experience proved what I (and I suspect others on the board) knew from the beginning: A national system of rail passenger service is an essential part of a balanced transportation system in the United States, but like the subsidized airways and the subsidized highways, it cannot operate without governmental subsidies.

George Warrington resigned as the end of our financial rope appeared near, and we were extremely fortunate that David Gunn was available to succeed him. David came to the job with impeccable credentials. He had been the top executive on subway systems in New York, Washington, D.C., and Toronto, Canada. He had a period of employment with the Illinois Central Gulf Railroad, one of the Class I railroads. He was intimately familiar with all phases of the operation of a railroad and especially of a successfully operating rail passenger system. But perhaps his major asset for Amtrak was his credibility because he is articulate, knowledgeable, and straightforward. Even Senator John McCain, leading opponent of subsidies for Amtrak, remarked that David's first appearance before a congressional committee in his role as president of Amtrak was "a breath of fresh air." In simple words, David Gunn told the committee plainly that annual appropriations from the federal government are essential for the operation of a national passenger rail system, and he supported that position with a recital of facts that were indisputable.

My confidence in David Gunn began early. Because of a schedule conflict, I had been unable to participate in the board's interview of him during the selection process, but I did have a private chat with him before his interview with the board. Besides his experience with subway systems and railroads, his obvious knowledge and impressive straightforwardness convinced me that he indeed was the breath of fresh air later described by Senator McCain. I told him after a fifteen-minute conversation, "You have *got* to take this job!"

Fortunately for the future of rail passenger transportation in the United States, the Amtrak board agreed with my appraisal, and again fortunately, David Gunn accepted the job when it was confirmed in board interviews that the board recognized and would stand behind his conviction that Amtrak must be subsidized by the federal government as an essential public utility comparable to our systems of highways and airways. A three-legged stool needs three legs—air, highways, and passenger rail.

But Bush appointees to the board fired Gunn in 2005 in a dispute over disposition of Amtrak's Northeast passenger corridor. Fortunately nothing has come of the proposal by the Bush administration to separate that corridor from the rest of Amtrak, and Congress continues to subsidize Amtrak at approximately $1.2 billion or more per year, essentially overruling the Bush administration's desire to phase out Amtrak.

My five-year term on the Amtrak board expired in September 2003, and there was no chance of reappointment by the Bush administration. My strong support for a national rail passenger system and for the needed federal subsidies was in direct opposition to the Bush position, which is that it would like the country to wash its hands of Amtrak. The administration's budget recommendation through fiscal year 2004 was just about half the needed amount. David Gunn was successful during his tenure in convincing Congress to appropriate sums considerably higher than the Bush recommendations— though still not enough.

The issue came to a crisis during 2005, when the Bush budget for the fiscal year beginning October 1, 2005, recommended exactly zero for Amtrak, but the U.S. House of Representatives voted to subsidize Amtrak's October 2005– October 2006 fiscal year at approximately $1.2 billion. The Senate agreed with the House, and that essentially overruled the Bush administration.

My optimism that Amtrak will survive and ultimately thrive is supported by my confidence in the strategies begun by David Gunn. Even with the absence of Gunn and even in the face of Bush administration efforts to eliminate the long-distance portion of Amtrak, the nation's railroad continues to be supported by Congress. The Bush proposal to sell all or part of the passenger business to nonexistent prospective buyers has died aborning, and it is heartening to note that Amtrak passenger travel in the past five years has grown from 20 million to 25 million, a 20 percent increase.

Equally encouraging for the national transportation system is that several long-distance truck carriers are entering into partnerships with Norfolk Southern Railroad and other railroads to move trucks from crowded interstate highways to less costly movement by rail; trucks are moved long distances on special railcars at lower costs than on crowded interstate highways, and short-distance deliveries can be made by truck from the rail destination.

I have for years advocated that part of the existing transportation trust fund, which comes from a special tax on fuels, be used to pay for capital improvements to rail infrastructures. Freight railroads, which own most of the infrastructure, have not been able to earn sufficient funds to pay for the needed capital enhancement. Investments from the trust funds would increase rail capacity, a prerequisite to efficient operation of freight (including trucks) and passenger systems on the same tracks. Such investment is, in my opinion, ultimately coming because it's cheaper to upgrade railroads than to acquire land and build more lanes on interstate highways, and a much more efficient transportation system will come from the expenditure of the same bucks.

Youngish Elder Statesman Finds New Opportunity Times

My varied career since 1975, when I left the State Department, reminds me of an expression heard during the Depression years of the early 1930s: "He can't keep work!" For one reason or another, new opportunities kept finding me for the rest of my career, and though sometimes I went looking for them, they never failed to pop up.

I urged my prospective partners at the sophisticated Washington, D.C., law firm of Hogan and Hartson to be aware that I was perfectly capable of doing legal work, but that I was not confident that business would just naturally come to me as a partner—even as a former governor of Virginia. They should have understood—and I think they did—that they would have to provide the business on which I would work. I did not intend to be a "rainmaker."

This was consistent with my indoctrination to the practice of law: not soliciting business or clients was a hard-and-fast ethical rule for lawyers back in the 1950s. Solicitation in those days was not only unethical but indeed, possibly *illegal.* But the profession was changing. Law firms were becoming commercial operations, and "merchandising"—hustling business—was becoming an important element of practice. I simply didn't fit the new mold, and it was easy to use the 1978 Senate campaign as an occasion to part company with Hogan and Hartson.

After the failure to gain the Senate nomination in 1978, I moved on to be vice president and general counsel of the American Council of Life Insurance at the invitation of Blake Newton. As I related earlier, that career experience was interesting and challenging as long as his tenure as president and his influence on policy continued. I was less enchanted when the ACLI policy morphed into a more traditional, less idealistic lobbying approach: create a huge political action committee, contribute huge sums to incumbent members of important committees, and buy yourself a Congress. My disenchantment coincided with management changes at ACLI. The new boys were eager to curtail expenses by downsizing staff, so I was able to negotiate a somewhat golden parachute with a nice annuity for life plus health insurance for Jinks and me for life.

I then joined the small law firm in Washington to which Blake Newton had gone when he left ACLI—Zuckert, Scoutt and Rasenberger. It was an extremely congenial setting, and it was from there that I did the Metropolitan Washington airport transfer work for which I was retained by the U.S. Department of Transportation. Also during that time I was elected to succeed Blake Newton on the board of the Jefferson-Pilot Life Insurance Company— a very fruitful investment of my time.

A fellowship at Harvard's Kennedy Institute of Politics was offered in the fall semester of 1988, so Jinks and I moved to Cambridge, where I conducted student seminars. There I not only enjoyed revisiting the law school but also audited a civil rights class conducted by a very aggressive African American, Derrick Bell. At the same time, Jinks attended some classes about China before leaving for an adventurous China vacation later in the year. The formal and informal associations with students and academics during those four months at Harvard were more than pleasant, and provided a challenging intellectual interlude. It was there that we met, and became fast friends with, Matt and Martha Reese. He was a semi-retired Democratic political consultant who spoke the same moderate political language as I. Jinks and I both felt invigorated from our experience there and open to new horizons.

In 1982 or 1983, Governor Robb instigated the Center for Innovative Technology (CIT). Its purpose was to encourage the creation of job opportunities in Virginia, based on products or processes that were being developed from research conducted privately or in our major universities. By the end of 1988, the center existed, but two of the first presidents were inadequate or failures. Ronald Carrier, president of James Madison University, was serving as CIT's interim president at the request of then-governor Baliles. A search for a permanent replacement was under way just as I finished the fellowship at Harvard. The timing was perfect for me, and with support from Governor Baliles and some members of CIT's board who knew my record, I was chosen for the post in December 1988—opening up yet another "Opportunity Time."

My assignment at CIT was largely political; I helped convince the legislature, especially during the Wilder administration (which recommended zero budget during the second year of the 1992–94 biennium), to continue CIT's funding. That was easy. Senator Hunter Andrews, a very powerful chairman of the Senate Finance Committee, had been chief patron of the bill creating CIT, and he was a believer. In addition, CIT had some significant successes during those early years of my presidency. We were able to provide critical financial help to Orbital Sciences Corporation in connection with one of its first rocket launches. That start-up company hoped to prove that launching space vehicles from aircraft was a better way than elaborate launches from the ground. Today Orbital, a very successful organization, employs several thousand employees.

In its early stages, the Jefferson Lab in Newport News received aid and encouragement from CIT. It created and maintains an underground raceway in which electrons are accelerated to a speed of almost 186,000 miles per second before bombarding test materials. I described it in my promotional speeches as the "doggondest demolition derby ever seen." It goes to the heart of particle physics and has attracted highly trained researchers from all over the world to conduct sophisticated experiments on their "racetrack" in Newport News, Virginia.

We even had a hand in developing the Internet. DARPA (an acronym for Defense Advanced Research Projects Agency—an independent research arm of the Defense Department) had subsidized experiments with computer communications in which the University of Virginia participated, and we gave financial support through the university to those trials. The present Internet grew out of DARPA's original investments.

I had agreed to stay five years as CIT's president, and I extended that commitment by one year at Governor Allen's request. He expressed confidence in me and asked that I stay on until he had moved further along in putting together his new administration.

It was Opportunity Time once more when in 1995 I joined the Richmond law firm of Mezzullo and McCandlish, P.C., where my idealistic son-in-law Tim Kaine was then a partner. It is an understatement to say that this association has been extremely pleasant. The firm grew rapidly for a while, probably too rapidly. A group of dissatisfied partners left, followed by several firm name changes, ending up now as McCandlish Holton; the firm is comprised of about twenty-five lawyers and a supporting cast. I contend that my principal contribution is to increase the average age of the membership—most of the others are in their forties or younger, and I'm given an opportunity to advise or assist once in a while. The firm does trial and international work, assists health care providers, and maintains an intellectual property and very significant immigration practice. The group is stable, successful financially, and increasingly recognized as a first-class professional organization in Richmond and beyond. Very importantly to me, a congenial atmosphere prevails, and it is indeed a privilege for me to play my elder statesman role there. Happily, I am not expected to be a rainmaker!

All in the Family:
19 Governor Kaine's Win

I visited our daughter Anne at the Harvard Law School during a business trip to Boston in 1982. We stood together at the back of one of those large theater-type classrooms in Langdell Hall, then the principal academic building at the law school.

"You see that tall, curly-haired boy standing next to the teacher's desk down in front?"

"Yes," I replied, my eyes following her direction. I tried not to stare.

"Well, he's the one. He doesn't know it yet, and I do have some competition in Kansas City, but I'll take care of that."

The curly-haired Tim Kaine had come to Harvard after obtaining his undergraduate degree from the University of Missouri and was scheduled to graduate from law school in 1982. He decided, however, to spend a year as a Catholic missionary in Honduras. When he returned to Harvard, he was in the class that would graduate in 1983—Anne's class. Her prediction came true, and their decision to marry came before they graduated, along with the decision to make Virginia the site of their life's opportunities. Their wedding was in St. Elizabeth's church in Richmond in 1984.

When Tim Kaine and Anne completed clerkships with federal judges (she with the U.S. District Court in Richmond and Tim with the U.S. Court of Appeals for the Eleventh Circuit in Atlanta), they put their law degrees to work in areas of public service: Anne went to Legal Aid; Tim went successively to two private law firms in Richmond, in each case reserving the right to apply a substantial portion of his time to pro bono cases.

It was therefore no surprise to me when Tim told me in 1994 that he planned to run for Richmond City Council because he believed he could help improve the performance of the governing body. It did indeed need improvement. I had no argument there, but shorthand for what I told him was, "You're crazy!"

I thought the existing council was in such a mess that it would be impossible for one person to make much of a difference. After years of observation, I had also reached the conclusion that municipal governments are inherently the burying grounds for otherwise promising political careers. The tasks are nearly impossible, funds are never sufficient, every dissatisfied constituent is as near as the local telephone, dissidents scream loudly, publicly, and incessantly, while voices of those in accord seldom rise above a whisper.

But Tim proved me wrong. He ran; he won; he reorganized the parliamentary structure of council; he brought together the deeply divided members of a mediocre (at best) governing body. Twice an adoring membership of council, a majority of whom were African American, unanimously elected Tim as mayor of the city, tangible evidence of Tim's almost miraculous ability to focus the efforts of folks with diverse views on desirable common goals. It had been years since a white person held that job. In a short time, substantive and positive accomplishments came about, almost universally attributed to his leadership.

In Tim's seventh year on council and in his third year as mayor, one person's tragedy became opportunity for another. Emily Couric, a Democratic member of the Virginia Senate representing Charlottesville, was diagnosed in July 2000 with terminal cancer. Prior to that, it had been increasingly clear that Emily's announced plans to seek and win the Democratic nomination for lieutenant governor of Virginia would be fulfilled. She was capable, visible, popular, experienced, and enjoyed high name recognition throughout Virginia— both on her own and as the sister of Katie Couric, then the NBC-TV star of the *Today Show*. It appeared that Emily's candidacy would be unopposed, at least for the nomination. When she learned of her impending demise, she did her best to transfer her aura to Tim Kaine, making clear to the public her hope that he would fill the shoes she might have worn.

Anne gave his candidacy full support. "If you're going to try, go all out!" was her attitude. Tim did go all out, though at the outset winning looked all but impossible. Alan Diamonstein, veteran Democratic member of the House of Delegates from Newport News, would seek the nomination. Jerrauld Jones, also a longtime member of the House of Delegates and one of the leaders in the black caucus of that body, would be another candidate. Most of the Democratic establishment—long in control of the General Assembly and getting pretty shopworn—was skeptical of Tim's candidacy. He had never been a Democratic candidate (his candidacy for city council had been nonpartisan); his views on gun control were only partially known but already suspect;

he personally opposed the death penalty. "Too liberal," harrumphed some senior officeholders and Democratic lobbyists. Tim's support while mayor for "Project Exile" (an effective deterrent to gun-related crimes), his campaign promise not to seek further gun control legislation if elected, and his assurance that if governor, he would carry out the death penalty laws of the Commonwealth were not sufficient to gain active support from these leaders. An exception was Vic Thomas, a very senior delegate from Roanoke. An avid hunter, fisherman, and environmentalist, he was enthusiastically behind Tim from the beginning. His influence with some of the sporting and National Rifle Association voters provided critical support for Tim. As it turned out, a majority of Democrats who voted in the primary apparently thought it was time for fresh, new leadership. Tim was nominated as the Democratic nominee for lieutenant governor.

Mark Warner, a wealthy businessman from Alexandria who had never held public office, was unopposed for the gubernatorial nomination. His only previous campaign experience (largely self-financed) had been a run for a U.S. Senate seat against the unbeatable incumbent John Warner in 2000.

In the general election of 2001, Mark Warner beat lackluster Mark Early, the Republican candidate for governor, and Tim beat Jay Katzen, the Republican candidate for lieutenant governor, whose right-wing views were extreme to the ultimate degree. And the electorate's increasing disillusionment with Republican leadership had peaked because of the sad state of Virginia's fiscal affairs. Voters believed the financial problems of the state had been caused in large part by Republican governor Gilmore's car-tax refund legislation, and this background provided a groundswell of support for the successful campaigns of these two promising new Democratic leaders.

The new leadership did not disappoint. The prestige of the new governor Warner got a big boost when, with Virginia Senate support (in which Tim, as its presiding officer, participated), he was able to break a stalemate caused by the obstinacy of the House leadership and pass tax-reform legislation. This reduced some sales tax on food and enhanced general fund revenues (euphemism for increased taxes) by approximately $1.4 billion. These dollars enabled the Commonwealth to make appropriations for essential needs too long neglected because of lack of funds. Most importantly, these revenues eliminated the possible reduction of Virginia's Triple-A bond rating, which Moody's and some other rating agencies were threatening because of the existing mess of Virginia's fiscal affairs.

Governor Warner ended his term with favorable poll ratings of over 70 percent, and Tim gained standing with the voters because of the open and enthusiastic support he had given to Warner's programs; he was unopposed for the Democratic nomination for governor in 2005. Admitting to some father-in-law prejudice, I was glad to find myself not alone in finding him bright, knowledgeable, articulate, and genuine. To those qualities must be added that he is a phenomenal campaigner. Perhaps it should also be added that the stars in 2005 were aligned right. He won, and daughter Anne resumed her residence in Virginia's Executive Mansion. I joked, "Our family isn't greedy—we just want one governor in every generation." To grandson Nat: "Stand by!"

There were many factors that brought support for Tim during his gubernatorial campaign. Not the least of these was that voters were increasingly disillusioned with Republican leaders of the U.S. Congress and with the Bush administration, and that the popular Governor Mark Warner campaigned vigorously for him. But above all, Tim had worked effectively during his four-year term as lieutenant governor. His promise, carried out and well received, to visit every school district in the state during his four years in office gave credence to his support for public education and helped enhance his name recognition. His Republican opponent lacked charisma, and the negative campaign directed by professional political consultants backfired and then fizzled.

I myself had great fun actively campaigning for him toward the end of the campaign. I joined Mark and Tim on a Southwest Virginia twelve-stop foray the weekend before the election and bragged to Democratic audiences that I had made twenty converts to Tim's candidacy. Mark added to that, "If an eighty-two-year-old *Republican* can get twenty voters, surely each of you Democrats can get ten!"

Governor Tim Kaine will certainly be challenged during his term, particularly by an intensely conservative group of Republicans who control the House of Delegates, and who will embarrass the Democratic governor at every opportunity. They refused, for example, on specious grounds, to confirm his nominee for secretary of the Commonwealth. They adamantly opposed Tim's early recommendations (supported by the Senate) to provide a recurring source of revenue to help alleviate congestion in Virginia's transportation system. An ongoing stalemate on the transportation issue between the conservative Republican House leadership and the more pragmatic Republican Senate threatened to distract the governor from leadership opportunities for innovative programs in education, health care, and immigration, among many others, during the remaining years of his term.

My own view is that the extreme positions supported by the House Republican leadership are passé because Virginia's electorate is increasingly less conservative. Voters expect a reasonable approach to governance by their elected officials. The elections of Mark Warner and Tim Kaine support that view. A reasonable compromise on transportation revenues appeared for a time to free Tim to focus his leadership on solutions to some of the state's other pressing problems; the levy of severe penalties for traffic violations—designed to raise money for transportation needs—has, however, met serious constituent opposition. More legislation will therefore be required in early 2008—after significant elections in November 2007. I know that Tim is optimistic; his enthusiasm almost bubbles. He will be able to bring these elected prima donnas (all elected officials are prima donnas!) together and successfully conclude one of the truly outstanding gubernatorial terms in Virginia's history.

Afterword

While writing this memoir, I've welcomed yet another opportunity: it's pro-vided a reason to indulge in some retrospection and introspection about both my public life and my personal life, although it's hard to say where one began and the other left off.

As for my public life, I remember chuckling a bit a few years ago when reading comments about the "premature end of my political career." In his book *The Color of Their Skin,* Bob Pratt speculated that "there could be little doubt that his support of desegregation's end . . . ended his political career." And my good friend Jay Wilkinson, in his chapter about me, "An Idealist's Demise," in his book *The Governors of Virginia, 1860–1978,* postulates that "his demise was partly the result of commendable convictions: to light Virginia a new way in matters of race."

I have another take on that picture, being the only one who can really know what my goals in life have been. Jinks had it about right when she told the press back on election night 1969 that I would rather be governor of Virginia than president of the United States. What more could you aspire to after being elected governor of Virginia? My awe of that position is such that there is no way up from the top. Ned Breathitt, a former governor of Kentucky, expressed the same thought, once saying to me: "We don't need another mountain to climb; we've already done it." So if there's no political career after governor, so what?

Today I am still amazed and humbled about my place in history: The seventy-first governor of Virginia! *Virginia!* We Virginians like to reflect on and emphasize our legacy. Virginians inspired and led the American Revolu-tion: Patrick Henry, Thomas Jefferson, George Mason, and George Washing-ton. James Madison, with help from a New Yorker and some others, wrote the

Constitution. Chief Justice John Marshall gave it its most important early "spin." We're proud of all that heritage.

However, like the rest of all proud Virginians, I prefer to skip over some of the less admirable later events: our part in the preamble to the Civil War—Virginia's secession, an act designed to destroy the United States; the adoption of the Virginia Constitution of 1902, a document that effectively nullified the Fifteenth Amendment right of all U.S. citizens to vote regardless of race, color, or previous conditions of servitude; and of course, coming up to my own day, Massive Resistance to school integration, a phenomenon whose purpose was to overrule the decision of the U.S. Supreme Court that rendered unconstitutional the doctrine that permitted separate public schools for African American children.

A governor of Virginia in my day could have cast his lot with the firebrands—Maddox of Georgia, Barnett of Mississippi, Wallace of Alabama—and shaken a metaphorical fist at Washington. The short-term political cost might have been lower. I chose to proclaim with my family by word and deed—in contrast with actions of other southern states and in contrast with some of those darker moments of the history of Virginia and the South—that Virginia would comply in letter and spirit with the fundamental law of the United States. I chose to set Virginia on a course to become in all respects a model of race relations. If forfeitures of additional elective office was the only price I paid for having made those choices, then indeed I got a bargain.

As for my home front, I got more than a bargain. Jinks and I are now in our fifty-fifth year together. It has been a partnership of two strong people, each of us very active in our own spheres, with my concentration on political activity and hers on important civic and charitable activities in all the communities where we have lived. Most important to us is having been blessed with four equally strong offspring, professionally trained and happily married, who have provided us with nine wonderful grandchildren—so far.

Each of the four is civically responsible and fully aware of the satisfactions and challenges of public service. I am deeply thankful to be able to say that the naysayers who predicted disaster in 1970, when we sent the children to integrated schools in accordance with busing decrees, were wrong. Completely wrong.

Our oldest child, daughter Tayloe, earned her M.D. at the University of Virginia in 1982 after graduating summa cum laude from Dartmouth College in 1978. She married Jon Loftus, whom she had met at Strong Memorial Hospital in Rochester, New York. He was a medical student when she was there for her residency in internal medicine. Tayloe is director of clerkship training in internal medicine at the medical school of the State University of New York in Syracuse; she also has a clinical practice there. She is the president of the national organization of clerkship directors. Jon is a plastic surgeon specializing in hand surgery.

Jon and Tayloe have three children: Elizabeth, who was eighteen on her birthday in 2006, was admitted to Cornell's early-decision class of 2010. She plans to study veterinary medicine with special emphasis on the care of large animals. (She is a well-trained horsewoman who has owned her own horse since early high school.) David, now seventeen, is a superb skier and the valedictorian of his graduation class at a sports academy in Lake Placid. Little brother Carter, aged fourteen, is a dog lover, owning two golden retrievers and a Newfoundland. A talented piano player and holder of blue ribbons as a horseman, he attends public school in a Syracuse suburb where, like his two older siblings, he is an excellent student.

Our second child, Anne, graduated magna cum laude from Princeton University in 1980. She enjoyed a little game with the challenge of admission to law school; she applied to several and was accepted by all except Yale. Anne tried to get me to tell her which one to choose, but even when she pushed me, I would go no further than to say, "Anne, there is only one Number One." She got the point, went to Harvard, and there selected Tim Kaine, a classmate from Kansas City, to be *her* Number One. She brought him to Richmond, and made a Virginian of him. During the next twenty years, she provided legal services to low- or no-income clients through Legal Aid. She then spent seven years as a judge of Richmond's Juvenile and Domestic Relations Court. She is now the First Lady of Virginia. Tim practiced in private firms, where he did a substantial amount of pro bono work. He was elected governor of Virginia in 2005 after having served on the city council and as mayor of Richmond, and for one four-year term as Virginia's lieutenant governor.

All three Kaine children attended the new Linwood Holton Elementary School in Richmond. Nat, who is seventeen, and Woody, fifteen, attend the Maggie Walker Governor's School. Twelve-year-old Anella moved into the Binford Middle School in September 2006. Both boys served as pages in the General Assembly, and Anella is a likely candidate for paging when she reaches fourteen. The scholastic record of these three is equal to that of their New York cousins.

Number three child, and the last of our four to marry, son Woody (Abner Linwood Holton III) graduated from the University of Virginia in 1981, where he was editor of the editorial page of the prominent student newspaper, the *Cavalier Daily*. He earned a fellowship for his graduate work at Duke University, from which he earned a Ph.D. with a specialty in colonial American history. He worked for nearly twelve years to expand his doctoral dissertation into a book, *Forced Founders*, the publication of which brought him invitations to join the faculty of both Bates College in Maine and the University of Richmond. We were of course pleased that he chose the latter, where he attained tenure in the spring of 2004. His second book, *Unruly Americans*, came out in 2007 and was named a National Book Award finalist.

Woody met his bride, Gretchen Schoel, as she was completing the work on her doctorate at the College of William and Mary in Virginia. Their marriage took place on a family farm near Vicksburg, Mississippi, on April 16, 2005. Their first child, Beverly Ferris Holton, arrived in June 2006.

Our baby, Dwight, was born in December 1965, about a month after the conclusion of my first campaign for governor (and about six years after our first covey of three, who had come in pretty quick succession). Probably all of us assumed that if the new arrival were a boy, he would be named for Jinks's grandfather, Bishop Robert Carter Jett, the first Episcopal bishop of Southwest Virginia. But, after several hours' exposure to President Dwight Eisenhower when he campaigned in Virginia for me in 1965 (as I've said earlier in this book), the first three siblings proposed to their mother: "Mama, if we have a little brother, why don't we name him for that nice man instead of your grandfather—somebody we never knew?"

And so it was that *Dwight* Carter Holton graduated from Brown University in 1987, destined perhaps, because of his name, to leap immediately into the political world. Right after graduation he campaigned as an advance man for Michael Dukakis in the 1988 presidential campaign and then ran the travel schedule for Douglas Wilder's campaign for governor of Virginia in 1989. He served for a time as deputy secretary of health and human services in the Wilder administration. He then traveled around the world with a side trip to climb Mount Kilimanjaro in Africa. The Clinton campaign lured him away from a beach in Vietnam to be in charge of the balloon drop and other backstage logistics at the Democratic National Convention that nominated Bill Clinton for president. After the 1992 presidential election, he worked in the White House with Hillary Clinton and Ira Magaziner on a health care program. Toward the end of President Clinton's first term, he entered law school at the University of Virginia. For one year following law school, he clerked for Judge John Gleason in the Eastern District of New York in Brooklyn; for several years thereafter, he prosecuted violent criminals as an assistant U.S. attorney in the Eastern District of New York.

In 2000, Dwight married Mary Ellen Glynn, a graduate of Northwestern University who was serving at that time as spokesperson for Richard Holbrooke, President Clinton's appointee as U.S. ambassador to the United Nations. Their first child, a boy, and our first *Holton* grandchild, was born in July 2004, joined by a sibling, Fiona Bright Holton, in August 2006. Terence Oliver Linwood Holton's names come in order, first for Terence, Mary Ellen's brother; then for Oliver W. Hill, a prominent African American civil rights lawyer, whom Dwight adores (Oliver's first cases were on behalf of African American public schoolteachers who were being paid discriminatory salaries because of their race in the 1930s); and finally, for me.

A visiting teaching position at Lewis and Clark Law School took Dwight and Mary Ellen to Portland, Oregon, in 2002. Mary Ellen did a six-year tour as the communications director for Oregon's governor, and in spite of his Democratic proclivity, Dwight was retained as assistant to the Republican U.S. attorney in Portland, where he now prosecutes white-collar criminals.

As our sunset years approach, Jinks and I plan to continue catching our share of croakers and Norfolk Spot for some years to come, with no concern about a family legacy. Our genes are jumping around inside that spirited group of four and their offspring, who follow us. They are blessed with talent and inclination and will be doing good works for a long time. We are proud.

And we are proud, too, of what we have been able to do with the opportunities that have come our way. Following her mother's example, Jinks has concerned herself almost constantly over the years with community service. She magnified our joint efforts through her work with Habitat for Humanity, having helped build houses from Prague to South Dakota. She has worked to get help for disadvantaged families, to find ways to help children with special needs, and has actively supported care for the environment. But hardly least, Jinks gave full support to my own public service through a political life. We look back gratefully, seeing that some of our work as a team will live on:

- My major political goal was accomplished. There is in place in Virginia a vibrant two-party democracy: Republicans control part of the legislature, Democrats hold the governor's office, and voters control. No more can a one-party political machine impose its unopposed will on the destiny of Virginia;

- The tone set in race relations in Virginia, especially in equal job opportunities, will contribute to interracial harmony for generations;
- Jobs derived from consolidation of the port of Hampton Roads continue to increase, sustaining better lifestyles for thousands of families;
- From their pilot beginning at Mary Baldwin and Mary Washington colleges, Governor's Schools are ongoing, providing education for gifted students statewide;
- Emphasis on environmental issues—which began with the creation of the Council on the Environment and was followed in my term by governmental recognition of Earth Day, the elimination of untreated municipal sewage from Virginia's rivers, and acquisition for preservation of Grayson Highlands and False Cape state parks—has brought intense interest and tangible support for wise use and protection of our natural resources;
- The National Center for State Courts now sits in Williamsburg, adjoining a world-class physical facility for the Marshall-Wythe School of Law, which now ranks with top law schools in the country;
- Washington National and Dulles airports, far more efficient and accessible now that they have been transferred to a unified authority, may not last forever in their current incarnation, but they will be serving an ever-expanding urban area for a long time to come;
- The structure of Virginia's government was reorganized through the instigation of a governor's cabinet with ongoing improvement in communications with over one hundred major agency heads.

These are contributions Jinks and I remember with a sense of satisfaction and pride. Two personal anecdotes reassure me that we were on the right track.

One day in the early 1980s, Jinks and I were walking with a group down Urbanna's main street during the famous annual Oyster Festival. A young gentleman walking in the opposite direction, happily—and at least partially in his cups—blurted out loudly as he passed us, "There's that old son-of-a-bitch Holton! Best damn governor we ever had."

The second incident, not quite so humorous, followed not much later the same day. An old black man, rather stooped, got my attention and signaled that he had something he wanted to say to me. I bent down to hear his words, spoken barely above a whisper:

"First governor of *all* the people."

Appendix

Inaugural Address of Linwood Holton, Governor,
to the General Assembly and the People of Virginia,
Saturday, January 17, 1970

Mr. Speaker, Mr. President, Members of the General Assembly, My Fellow Virginians:

Much has been said and written today as the date of the inauguration of a Republican as governor of Virginia. And, indeed, there is much of history in this occasion. I am a Republican, and I welcome the advent of a two-party system in our Commonwealth. But the campaign is over.

The time for partisan politics is over. It is time now for leadership, for action, for progress through unity.

The unity of Virginia is demonstrated by the former governors of our state who are participating in this Inauguration. I am honored by their presence and will endeavor to serve our Commonwealth in the future as they have served it so loyally and well in the past.

I turn today to all Virginians, whatever their political persuasion, and say: Let us act together.

I do not ask you to join me in a *Holton* program. I ask all of you to support a *Virginia* program for the 1970's.

I seek the help of all Virginians in this endeavor, no matter where they live, what they may do, what age or race they might be, or what political philosophy they might hold.

At the dawn of the 1970's it is clear that problem-solving, and not philosophical principles, has become the focal point of politics, both in Virginia and in the nation.

No longer can we be divided into opposing camps of political philosophy. No longer is there complete disagreement between "conservatives" and "liberals" about the problems confronting us or the need for their resolution. Old cliches have now blurred and old dogmas have died.

The common belief is that state government must act, that the future of states' rights rests upon the success of state efforts. No more must the slogan of "states' rights" sound a recalcitrant and defensive note for the people of the South. For the era of defiance is behind us.

In its place is the challenge posed by the late 20th century. Moreover, it is evident that the federal government alone has not coped and cannot cope with this challenge. So much of the national government's attention must be given to our commitments abroad; and even its massive domestic programs have failed to halt the decay of our cities, the exploitation of our rural resources, the rising crime on our streets, and the befoulment of our environment.

John W. Gardner, chairman of the Urban Coalition, recently spoke on the nation's apparent incapacity to launch meaningful solutions to its problems. "We know our lakes are dying," he said, "our rivers growing filthier daily, our atmosphere increasingly polluted. We are aware of the racial tensions that could tear our nation apart. We understand that oppressive poverty in the midst of affluence is intolerable. We see that our cities are sliding toward disaster. . . . But we are seized by a kind of paralysis of the will. It is like a waking nightmare."

The great task of state government is to dispel this nightmare, to overcome this paralysis of the will. We are fortunate in Virginia. Environmental decay has not yet beset us as it has the great cities of the Northeast and Southern California. There is still time here to see that Virginians have both material progress *and* a dignified, enjoyable and lastingly productive place to live.

This administration intends to move forward immediately on all fronts against the deterioration of our environment. We are determined to make the quality of our air and water, the safety of our streets, the core of our cities, the development and preservation of recreational areas top priority public concerns.

We intend further to continue the development of our educational system at every level. We must see that our youth are prepared for the complexities and changes their generation will face; and we must engage them actively in the identification of major concerns and in finding solutions to those problems. We must make our highway system adequate for the demands of a mobile population, and we must find some way to save our urban areas from traffic strangulation. We must develop fully the potential of our great natural harbors and waterways. We must offer every incentive possible to persuade industries to locate in our rural areas so that their young people will not migrate to cities already overpopulated. We must seek a new partnership with the federal government to insure that Virginia will receive the full benefit of federal funds and programs available to it.

Most of all, we must begin long-range planning now for a future in which our population will reach new heights and our public concerns new dimensions.

The durability of our nation and civilization will be in the end determined by how we have responded not only to external problems but, more importantly, to our problems from within. One of the foremost of these is obviously that of racial discrimination.

Here in Virginia we must see that no citizen of the Commonwealth is excluded from full participation in both the blessings and responsibilities of our society because of his race. We will have a government based on a partnership of all Virginians, a government in which there will be neither partisanship nor prejudice of any kind.

As Virginia has been a model for so much else in America in the past, let us now endeavor to make today's Virginia a model in race relations. Let us, as Lincoln said, insist upon an open society "with malice toward none; charity for all."

To succeed, this quest for an open society must involve all of us, not just the leaders of government. We earnestly ask the active participation of our business and professional leaders, the heads of our schools and universities, our labor chiefs and legislators, our local governments, leaders of minorities, and all individual citizens. Let our goal in Virginia be an aristocracy of ability, regardless of race, color or creed.

It is now almost 200 years since Thomas Jefferson and George Washington, Patrick Henry and James Madison inspired the birth of our nation. All through the early years of our Republic, it was Virginia which guided the nation's destiny. For long after the Civil War, Virginia's people had to overcome the hardships of poverty and defeat. But they succeeded.

Today a new vigor, similar to that of 200 years ago, has caught our people. It is an honor to become governor at such a time. We accept a challenge which Daniel Webster once expressed in these words:

"Let us develop the resources of our land, call forth its powers, build up its institutions, promote all its great interests, and see whether we also, in our day and generation, may not perform something worthy to be remembered."

This challenge summons us forth again today, and, with God's help, we shall succeed.